FREDERICK MARX

Rites to a Good Life

Everyday Rituals Of Healing And Transformation

First published by Warrior Films 2021

Copyright © 2021 by Frederick Marx

All rights reserved. No part of this publication may be reproduced, stored or transmitted in any form or by any means, electronic, mechanical, photocopying, recording, scanning, or otherwise without written permission from the publisher. It is illegal to copy this book, post it to a website, or distribute it by any other means without permission.

Frederick Marx asserts the moral right to be identified as the author of this work.

Frederick Marx has no responsibility for the persistence or accuracy of URLs for external or third-party Internet Websites referred to in this publication and does not guarantee that any content on such Websites is, or will remain, accurate or appropriate.

Designations used by companies to distinguish their products are often claimed as trademarks. All brand names and product names used in this book and on its cover are trade names, service marks, trademarks and registered trademarks of their respective owners. The publishers and the book are not associated with any product or vendor mentioned in this book. None of the companies referenced within the book have endorsed the book.

First edition

ISBN: 978-0-9984062-5-1

Cover art by Michael Birnbaum
Editing by Ryan Cove
Illustration by Don Huff

This book was professionally typeset on Reedsy.
Find out more at reedsy.com

With the prayer that all teens everywhere get initiated and mentored into adulthood...

Our task today is to help the man who has come to the end of his tether, by revealing to him the latent content of his deepest and most essential experiences, by opening the door to the basic truths and laws of life, and above all by showing him a way to acheive by practice a lasting attitude in consonance with them, without which there can be no progress in faith and no inner ripening.

KARLFRIED DURKHEIM
HARA, THE VITAL CENTRE OF MAN

Contents

Foreword	ii
Preface	vii
Other Works by Frederick Marx	ix
Introduction	xi
1 The Story of Rites of Passage	1
2 Initiating Teens	30
3 The Mature Masculine (and How It Serves Women!)	67
4 Mentorship and Eldership	90
5 Bringing the Sacred Back to the Everyday	118
6 Parents	132
7 Community	149
8 Nature	176
9 You as an Individual	193
10 Contemporary Challenges and Future Speculations	200
11 Covid-19 and our Planetary Rite of Passage	218
Thank You For Reading My Book	232
Acknowledgements	233
Appendix I: My ROP Teachers	234
Appendix II: Rites of Passage for Teen Boys in the United...	237
Appendix III: The Ten Best Practices of Mentorship	240
Appendix IV: Desired Qualities of a Mentor	242
Appendix V: My Mentor Harold Ramis	244
Appendix VI: 2012 Mini Vision Fast at 3 Creeks - FM Journal	250

Foreword

I grew up in a family where it was always important that whether you had money or not, your gift of time was very important. My father drilled that into every one of us. He always used to say, "Whether you become an astronaut or a medical doctor or a musician, find a school and go teach." That was something that he always told all of us. As a result today I'm teaching. **Chike Nwoffiah**

I should never have written this book. That's what my judging mind tells me. It tells me I could never do justice to all that my teachers, including Chike Nwoffiah, have taught me, much less add something new to the Rites of Passage (ROP) conversation or surpass them in some way.

I'm not a Ph.D. I'm not a social scientist, a cultural anthropologist, a scholar, a medical doctor, a licensed psychologist or therapist, a philosopher, a professional advisor or some kind of guru. I'm an artist. By trade, I'm a storyteller. I tell stories primarily through films, occasionally through song and increasingly through writing.

But I've been initiated by life. I'm a close observer of life as I've seen it lived by myself and others. Gratefully, I've learned not to pay overdue attention to my judging mind. I've also learned that if I share some of what I know, and do it in a good way, recognizing my teachers, calling out their names as I stand wobbly on their shoulders to sing to the horizon they have opened for me, I will fulfill some of what my own life has called me to do. Maybe now it is incumbent on me. These are the things I have to teach. After 20 years of close study, maybe it's my turn.

I feel a deep sense of urgency. With the dramatic changes that will occur across the planet in the coming years due to climate change, given how those changes will ripple across all sectors of human society – governments, economies, every kind of institution - it is essential that we consider, resurrect and reinvent as many of these historical indigenous practices, these wisdom filled traditions, as much and as soon as possible. Time is pressing. The United Nations, not a body known for its extreme radicalism, says we have ten years left before we descend into irreversible disaster.

This is an unusual book. You will see quotes from filmed interviews I have done with my teachers. Some of these quotes have been edited slightly to fit this new context. You will see me dialoguing with, responding to, and in some cases contradicting or being contradicted by my teachers' quotes. Sometimes these quotes are self-sufficient; they stand alone in their brilliance. Sometimes you will hear some of my teachers' stories intertwined with mine. You will see parts of my own films, blogs, talks, essays and curriculum guides interwoven with new writing. If you do nothing more than investigate further some of the teachings of these wise and remarkable women and men, I will consider my job well done.

Along with those quoted and named teachers, I draw on a wealth of resources from those only sparsely quoted or altogether unnamed: Carl Jung, Joseph Campbell, Robert Moore, Robert Bly, Mircea Eliade, Malidoma and Sobonfu Some, Gigi Coyle, Jack Zimmerman, Joan Halifax, Martin Prechtel, Louise Carus Mahdi, Steven Foster, Rabbi Goldie Milgram, Luis Rodriguez, Howard Thurman and so many more. My role, as I see it, is to take some of their wisdom and distill it into the why and the how of ROP - what's actionable in this day and this time, in these circumstances and why it's necessary.

In some ways it's a fool's errand to even try to write about these things. There are no codes. There are no rules. Initiation and mentorship are not science. This is art. It requires creativity. The very notion of an ROP handbook is, in effect, a contradiction in terms, an oxymoron. In the course of this reading, there are many times when I say, "It is effective to do it this way. But it is also effective to do it the other way." Seeming inconsistencies abound. ROP success can only be measured by the result, not by the path taken. Is the individual truly transformed? As I discuss in Chapter Three, rituals are not ceremonies. They don't work by prescription the way recipes do. At the end of Chapter Two I point out various ways and means of recognizing ROP success. If Initiates have a new sparkle in their eyes, walk with greater confidence, smile and laugh more easily, speak in more measured, thoughtful tones, that is success. Transformation has begun.

This book generalizes. It makes broad statements about human beings. This is ironic since one of the book's great themes is discovering and appreciating the uniqueness of each individual. Wherever I've made a grand generalizing statement, I've tried to temper it with some of the circumstances I know that work against it. So, there is a "Yes, but…" quality, a back and forth, to much of what you'll read here.

The chapter headings have limited utility. There are subjects I address in almost every chapter that might have easily been placed in a different one. It's hard to separate these things. Many of the distinctions I have made, incorporating a given subject in one chapter but not another, are somewhat arbitrary. Community and Mentorship are deeply interwoven. Parents and Initiating Teens are almost two sides of the same coin; they could have been written about together. But I chose to separate these various subjects, these different categories of understanding, because I wanted the book to be maximally useful to you, the reader. Not everyone will read the book cover to cover. I broke the subjects down into easily distinguishable categories for those readers pressed for time or with limited interest.

As you've already seen, I use the term initiation synonymously with Rites of Passage. For ease and variation, I also use the acronym ROP interchangeably with Rites of Passage. When I do, please note that it can denote either a single Rite of Passage or multiple Rites of Passage. I also capitalize the term and other key related terms to clearly distinguish my meaning from everyday usage. "Elder," for example, is often capitalized to differentiate it from "elder." There's a real difference between maturing enough to share deep wisdom in a generative way versus simply growing old.

There's a clear gender binary quality to this book: he/she; man/woman. I apologize to those who identify as non-binary. This book is addressed primarily to the vast majority of people who don't live in that world. Meanwhile, I'm working hard to get educated and up to speed on non-binary issues.

Even though I typically refer to "masculinity" in the singular, I also appreciate how there are many different "masculinities." One size does not fit all. When I talk about "Mature Masculinity" in Chapter Three, I fully recognize that the qualities I describe may only apply to myself and the many men I know (nonetheless including gay and transgender male friends). I've spent a lifetime trying to re-appropriate the terms "man" and "masculinity" away from the John Wayne model I grew up with, toward something richer and far more rounded - what I know to be good and true and noble about men. But I fully accept that those definitions and terms may be restrictive and inapplicable for others.

This is not a book about religion, though it occasionally addresses specific religious practices and traditions. Does religion make for an important ingredient in many different ROP? Absolutely. Do religious rituals positively impact Initiates and enrich their life journeys? Most often, yes. But I see applicable religious practices as a subset of ROP. I see ROP as more broad and more universal. Here, all beliefs and non-beliefs are welcome. The aim is to appeal to those who presently practice religion as well as those who have been put off by religion. The focus is on everyday modern *culture*, how there's still room in our hectic lives for sacred ritual, with or without the overlay of religion.

I'm also clear that this book is directed mostly toward Caucasian people of a higher-class standard with educational privilege. In many ways, they are the people most in need of ROP. They're also the ones largely privileged enough to have the time and money to contemplate what ROP might do for them and their families. Unless I specifically mention indigenous people and their historical practices, most of the cultural assumptions made here are "the Global North" - people largely of the Northern Hemisphere, or of the so-called "West," of the so-called "Modern World." Primarily countries that are more technologically advanced, where the standard of living is higher, like Western Europe, Canada, the U.S., Iceland, Japan, South Korea, Singapore, Australia and New Zealand. I am not addressing 50% or more of the world's population who survive on $2 a day or less. Not because they don't deserve ROP, but because they're more likely to still have them in place. Those cultures are far more likely to be much closer to their indigenous roots.

Even in the U.S., most low-income and people of color already have a deep sense of community because they have to rely on supportive friends, neighbors and family to survive. Many already know firsthand the extremely limited capacity of the so-called "nuclear family." They know that real thriving occurs only with extended family. Many deeply spiritual or religious people already understand the need for ROP for young people because their community already provides it. Many LGBTQ folks understand their strength is in numbers because their very survival may depend on it.

The focus of much of my life's work has been on teen initiation and Mature Masculinity. But I wanted to write a handbook that would be useful for all the genders (and, with any luck, maybe even non-binary genders), throughout all the different phases in a normal human lifespan. So even though there is a direct focus on teens in Chapter Two and boys becoming mature men in Chapter Three, I hope the book will prove valuable to anyone at any point in their life's journey.

200 or more years ago, this book never would have been necessary. These practices would have been so deeply woven into the culture, into all cultures, that no one would even question them because everyone would already know them. They would be as fundamental to life and as natural as breathing. Now we live in a time of cultural depletion, when it's urgently necessary to call forth and name what previously were commonplace understandings. In 100 years, or hopefully sooner, this book will be of no value whatsoever because people everywhere will have long rediscovered and successfully reinstated these practices and, like crowds pointing at the sky in recognition of coming rain clouds, everyone will simply nod and say, "Of course."

Preface

We live in a culture that could be characterized by the absence of the sacred. Our education, our business, our healthcare, our transportation, our media and entertainment most often lack a sense of connection to the vast, tender, powerful, mysterious, sacred nature of life.

And even when we have a personal brush with the sacred, when someone near us dies, when we take special time in the high mountains or connect with a moving work of art or are present for the birth of a new child, the compelling sense of sacred mystery can quickly fade as we resume our quotidian chores.

This absence is exacerbated by our divisive political discord, our racial and economic divisions and injustice, by our unattended trauma, both individual and collective.

Yet underneath, when we get quiet and honest, there is in almost everyone, a longing for deeper connection: to our self, to the earth, to the community around us, to life.

This deep connection to the sacred, and to your own unique gifts and courageous place in the world is what *Rites to a Good Life*, and Rites of Passage reminds you is possible.

My own high school and university education did not provide this, nor did it help me learn to handle my own fears and pain, longing and love. Somehow I knew I needed this. I volunteered for the Peace Corps and then in my early 20s, I ordained as a Buddhist monk in a remote Thai forest monastery near the borders of Laos and Cambodia. With ocher robe and shaved head, every morning at dawn I would walk barefoot for miles to collect alms food offered by lay supporters from poor local villages.

I learned to trust that there would be enough food, that I would not starve.

I learned to steady myself in meditation amidst the monsoon rains and the tropical heat. I grew up and matured in ways that my Western education never offered.

In *Rites To a Good Life*, Frederick Marx shows us the possibility of finding this transformation and courage in our own culture. The text is filled like a banquet with rituals, stories, medicines, quotes and models, recipes for genuine growth and transformation.

Sometimes these rituals focus on grief, as the Elder Mircea Eliade tells us, "…tears are required for sacred space to appear." Other times they focus on joining the community in movement. The playwright Moliere explains, "All the ills of mankind, all the tragic misfortunes that fill the history books, all the political blunders, all the failures of the great leaders have arisen merely from a lack of skill at dancing."

While a collective process, often these rituals of initiation and Rites of Passage also require time alone, difficult trials, testing of limits, facing oneself. They all require strong and steady mentors. All our children need them, the children in the poorest and most marginalized communities who deal with the deadly streets, and the prosperous children who deal with the deadly white fog of the suburbs. All need to be initiated and mentored, their gifts seen, honored and acknowledged.

Rites to a Good Life is a call for us all to reflect on our own personal journey and its place in the culture and cosmos around us. It is not just for our youth. We need the gifts of these Rites at every stage of life and we need ways to continually renew our connection to our deepest purpose and the sacredness of life.

I hope this book inspires you to do so.

Read it slowly, take notes, turn down the corners of pages, let it be a reflection, and inspiration, a mirror held up to your own journey. And then take the medicine of Rites of Passage and meaningful Ritual, and bring it alive in your life.

Many blessings,
Jack Kornfield, Spirit Rock Center 2020

Other Works by Frederick Marx

Other books by Frederick Marx

At Death Do Us Part

Films by Frederick Marx

Veterans Journey Home (a five part series)

- *Kalani's Story*
- *Leaving it on the Land*
- *Solutions*
- *On Black Mountain*
- *Ben's Story*

Rites of Passage
  The Tatanka Alliance
  The World as it Could Be is Within Reach
  All Must Be Documented!
  Journey from Zanskar
  Boys to Men?
  The Unspoken
  Joey Skaggs: Bullshit & Balls
  A Hoop Dreams Reunion
  Hoop Dreams
  Higher Goals
  Inside/Out

Hiding Out for Heaven
Dreams from China
House of UnAmerican Activities
Dream Documentary

Introduction

When a culture doesn't provide formal Rites of Passage or initiations, people find their own. Or they don't find them and never really find the traction of their life. And when a society or culture doesn't attempt to create circumstances in which that can be worked on creatively, then you get usually destructive versions of them. **Michael Meade**

I think the greatest crime of the last two centuries has been the countless millions of children who have been brought into this world but never taught to discover their unique purpose in this life.

In the past, in villages across cultures and around the globe, it was common to be taught why you were here, what your purpose was and how you could best contribute to your community. That was an automatic part of growing up. You were taught those things at your initiation into adulthood. And you were supported by your peers and Elders in making necessary adjustments as you grew older and your life circumstances changed.

In the modern world at the dawn of the industrial age, purpose was largely confined to what Karl Marx called "wage slavery." Children were raised to work in the factories. If they were schooled at all, (many went to work before they reached the age of ten), they were schooled in ways that maximized their value to become the administrative class: clerks and shop attendants, bureaucrats and accountants. The lucky ones worked on farms or learned crafts with their skilled artisan parents. They were lucky because, even though the work was extremely difficult, they were being mentored by their parents and others, learning useful skills. They were also lucky because their long apprenticeships doubled as Rites of Passage, initiating them into a greater measure of economic self-sufficiency and bequeathing them intimate knowledge of the rights and responsibilities of adulthood.

In the modern world we inhabit today, young people are largely abandoned by their elders and their community, left trying to figure out for themselves who they might be in their deepest essence and what unique gifts are theirs to share. The result? We have a worldwide teen crisis on our hands. It is estimated that the costs to society for teen dysfunctions – both behavioral and medical – is close to $500 billion per year in the US alone.[1] Pregnancy and STDs, school dropouts, drug and alcohol abuse, violence against self and others, including cutting, rape, and suicide, gang violence and gang crime, property crime and theft, traffic accidents, depression, ADD, ADHD, anorexia, bulimia, overeating and Type 2 diabetes. This is not an exhaustive list; it goes on and on.

Why do teens do this? Is it because they're inherently bad? Is it just bad parenting? No. Though family, genetics and biology can predispose certain people to some of these dysfunctions, all of them have a strong, if not decisive, cultural determinant. It's because teens unconsciously push against the confines of their own bodies, the rules of parents and society, and the capacity of their own minds and willpower to discover the true limits of their potential. They also have "shadows,[2]" the unconscious stories they tell themselves about who they are that fuel the coping mechanisms they adopt in order to survive a dysfunctional culture. They must become acquainted with those shadows. If they don't, they will act out and become a danger to themselves or others. They need to be initiated into adulthood.

And that's just teens. The cost to society for not supporting *all* humans through *all* the passages in their lives is immeasurable – into parenthood and

---

[1] As estimated by Andy Mecca, founder of the California Mentoring Foundation.

[2] "Shadow" is a term first coined by psychologist Carl Jung to characterize our human blind spots. It comprises all the things we hide, repress, and deny – all the dark truths about who we are. It can also be called our "Limiting Beliefs:" 'I'm not loveable. I don't deserve happiness. I'm better than everyone else. I must be perfect." There are hundreds of forms. *All* human beings have shadows. *If people have no awareness of their shadows they will be ruled by their unconscious fears and appetites.*

family making, into career building and making an occupational mark, into Eldership and the inevitable decline of the body, into illness and eventual death. Stop and consider the costs of all the dysfunctional behaviors that exist in the world. Warfare and addictions are only two of the top ten. When life gets hard and there is no effective instruction on how to deal with challenges, humans naturally turn to acting out or self-medicating. A friend of mine says that life affords us two choices: initiation or addiction. I think that's an overstatement but there is some truth there.

My own journey on the path of the Mature Masculine began when I was nine. My father died suddenly of a heart attack when he was 41 years old. I was in shock. On our way to the funeral, my uncle put his hand on my bony shoulder and said, "Well, Freddy, you're the man of the house now."

Nowadays we might laugh at the inappropriateness of such a statement. But his words didn't seem inappropriate to me. I wanted to be that man, to care for my mother, older sister and younger brother. I wanted to live up to that responsibility. I thought my father's untimely death and my uncle's recognition somehow combined to anoint me a man. It would be many years before I understood the childish conceit of that idea. I was no more a man than my sister or brother or mother. But that moment planted a seed in me, one that would continue germinating throughout my lifetime. How to become the man of integrity and honor I yearned to be? How to hold responsibility for the wellbeing of those I love? What, in fact, does it mean to become a man?

Throughout my teen years, I drank, did drugs, and somehow managed not to physically harm others or inadvertently kill myself. But no men materialized to show me how to become that man. Coaches, neighbors, relatives, certainly not my uncle. No one offered me that much needed mentorship. No one offered me a pathway to manhood, an initiation. Though I had good friends and a supportive social circle, I felt alone, hermetically sealed by the silence I couldn't articulate and the need I couldn't name.

This book is partly the logical product of my personal and professional work to understand my own adolescent life and others'. It is also an exercise in active mentorship, reaching out to "father" those who themselves may never have been fathered, whether at all or effectively, which is to say, many of us.

This book also aims to play a small part in our planetary initiation. An initiation that accesses and re-empowers the wisdom of Elders and unleashes and empowers the capacities of youth. I aspire to activate readers, regardless of age and station in life, to begin to co-create Rites of Passage and mentorship programs for people in their own communities. I offer many practical rituals for healthy and wholesome living. You will find them throughout, but there are helpful lists in the back of each chapter titled "What You Need to Do *Now*" along with space for taking notes. I nod in gratitude to Dane Zahorsky who first drafted some of these ideas with and for me in the "ROP Toolkits" that my company Warrior Films published some few years ago.

I hope to elevate teen initiation from the counter-cultural underground into the international mainstream. The big goal? **Every person on the planet receives the mentoring and Rites of Passage they need in order to fulfill their greatest human potential.**

1

The Story of Rites of Passage

My father said, "This whole thing about life, in the end, is going to end up as stories, so you have to create stories, you have to create memories for your children." I celebrate him every day because without him, the Rites of Passage program that I run wouldn't have even started. Although he's now passed on, he was there every step of the way and helped mold my program, be my wisest counselor and advisor, and up to today, I know that he's always guided it. So, when I had my son, I gave my son my father's name." **Chike Nwoffiah**

What follows is the "Half Boy Story," as told in a live presentation by Michael Meade, and slightly edited. According to him, the tale originated in Borneo about 10,000 years ago.

Once upon a time, once in the old time, when people had time, once before time got captured and put into little circles and got strapped to people's wrists. Once, when time would flow more like a river than tick like a clock, once back in those times, there was a village. In the village there was a woman who became a mother. She became a mother by giving birth to a child. It was her first child that she gave birth to and so it was the first time she became a mother. But I have to tell the truth about this child. I have to tell the whole story of the child because the child that was born to that mother was really only half of a child. The child that was born was a half boy.

What I mean to say is there was a left foot and there was a left leg and there was the left side of the body and there was the left shoulder and the left arm and there was the left side of the head and there was the left eye looking out from the left side. But on the right side where you would expect all of the same things to be, there was nothing, and maybe because of that the child came into the world weeping and crying and maybe because it was only half of a child and maybe because it was lamenting so seriously people didn't like to look at it and so they moved away. And when the people moved away that half boy lamented all the louder and screamed all the more. And maybe because of that the people moved further away and because the people moved further away the half boy lamented even more wildly into the world.

And somehow, despite being half, that boy grew and as he grew his lament and his cry at the world also grew and eventually he reached the age that people call an adolescent, and I have to tell you at that point even his own family turned away from him and that caused him to lament all the more seriously. And then it occurred to him that if he stayed there in that village things would always be the same as they had been so far, people would always see him as that half boy and so it occurred to him to leave. And soon after that occurred to him, on the next day when the sun rose up in the east, the half boy gathered himself and went on his way out of the village.

He went towards the road that left the village and went out into the wide world and he pulled himself up to the line that separated the village where he was born from the wide world beyond, and I have to tell you that as he crossed that line and left the village, there was no one there to say goodbye. There was no one there to wish him well. There were no people there to stand and sing the songs the way people used to when a girl or a boy left the village to go out into the world and find themselves. There was no one there at all and so the half boy dragged himself across that line and out onto the roads of the world and he dragged himself down the road the way a half person dragged themselves through life and he was going along in that way - for a short time, for a long time, for whatever time it was - when he came upon another road that crossed the road he was on and the road that crossed in front of him was made of water. What people called a river.

And so the half boy dragged himself up onto the banks of the river. And there on the banks of the river he looked down along the bank and he saw something coming towards him, down the riverbank, and so he squeezed his one eye down hard and looked as best he could and as he looked that thing that was coming towards him was growing larger. And pretty soon he could make out that it was another person coming towards him, although actually as he looked he could see it was another half person coming towards him. That is to say the person coming along had a right foot and a right leg and the right side of the body and the right shoulder and the right arm coming out of that shoulder and the right side of the head in which there was a right eye and the right eye was looking right at him and he was looking back with his left eye and pretty soon the right half was coming up close to the left half and you may think that because one was the right half and one was the left half that they immediately joined together and lived happily ever after. But this is not that kind of story.

When the right half came in proximity of the left half the two of them began to argue; the two of them began to struggle. They entered into a heated conflict so much so that the conflict that they began raised up the dust of the earth and began to obscure even the brightness of the sun. And pretty soon in the intensity of this struggle these two halves, the one with the other, the two of them rolled right into the river and when they hit the water of the river, the intensity and heat of their conflict caused the river itself to boil up and pretty soon wave piled upon wave, and at the peak of the waves there developed a foam where the waves, heated up, met with the air. And then after a while the waves subsided and the river began to grow quiet and after a time, the river flowed the way it does any day in the world and if you arrived at that point and looked around there would be no evidence of the half boy, the left half or the right half. There was nothing but the flowing of the river through the earth.

Down in the bottom of the water again, the right half and the left half had conflicted so seriously. They had fallen into the deep waters of life and disappeared from the sight of the world like young people that disappear into a detention center or fall into addiction or wind up doing some secret behavior that no one knows about. And after a time - a short time or a long time, nobody knows - the river began to boil up again and waves began to pile on top of waves and soon enough from those waves in the river there came a boy. It was the half boy coming back from the depths of the water. Only now he had a left side and a right side.

Now he had a left half and the right half. But because this was new - to be looking at the world with two eyes - and because it was new to be going on the earth with the left foot and a right foot, the half-boy, turned whole, was disoriented and he was stumbling about. He was confused, not knowing how to act or what to do. And it was while he was in this state of stupefaction and confusion that it happened that he saw a village nearby and so he began to stumble in the direction of the village. And as he approached the village he could see that there was an Elder sitting right on the edge of the village with one foot inside the line of the village and the other foot outside the village and he stumbled up to the old person and said "Listen, I've been in a huge conflict. I've been in a great battle. I fell into the river and now that I've come out, I'm not sure where I am. I don't know where I've come to. I don't know this place that I'm at."

The Elder sitting there said, "I can tell you exactly where you are. I can tell you where you have arrived. You have come back to the place where you started from. You have come back to the very village where you began. And I can tell you this also: no one has been dancing in the village since you left. But if you and I were to enter the village dancing together, you with your youth and me with my years, if we were to enter dancing together then the whole village would begin to dance again. Would you try it?" So, the half boy said, "What the heck. I'll do it!"

And so the two of them entered the village, the half boy doing those kinds of pretty, quick-stepping, high-leaping things that young people will do on the occasion when they find themselves with two feet and the Elder doing those kind of I'm-going-to-keep-this-going-slow-because-I-hope-to-last-out-the-whole-night-and-live-a-long-life kind of steps. Entering the village with those two dances going on, just as the Elder said, caused everybody to pay attention and pretty soon people were coming out and it was the children of course who joined the dance first because they loved something as exciting as that.

And after a while, the old people began to dance, remembering how life dances even inside the old collapsing bodies, and after a while the adults – giving up the deep concern over taxes being due the next day – they came out and danced too. And then finally, last of all, the rest of the youth, realizing that this was an unusual occasion, came out and they began to dance as well. The entire village all danced together and they danced all night long in a delight of dancing. And some people say they're still dancing now. And other people say, that actually, after a night of dancing everyone was tired. And it happened then that a young woman was about to give birth to a child and it was the first child that she was going to give birth to and when the child was born, she became a mother at that moment. But it also was said that she gave birth to half of a child and that child entered the world screaming and crying and perhaps because of that, the people forgot their dance and they all decided to look away and that caused the child to scream louder and louder and the rest of the story you can imagine.

Myself? I think that both things are true. I think somewhere just beyond the line of the usual attention of the culture there is a whole village that is all dancing together and I also think that each day there *are children born that are seen only as half and have to cry their way into the world. That's how it seems to me. I'm not sure. My only job is to tell the story the way I learned it. To tell the story the way the old people told it when they first started telling this story and tried to educate or offer some knowledge through the story. And tell me this: If those old people don't know something about dancing, something about being half and half in life, if they don't know, tell me this, who does?*

Our world is made of stories. The stories we hear as babies and toddlers, the stories we read as children, the stories we tell ourselves as teens and young adults about how the world works, and, throughout our aging, the stories we tell ourselves about how our lives have gone.

Stories teach us what we need to learn about life. Stories awaken in us the understanding of where we've been and where we need to go. Stories call out to our lives and say, "I know you, friend. Come with me…"

Narrative is what makes meaning possible. Isolated facts and data points have no particular relevance unless and until they're woven into story. No stories are more important to me than stories containing the archetype of initiation, of Rites of Passage. Many of the world's best and most popular stories do: The Odyssey, The Mahabharata, the Bible, and King Arthur, to name a few. Stories mentor.

All the world's key spiritual and religious figures had their own Rites of Passage. Jesus fasted for 40 days and nights in the Judean desert before undertaking his life ministry. The Buddha sat under the Bodhi tree for 49 days and nights (some say six, some say three) before realizing enlightenment and undertaking his life's teachings. The Prophet Muhammad, peace be upon him, withdrew regularly to a cave called Hira for days of fasting and prayer before receiving his first divine revelation and eventually undertaking his ministry. Although they are rarely thought of as Rites of Passage, these are some of the best known and most widespread stories in the world. They serve as models not only for achieving liberation, but also for realizing one's life purpose.

But stories can also be prisons. They can trap us into thinking only in predetermined ways about what life can be. All too often the stories that we tell ourselves about how our lives have gone fit this notion. "It has always been thus, so it will certainly be that way again…" Not every story is a good story, one that's productive and conducive to human growth. It is important to sound this note of warning before we continue. We must become discriminating listeners to discern whether a story serves our ongoing lives with wholesome openness and flexibility or entraps us into repeated patterns, which are all too often negative ones.

> *You can never tell the same story twice. You can't get it again, as the storyteller you can't say it with the same words, and the same emphasis. As the listener you can't hear it the same way ever again. And so, a story is a unique thing, and our rituals are the same. You can never do a ritual the same way.* **Jim Horton**

ROP can most simply be defined as an intentional, transformational shift from one phase of life to the next. I think of them as cultural ceremonies and rituals that actuate and/or commemorate life passages. The term was first coined by cultural anthropologist Arnold Van Gennep in his 1909 book of the same name, *Rites of Passage*. Most "modern" people believe transitions just happen naturally. Biology drives them and at some point, children automatically become adolescents, teens inevitably evolve into adults, adults inexorably age into Elders, and Elders eventually die. Yes and no. Physiological shifts will occur naturally in the human body. But they are not all that can or will drive transformation from one human life stage to another. Biology is not sufficient for accomplishing psychodynamic change. The *quality* of those changes, even the transition into death, is determined not by biology but by the practices of culture and community. If the psyche doesn't shift along with the human body then humans will remain locked or suspended in "immature" states of being - states that will suspend their passage into the next human growth phase.

There are a minimum of seven key passages in the average person's normal human lifespan:

1. Birth
2. Baby to childhood
3. Childhood to puberty
4. Adolescence to young adulthood
5. Young adulthood to middle age (sometimes defined by parenting)
6. Middle age to Eldership
7. Eldership to death

Some would argue there are more. Certainly, there are key transitions in the average human life that can begin a Rite of Passage: getting married, becoming a parent, dealing with extreme illness, losing a loved one. All of these passages are best accomplished through a conscious recognition of the transition, the support of community and application of appropriate ritual. I refer you, dear reader, to the elegance and depth of Bill Plotkin's work, particularly *Nature and the Human Soul*, should you want to learn more about these stages.

> *I saw again and again in studies of indigenous cultures it wasn't that they created ceremonies to impose something on people. Instead, it was seeing these life transitions and seeing natural changes that happen in humans as we grow and as we die and as we're born, and recognizing that they needed ceremonial ways to help guide what was already happening. I don't understand why it is that the human psyche so desperately needs ceremonial markings, but it is like magic. It's one of the things that we have taken out of our culture.* **Meredith Little**

That's our task in a nutshell. To recognize all the life transitions that someone is going through and fashion accompanying rituals to sear the meaning of that shift into their soul. By acquainting humans with and keeping them in alignment with their soul's purpose, doing so might not only save the individual, as they learn to live out that purpose in the public sphere, it could help save the planet.

I like this more elaborate definition of ROP from David Blumenkrantz. Though written only for ROP involving youth, the definition works equally well for any life stage.

> *The degree to which a series of activities are a Rite of Passage is directly proportional to a community's acceptance and participation in the activities, and the youth's perception and belief in the activities as fulfilling their conscious and unconscious needs for transformative experiences. That is, a modern-day Rite of Passage is achieved when parents and the community create and participate in experiences that are perceived to be transformative by youth and, in fact, offer them increased status within the community and facilitate their healthy transition through adolescence.* **David Blumenkrantz**

The practices of ROP across time are too numerous to begin to list, but here are a few examples of ROP from adolescence to young adulthood that have survived into the modern day. Certainly, you will learn of others as you read this book.

- Vision Quest or Sun Dance (Native American).
- The big game hunt (traditional for some African peoples).
- Adult male circumcision (also traditional for some African peoples).
- Hitting a wasps' nest with a stick and paying the price (Kayapo people of northern Brazil).
- Capturing and taming a wild reindeer (Nenets people of Northern

Siberia).
- Climbing giant trees to retrieve honey from bees nests (Baka people of Central Africa).
- Jumping on the backs of wild bulls (Hamar people of Ethiopia).
- Monastic retreat (Asia). It's common in Thailand for young men, usually aged 19, to spend a year in a Buddhist monastery, shaving their heads, wearing robes and devoting every day to service.
- Mormon Missionary Service. People younger than 25 usually serve for 1-2 years in a foreign land.

It's possible to recreate ROP through powerful workshops like the ManKind Project's (MKP)[3] New Warrior Training Adventure (NWTA), intentional communities like Pacific Quest, wilderness experiences like Outward Bound and camps like ReTribe.

> *I think about young men on the island of Vanuatu. They tie vines to their ankles after erecting this tall scaffolding out of logs. Then they climb to the top and jump off. The test is can they actually tie those vines and make them just long enough that they're tucking their head and brushing their shoulders on the ground. But not too long, right? Not any more on the ground than that because they're diving off headfirst. To me that's an incredible test of bravery.* **Darcy Ottey**

The structural similarities of initiation rituals are universal and must involve a minimum of three distinct stages: Separation, Ordeal and Return. Separation usually entails the complete disruption of the person's ordinary life - the removal from everyday affairs, surroundings, and support, and the

---

[3] A non-profit organization founded in 1985, the Mankind Project is an adult men's ROP that has grown from a weekend workshop in Milwaukee, WI to an international organization located in 25 countries, spoken in ten languages, with over 80,000 men initiated.

re-placement into an isolated location, usually in nature. The Ordeal usually includes some test of physical stamina that induces a heightened emotional and psychological state. Initiates are instructed to seek an awakening to their life's purpose or mission, a revelation to their place in the order of things, an illuminated direction for their lives. Finally, the Return, usually led by Elders, reunites the Initiate with family and community. With Reintegration, the Initiate's newfound sense of purpose and emotional grounding now guides and deepens connection to family, community and society.

Let's take a closer look at each one. Separation, also called Severance or Descent, is about suspending the relationship the Initiate has with everyday life. The familiar is suddenly replaced by the wholly unfamiliar. All the trappings of daily life, all the creature comforts – the foods we like, the clothes we wear, the environs in which we eat, work and rest - are cut. All our habits are interrupted: of waking, exertion and sleep. All of our relationships - with parents, siblings, relatives, neighbors, friends, fellow students, co-workers - are disrupted. No more cell phones, computers, TV or video games; no more alcohol, tobacco, recreational drugs or sex; no more familiar bed, electric lights or toilets. Everything is upended. Familiar places are gone. Separation is complete from all the old patterns, habits and routines. In order to be introduced to the new we must first sever from the old.

> *Pacific Quest is remarkable in terms of the similarities with a traditional Rite of Passage. That image of men coming in the middle of the night and taking a young person. In Pacific Quest they're called Intervention Transporters.*
>
> *They come in the middle of the night and say, "Your parents have decided that you're going to go to this program in Hawaii and you need to come with me right now." I can only imagine what your typical American sixteen year old thinks in this day and age. When they've had no boundaries before and some big beefy man that they have never met comes and says, "You're coming with me and we're going to get on*

a plane and go to Hawaii." "No, I'm not fucking going with you." "Well, yeah, you are."

And then the young person flies across the Pacific Ocean to this island - the most remote landmass on the planet. I mean, that is a pretty profound Severance, you know, from their previous identity and everything they've known before.

And I'll say to the students, "You're dressed now in blue sweatpants and an orange fleece jacket, and eating this totally foreign food, and your phone's been taken away from you, and you're not going to see your friends for God knows how long. And, that's what's been happening to young people for millennia. And very few of your peers are going to have that experience."

It's an essential enactment of this profound human story of what's going on emotionally, even though it's not, for most kids in our culture, going on physically. They are being ripped away from their parents.
Darcy Ottey

For initiation to work, even our sense of time must shift. The Greeks had two different words for time: Chronos and Kairos. Chronos is the linear, "everyday" time that most modern people conceive of and think is the sole way to define and experience time. The 24-hour day, 52 weeks, 12 months, 365 days a year. But Kairos is an equally valid, wholly different way to define and experience time. *"Once before time got captured and put into little circles and got strapped on to people's wrists,"* as Michael Meade put it. Call it sacred, or cosmic, time: the time it takes for flowers to know when to bloom in Spring, the time it takes for a star to die, the time of a given human life, the time it takes for trees to know when to drop their leaves in Fall, the time for salmon to know when to return to the spawning ground, the time that opens during human experiences of mind-altering substances or in moments of great epiphany or insight, or in deep meditation.

Chronos and Kairos are not contradictory, they're complimentary. Chronos and Kairos are simultaneously ever-present. Our only task is to choose which one to tune in to. More accurately, since Chronos is the absolute norm in modern society, and too regular an experience or too strong a perception of Kairos can be grounds for institutionalization, the challenge before us is to create the proper framework and conditions, with the guidance of ritual Elders, for humans to experience Kairos. One of the functions of Separation, leaving Chronos behind, is to make the experience of Kairos possible.

Kairos is a defining characteristic of the middle stage of ROP, known as Ordeal, Trial, Challenge, Threshold or Liminal Space. The metaphoric twilight zone, *"Betwixt and Between"* as Louise Carus Mahdi, Steven Foster, and Meredith Little put it in their book of the same name. Initiates should get some taste of Kairos. It's that time between worlds, the known and unknown, the sacred and profane, the mundane and the mysterious. The time between life and death.

An essential component of this middle stage of Ordeal is some kind of physical challenge. That physical challenge in turn generates an emotional, psychic and/or spiritual test. It can be fasting. It can be hunting a lion with a spear. It can be practicing silence and meditating for weeks. It can be taking psychotropic substances or drinking great quantities of alcohol in a safe, secluded environment guided by Elders, which is part of some Central American initiations. Whatever the proximate cause, we must take a journey to the underworld. We must enter into a new zone of being. We must confront the emotional baggage of the past, the wounds we received in childhood and continue to carry. We must question our life – all we have done and all we have yet to do. We must look death in the face and become familiar with it and all of our accompanying fears.

It's not a time to "make nice" or be "pretty." It's a time to get dirty and raw. It's a time of returning to fundamentals, to absolutes, of standing in the doorway between darkness and light, between good and evil, between on and off. Taking the measure of life's pulse and discovering it's probably more fragile than previously thought. That, in a myriad of ways, it can be taken from us in a second; yet paradoxically, also learning how life is stronger and more resilient than previously imagined. In the face of infinity, of endless time, of innumerable stars and planets in the sky, it's a time to recognize the complete and absolute insignificance of a single human life, and, again paradoxically, to awaken to the preciousness of every single human life and its limitless capacity to effect change, to make a difference for good in the lives of all beings, to bow with humility and stand up to serve the preciousness and wonder of this time, this place, this abundance. Ordeal insists we arrive at some understanding of how we are part of the fabric of life. An understanding that everything is connected to everything else, us no less, and that everything we do impacts others and that everything they do impacts us. It can be a dawning of the understanding of karma – the law of cause and effect. Every action we take, even every thought we think, has intended and unintended impacts that can reverberate throughout our lives and throughout the world in ways seen and unseen, perhaps for generations. The Ordeal can give us a taste of all that.

> *Everything in our egos, everything in our conscious makeup is going to want to resist change. Not everything, there's a part of us that is longing for this deeper connection with soul. But everything else says: "Don't rock the boat. I've got a good gig. It works. You know, I even make a living. People invite me to parties. DO NOT ROCK THE BOAT. Don't take the risk of losing everything." And then maybe there's an intermediate voice in us that says: "Well ok, maybe we can compromise here. Let's just hold on to this soul story lightly. But I'm not going to really let go of it, until I have the new story, and I feel like it's at least as good as the old story. Then I'll let go…" But it doesn't work that way; that's not the way initiation works. We have to go through this phase of the journey, which is The Liminal, betwixt, in-between stage, in which we are neither the old nor the new. And that takes a lot of courage and a lot of psycho-spiritual preparation, and for most everybody some pretty fierce ceremonies and practices to get that to happen.* **Bill Plotkin**

Most people will experience this trial as a mix of wonder and severe challenge, even extreme fright or horror. There is no telling what will arise for any given individual. The lessons we must learn are ours alone. But what is common for people is to return from ROP with a much deeper understanding of who they are, of where they have been and where they are going, of how mysterious and praiseworthy human life, and all life, is.

But we cannot and must not linger in this doorway. When our time is through, when our test is complete, we must quickly, consciously, even forcefully return to the overworld. If we don't, we risk becoming enraptured or injured. We might become entranced, stuck in the drama and mystery between worlds. We risk losing our lives or our minds.

This is a common problem with Veterans. Too many who return from service −especially, but not only, if there was combat involved − risk remaining psychically stuck in that war zone, perpetually entranced with the drama of war. When they physically return home, a handshake, a pat on the back, and "Good luck soldier! Thank you for your service!" are completely inadequate at accomplishing this transition. Even the military's transition programs, whether lasting one day or one week, where soldiers are taught how to get a job, find housing, reach out for counseling and medical care, open a checking account, etc., are woefully insufficient. What Veterans need are powerful rituals of Homecoming.

> *The journey of soul initiation does take several months at least, and probably a year or more in most cases. And for those who have gone through it in recent decades, in the Western world where there are so few Elders or initiators to help out, it's possible to get stuck in that initiatory journey, and spend the rest of one's life there, not quite being sure what is happening.* **Bill Plotkin**

Homecoming, also called Return or Incorporation, is the final stage of ROP and is just as essential as the others. We must return from our Ordeal to be embraced by our family, friends and community. We must tell our story, albeit in our own way and time, but with due intention. It is perhaps this ingredient of ROP that most underscores our interconnectedness, that, like the Lakota expression "Mitákuye Oyás'iŋ," we are indeed "all relations." The community must witness our passage story. Without it being told it can become toxic – a burden, a load too heavy to carry alone. Others must help shoulder the responsibility of all we have experienced – the good and the bad, because even the good can feel like too great a weight to carry alone, especially when those inspiring visions involve a call to leadership. It can be very lonely at the top and we need lots of help.

Telling our story in a safe, contained way, witnessed by non-judgmental, open-hearted people, especially Elders who can cogently reflect back to us what they've heard, is essential. That deeply compassionate witnessing accomplishes multiple ends. One is to relieve the burden of the Initiate carrying the weight alone. We need witnesses to hold the burden with us – in all its hardship and all its glory. That witnessing also allows Initiates to begin the process of transforming their experience into something positive. No less so with Veterans.

> *This is a practice traditional cultures did - ceremonially telling the warriors you acted in our name, for our protection. "I sent you; I paid the bills; I bought your bullets; you were acting in my name on my orders. Even if I disagreed with it, I'm responsible for you. So I willingly hear your story. I accept responsibility for your story. I carry your story as my own and I take the burden of blame and shame off you and willingly put it on my own shoulders. I will carry it as mine." And that transfer of responsibility lifts extraordinary burdens off our Veterans and you can see them change in the moment they hear civilians say this.*
> **Ed Tick**

No matter how shocking or horrible a Veteran's experience might be, it can become grist for the soul mill. In order to serve their future well-being, it *must* become grist for the soul mill. Future activities need to become living echoes of the horror they've suffered by directing all Initiates toward life and creation. The stories are legion of single Veterans returning to the families of their dead comrades and becoming surrogate fathers to the children of the deceased. In my own *Veterans Journey Home* film series, former Army Ranger Captain Matthew Griffin shares his vision of offering education to every woman in Afghanistan in order to help atone for his inadvertent killing of a woman and child. Former Marine Captain Kalani Creutzburg heals his own suicidal ideation and homelessness by founding a dog training sanctuary where other homeless Veterans come to live and work.

> *Veterans are the light at the tip of the candle, illuminating the way for the whole nation. If Veterans can achieve awareness, transformation, understanding and peace, they can share with the rest of society the realities of war. And they can teach us how to make peace with ourselves and each other, so we never have to use violence to resolve conflicts again.*
> **Thich Nhat Han**

Incorporation is also an essential part of Homecoming. We must incorporate our Ordeal experience. We must return to fully reinhabit the body. However far out we go during Ordeal, however liminal or transitory or otherworldly our experience, we must come back fully into this place and time, into Chronos. For the time being, we must leave the spirits, the visions, the animals and plants that spoke to us, the epiphanies, all behind. Without fully returning to everyday life, to the presence of the here and now, to living in and being grounded in the body, back in the mundane world, we are at risk of being disconnected, ethereal, spacey, dissociated or even crazy. Thank goodness the body has needs that must be tended to. It has to be fed, clothed, rested, emptied, toned and kempt. I myself know the challenge of this balance. I like to live in my head and explore exciting ideas for much of the day. Fortunately, the physical body calls me back to the demands of the physical world. This is necessary for maintaining equilibrium. Though we must maintain sensory memory of our threshold experience, of exactly how things felt – the fear, the hunger, the cold, the wetness, the loneliness – we must come back and fully inhabit our corporeal selves, resuming the simple patterns of everyday living.

Indigenous people understand that each human soul carries some unique skill or resource that benefits the community at large. The purpose of Homecoming is to begin to learn what each returning voyager carries in the way of good news for the collective. Some new insight they've acquired or skill they have passion for acquiring, some understanding of what might help the group, some vision of the future or valuable reframing of the past. There is some discrete area of human association that each individual is uniquely qualified to contribute to. They need to understand and to manifest leadership unique to them.

"Medicine" is the term Native Americans often use to refer to the unique gift that each soul carries. It's a beautiful term because it embodies the values of healthy community. No reasonably well-adjusted individual would ever withhold medicine from another. In their heart of hearts, most people want to do right by others. Sharing our medicine is how we do it. It's a two-part process. First, we connect to our raison d'etre, our fundamental reason for being. This makes us most fulfilled. We self-actualize. Second, and just as important, we must put that medicine at the service of our fellow creatures. Seeing how it impacts them, making their lives more fulfilled, more meaningful, better cared for and happy, we can then experience our greatest joy.

It astounds me how this basic truth is not taught in every family, school, religious institution and community group across the planet. Finding real and lasting happiness in life requires only one thing: putting our gifts at the service of other human beings. It's so simple! Seeing first hand that what matters most to us is of real use and value to others. We reduce their suffering. We observe how their happiness increases by virtue of our actions. Though it's not always easy to enact, it's not complicated. All we need to understand is where our gifts fit into the greater scheme. Rites of Passage help us identify that.

Everyone must come to know their place in the grand framework of community. Homecoming begins the process to help find it. In English, the phrase "know your place" immediately conjures up images of authority and subservience. As if feeling secure in the knowledge that one is where one belongs could only be determined hierarchically by receiving orders from above. It reveals how much of our language and culture is in fact determined by structures of power. But what we're referring to here is a more mysterious, even mystical brand of determination. Like figures in a mandala, each human being has a unique position to fulfill in relation to the creation of that perfect whole. The task of ROP is to help figure out what that position is so that the community remains in good balance, even in the midst of perpetual change. Each community needs to have its carpenters and plumbers, its teachers and shop owners, its doctors and herbalists, its artists and chefs, its gay people and transsexuals, its tricksters and priests - the entire rainbow of human manifestation and expression. There are no "misfits" because no matter how unusual a person's gifts, the presumption is that there's always a place those gifts are needed to complete the whole, to fulfill the mandala. The task of the community is to help each individual figure out where that is. Where is the perfect fit?

My friend Snake Bloomstrand says there are two fundamental questions that each guide must ask the Initiate: "What did you learn?" and "What are you going to do about it?" Related questions include: "How are you going to take action?" and "How are we all going to benefit?" Knowing the answers to these questions is especially crucial for young people. They must understand precisely how they are important and where, exactly, those gifts are most needed. They must have an abiding sense of "This is where I belong." Whether that place is a literal, geographic one, or a figurative one involving a path of apprenticeship and study. They must know in their bones "I can make a contribution here" and the community must be able to affirm it by saying, "Yes, we need that." This is the blueprint for belonging.

> *In parts of Africa, what they say is, 'In order to grow a bigger life, a person has to brush against death.' And some of the initiatory practices are severe enough that sometimes young people die. Actually die. And so it seems to me that to fashion something like that gets pretty serious... death is a real possibility.* **Michael Meade**

Death *is* a key component of ROP. Death, that thing that our culture hides and denies, is the very elixir we require in order to grow, to fully inhabit our lives. Initiates must open up to the possibility that during their Rite, they could die. In the past, Elders simply understood that some Initiates might die. Without the fear of death, in some form, the possibility of deep human transformation is minimal. Death helps drive the possibility of change. A tangible fear of death is necessary to fully acquaint human beings with the wonder of life. Fear by itself, and even more so the fear of death, heightens all of the senses. It deepens awareness. In the wake of dying, or possibly dying, the preciousness of all things crystalizes. Nothing can be taken for granted. Every rock, bush, speck of dust, blade of grass, bird, drop of water, breath and tear, cloud and star, becomes unique, irreplaceable and wondrous. Without this built-in appreciation for life, human beings start to take their own life and the lives of others for granted. All too often literally. The evidence of this gross misunderstanding is all around us. Just look at the huge numbers of suicides and murders. This is a monumental human error.

My late wife Tracy faced, and finally succumbed to the real thing. When we met in November 2002, she had experienced 11 months of surgery, chemo and radiation treatment for breast cancer. She knew her life would be short. It was the depth of her realization, and the beauty with which she carried it, walking each day with the fullest possible appreciation for the time she had, that attracted me to her. Our understanding of mortality was part of what drew us together. I proposed to her within four months of meeting. Partly because of the depth of her recognition of life's temporality, she extended her life another 13 years, many of them in a state of joy, even while living ten of those years with Stage IV Cancer.

The very cycle of life is dependent on death. Without death, there is no life. If it were not for dying plants and bugs and trees, the soil would not regenerate and bring forth new plants and bugs and trees. There's only so much room to go around on this planet, especially with the exploding human population. We need to die in order to make room for someone else. The same goes for resources. In the world we have now, most modern people assume they can consume any amount of the world's resources they choose as long as they have the money to pay for it. The average person in the "modern world" consumes 7-10 times his or her fair share of the earth's resources. The *average* person. But in a sustainable, sensible world, people would only consume as much as they know they can responsibly replace.

> *It is actually a very sacred act when you're growing your own food to be part of saying to an animal or to a bird or to a chicken, okay now is the time when mortality has come. We honor you. We always do it with prayer and with offerings. I think if young people actually were a part of that, they might actually grasp something about life and death that I think becomes very abstract in our society. Where, on the one hand, they're immersed in images of violence all the time where violence is made a game, where the video games are all about killing and shooting, where they are eager to join the military, some of them, because they think it's a great adventure. But where they never actually have to confront: what does it mean to have something that's alive one moment and dead the next? And what does that mean about death, that we're all going to have to face?* **Starhawk**

People of indigenous cultures often believe that when Initiates die during ROP it serves the greater good of the community. Perhaps something is unhealthy about those individuals. Perhaps sooner or later they would manifest destructive behaviors endangering everyone. For many of us in the West, in the modern world, ideas like that seem archaic, even heartless and cruel. Certainly, in our fearful and litigious world, safety at all costs is paramount and no loss of human life is acceptable. We do our best to create policies and protocols to mitigate against any form of accident or danger. But as the Buddha reminded us, there is no escaping all the sufferings of human life, including sickness, old age and death. We need only remember to appreciate how those frailties can awaken us to the preciousness of each lived moment. ROP help us do that and the fear of death is all that is required, not its actuality. Many people confuse the two.

> *It really began in the early 1970's when Steven [Foster] and I were working at the Suicide Prevention Center. I remember one night, when we were listening on the phone to people who were wanting to die and saying to each other, "You know, these people don't really want to physically die. They are trapped. They're caught and don't know how to transition into a new life phase or to make it good with what's happened."* **Meredith Little**

The Initiate's old self must meet a symbolic death in order to be reborn into something new. Without this symbolic death, nothing new is possible. For teens, their self-absorbed orientation to the world must die. "Me, me, me…" must be replaced by "Us, us, us…"

Introducing Initiates to the concept of bodily death acquaints them with the concept of "the eternal now" so they can appreciate the temporal preciousness of human life. It also teaches interdependence. Many modern ROP have some kind of a buddy system so participants look out for each other and become guardians of each other's safety. That's on the practical level. On the metaphysical level, it's common for Initiates to have an experience in which they realize how their life is deeply intertwined with others, whether family and friends, or those even further afield.

Our lives are made possible to a very real degree by those around us. To take the most extreme undesirable proof, consider how we take for granted that the strangers around us won't suddenly pull out guns and shoot us simply because they want to. The fact that mass random shootings occur more and more frequently, at least in the U.S., can deepen our appreciation of all the times random strangers choose not to murder us. At a more positive extreme, consider how our food, water, clothes, electricity, sewage and garbage collection, mail delivery and so much more depend on other human beings, most of whom are total strangers. ROP deepens our understanding of this interdependence.

I've never served in the military. One of the things that I respect most about Veterans is their commitment to one another. They have each other's backs. Not in a superficial way. If necessary, they stand ready to sacrifice their life for their buddy. Similarly, they know their own life is dependent on those in their squad. The depth of the trust and the bond they share is unique and beautiful to witness, especially for an outsider. The experience of mutual dependence has been drilled into their bones. It is a lesson that mainstream society can largely learn only through ROP.

One of the things I love most about my work with the ManKind Project (MKP) is the analogous role it has played in my life. Though we've never faced the kinds of trials that men and women in uniform have, those of us who are veterans of MKP have our own unique camaraderie and bonds. Those of us who might call ourselves Elders in this work have been through many of our own trials. When we sit around and "shoot the shit," what we often delight about each other's company is the sharing of our "war stories."

This soul connection was underscored early in my experience of this work through my friend Marty Feldman. Marty and I met during MKP's NWTA[4] in October 1995. We then sat together in a downtown Chicago men's support circle we call an I-group. In one of those early circles, Marty revealed to the nine of us that he had cancer and would likely not live very long. "You guys are going to be the ones to bury me," he said. He had a very young son at the time and it meant everything to Marty that the men in his circle would be there for his son and his family when he died. I felt

---

[4] NWTA stands for New Warrior Training Adventure. The New Warrior Training Adventure is a modern day Rite of Passage that the ManKind Project organized for men looking for an effective, pro-social initiation into Mature Masculinity. Over 80,000 men have participated in the NWTA to date.

privileged to accept some of that responsibility.

For adults, it might not be the fear of actual death that drives them through ROP. They might need to kill the notion of possessing something precious, to grieve the loss of a particular job, house, lifestyle, body, bank balance, relationship or partner. "I can't believe he fired me." "I can't believe they took our house." "I can't believe I lost millions in the stock market today." "I can't believe I put on 40 pounds." "I can't believe I, of all people, have diabetes." Those last words are the very ones that came out of my mouth when I was diagnosed with Type 1 diabetes at 41. "Why is this happening to me?!" I groaned. I was fit and slender. I couldn't believe it. Yet there it was. It took me about five years to fully accept it. I first had to go through a long process of fighting it through diet, more exercise, and alternative treatments before finally sinking fully into the grief and acceptance and accomplishing this particular ROP. That was around the time I met Tracy. My sense of mortality, combined with hers, helped bind us together. Without it, I'm not sure I would have been mature enough to recognize the tremendous gift that she was.

> *We don't even have an understanding of what a Rite of Passage is, and grief is a huge Rite of Passage. And so, you begin to think that you're crazy, you're not doing it right. Just with the understanding of what a Rite of Passage is, it makes people feel, "Oh, what I'm feeling is right and just keep going." And to have a culture to offer a meaningful way to help guide that energy would make such a difference.* **Meredith Little**

The old maxim that the truth will set you free is true. We have to be willing to turn, face and acknowledge the truth of our lives if we ever expect to live with comfort and ease. This means facing all the horrible things done to us as children. This means no longer protecting our abusers, sustaining the lie that "Everything is fine. There's no dysfunction in our house."

I was sexually abused as a kid. Admitting that for the first time in my life when I was in my first year of college, my whole life shifted. I never questioned any of the violence that I saw happening in the neighborhood because ultimately it meant to question the violence that I had experienced in my own household. And I didn't have language or the courage to do so. But when I exposed that deep secret, I learned it gives others permission to do the same. It creates kind of an opportunity for sacrament. And sacrament is the absolving of the sting that's connected to the transgression, so that one can actually do the proper analysis and inquiry without all the emotions that are connected to it. Once I exposed that secret, it set me on a whole journey: the experience of discovering the gift in the wound. **Aqeela Sherrills**

During natural disasters like the recent worldwide outbreak of COVID-19, it's common to hear people in denial. "This can't be happening," or, "This shouldn't be happening." Believe it. It's real. It's life reminding us we're not in control. ROP is exactly that kind of rupture with the "real world." Without this symbolic death, this dramatic shift in worldview, often brought about by shocking loss, by grief, losing what we had or wanted, our lives can never be re-contextualized, redirected. We must open to the possibility that this new reality is an opportunity to learn something different, for our own wellbeing, for our ascension to the next stage in our life, for our soul's growth. Without this letting go no growth is possible.

What I've since learned from living with diabetes is what a gift it is to be reminded how I have to stay awake 24/7, to monitor not only my blood sugar levels, but everything I eat. I must maintain vigilance. I tend to get lazy and want to go to sleep, literally and figuratively. My diabetes calls me back to perpetual awareness and attention. "Stay awake! Stay awake! Check your blood sugar!" My life is especially fleeting and deserves constant attention and care.

Our world today is in dire circumstances. Much of the exploitation, environmental destruction, racism, sexism and warfare are a function of uninitiated people, especially men, acting out their suspended adolescence in positions of leadership. This kind of leadership is about domination. This domination, this dysfunctional leadership, is leadership from those, the uninitiated, who unconsciously act out their own fears, projecting all evil onto "the other." Witness most of the leaders who presently run the world. Most blame someone else, usually an outside group, for what's wrong.

We need leaders who understand that real leadership starts with owning one's own projections and "shadows," facing first what is dark and scary *within* before looking outside. Real leadership is about service. Real leadership is conscious stewarding of the planet for the good of humanity. Real leadership is heart-full mentorship. It is not domination. Ultimately, initiation and mentorship are about creating this new kind of leadership – where all are leaders, servant-leaders, stewarding the planet for the good of all.

> *Our cultural and political leadership really suffers because a lot of those who are elected to high positions are not initiated into their own lives. And therefore, the decisions they make are often coming from the wrong place. And often they lack courage. That's something that you really see in modern leaders. They don't have courage for their own convictions. And they don't know how you sacrifice for something that is beyond your own interest, which is something that people used to learn from initiation.* **Michael Meade**

> *In a society where most people struggle with the goals of early adolescence - that's authenticity and social acceptance - we have people who don't achieve this deeper sense of identity, and so what they do instead is go after compensatory achievements. And for many people these compensatory goals are pathologically adolescent. Nothing wrong with adolescence, but it's kind of a patho-adolescence. They're compensatory goals like getting as wealthy as you can, getting as much control and power over others as you can. Winning in an aggressively competitive*

way, and having as many others lose as possible. Or another version of patho-adolescent goals is rescuing as many people as possible, rather than helping people develop their own strength and magnificence; having as many people be dependent on you as possible. **Bill Plotkin**

That we have an uninitiated President is something to think about. I have to contrast that all the time with Roosevelt. The number of intelligent decisions Roosevelt made during the war and the Depression. At the same time, Roosevelt had gone through his initiation; his legs were no goddamned good. And he went through an incredible amount of pain in order even to stand up.

The society with the greatest money in the world is being run by adolescents. That's heartbreaking. That indicates that you have more work to do than you would have imagined 20 or 30 years ago, when the lack of initiation is not noticed even in someone who is running for President. In a society that we call a primitive society, they would know immediately whether that man was initiated or not. And the women would know it. And they'd be horrified by some kid who wasn't initiated becoming a President. **Robert Bly**

What You Need To Do *Now*

For these questions, journal, write poems or stories, make any form of art that feels right for you to express your answers.
- What have your key life passages been? What extreme challenges have you faced, tossed up by circumstances beyond your control, that you have survived and learned something of significance from? The more you can bring these learnings into understanding your own life the more you will benefit. Make a simple list of the key lessons you learned from each trial. If you cannot think of a key lesson you learned from each

trial, it might be time for you to think deeply about what you could (or should!) have learned.

- What ROP have you personally witnessed that resulted in true transformational growth for the participant(s)? They could be ceremonies like weddings, funerals or Bar Mitzvahs, or they could be dramatic life changes like loss of a job or loved one, moving or getting diagnosed with extreme illness. Who has followed through on the promise of the event? What have they learned? Consider the things you can do now to drive the meaning of these events even deeper. It could be as simple as publicly naming the shifts or the growth you see in someone else. Or it could involve designing a simple ritual to augment and dramatize the shift you've witnessed.

- If you have aging parents or grandparents, arrange a time ASAP to do extended interviews with them. It's helpful to ask them anything that interests you about their life to serve as a historical record for your family. But using ROP as a framework will help guide their memories in ways that are constructive.

- If you have children of any age, ask yourself how the latest skills they've acquired is contributing to a Rite of Passage. Call it out and name it. Reflect it back to them: "You and your wife are having your first child. This helps mark your transition from young adulthood into middle age. I see it as a sign of your deepening maturity, your willingness to sacrifice for others, your want to create generativity. Congratulations!" "By helping Mr. Jones bring in his groceries I see you stepping into more responsibility. You're also underscoring how we rely and depend on each other as neighbors, which is essential for sustaining healthy community. Bless you!""When you clean up the house without my asking, you're taking one small step toward adulthood. You're building self-reliance and moving into greater autonomy. Yes, yes, yes!"

- Have you ever contemplated suicide, or do you know someone who has? Has anyone you know actually done it? What do you think really needed to die? What needed to be born? Consider framing a discussion with someone struggling with suicidal ideation in these terms. Support

them in finding a suitable ROP.
- Are there ROP practices or programs in your community you can support now? Challenge yourself, take a leap and reach out to them. If there aren't any already existing ROP in your community for you to support, perhaps you can reach out to others and create your own. The tools and resources you'll find in this book will help.

2

Initiating Teens

This is the phase of life in which most contemporary people get stuck and the phase in which most need the greatest support. Adolescence holds the key to our becoming fully human. **Bill Plotkin**

A Rite of Passage was a time for the young people to be taken away from Mother and Father, away from their cultural values, to cut the ties, to be dropped into the context of nature where the only eyes they saw themselves through was the land itself. To be pushed, their borders pushed, so that there was a significant and real challenge for them that cracked them open, and to get through, themselves, with nobody else there, to get through hard times. "What do I do when I'm lonely? What do I do when I'm afraid?" And the teaching that comes about how to do that, from their own nature inside themselves and from the land. And then, having succeeded, to come back to their community where it's not just celebrated a little bit, but really celebrated. The whole community celebrating that this young person has gotten through the hard times, has learned so much, has brought back wisdom for the community, and are welcomed as adults who are essential for the survival of the community. **Meredith Little**

Throughout history, across cultures, ethnicities and religions, men have initiated boys into manhood and women have initiated girls into womanhood. Bar and Bat Mitzvahs, Catholic confirmations, Boy Scouts, urban gangs, fraternity hazing, team sports all reflect – some for better, some obviously for worse – this need for initiation. Adults knew that two primary childhood fears stood in the way of maturity: separation from parents and fear of death.

The chain of generativity going back at least 50,000 years in the lives of Homo Sapiens is now broken. The wisdom passed from individual to individual, from generation to generation, has largely been lost. In indigenous cultures across the world, it used to be that young people were initiated into adulthood by the Elders as a matter of course. In fact, many indigenous cultures don't even recognize what we in the West call "adolescence." You're either a child or you're an adult. There's no in-between. The Rite of Passage, universally applied, is designed as a mechanism to usher all children across that threshold into adulthood.

> *The word "adolescence" apparently was coined around 1900 by Stanley Hall, who was the first person to receive a doctorate in psychology in America. And apparently, we didn't have that term before, and apparently, we didn't need it so much. It could be, in part, a sign of human evolution, of the development of our species. Something about our destiny as humans, or a place in the earth community, might require us, as time goes on, to take gradually a little bit longer to mature. So, it may be that late adolescence has differentiated from early adolescence, within the last several hundred years. And maybe even adolescence in general, has become more differentiated from childhood than it used to be.* **Bill Plotkin**

Initiation is a biological need, resonating within us as deep as the cellular level. It accounts for most of where teen pushback against parents and other authority figures comes from. Teens need to individuate. They push boundaries to learn the limits of their own bodies, the reach of their critical judgment and their connection to nature and to Spirit or God. This is how they learn who they are and what is unique about them. They learn how to live with pain. It's also how they become validated. To be initiated is to fulfill their genetic inheritance – to be brought into the community of adults, to take their seat at the village table, to be honored, accepted and treated as equals.

> *If I can't find a way to express my gifts and talents positively, I will go to the dark side to express those gifts and talents. And become very clever and resourceful in drug trafficking, very clever and resourceful in my gifts of stealing, very resourceful and clever in reporting to the gang leader, showing how courageous I am in killing someone. That's misdirected energy and it indicates that somehow we're not doing our job as parents and as guides. Somehow we're not doing our jobs in generating meaningful neighborhoods and communities and families.*
> **Angeles Arrien**

> *If we do not initiate the young, they will burn down the village to feel the heat.* **African Proverb**

Look around. A lot of villages are burning. Some literally, like the UK fires in 2011 that started as the London Riots then quickly spread to towns nationwide, largely led by frustrated teens. The examples of dysfunctional attempts of teens to initiate themselves are legion. Negative, anti-social ROP include:

- Rioting and fighting with police
- Speed drinking and over-drinking

- Committing violence
- Committing a crime
- Rape and sexual assault
- Bullying
- Street drag racing
- Fraternity and sports team hazing
- Gang-banging

These acts are not *moral* equivalents. But they are *equivalent byproducts* of young people's attempts to simulate proper Rites of Passage. They can be called *misguided Rites of Passage*. Young people do these things not because they're inherently bad or because their lives have taken a wrong turn, but because they *must*. We have to learn to *expect* teens to do these things. This is not abnormal behavior; this is entirely normal behavior. *These are attempts at self-initiation – unconscious efforts by the young to cross a threshold into maturity.*

We need to do more than put out the fires started by rioting teens. In intentional and controlled ways, we must *generate* the heat that will transform teens into responsible adults. It's not enough to teach them responsible behaviors, or worse, trick, coerce or bribe them into being responsible. We must steer them down a productive pathway to growing up. We must help direct them through the transition. We must take that roaring internal fire, all that youthful energy, that raw excitement and brilliance, and using the means of ROP, guide it toward productive, pro-social ends. We must initiate them into a cooperative, non-violent, inter-independent way of being.

It's *we* who are out of alignment with *them*. We're not accurately reading their needs and offering them solutions – properly guided and controlled Rites of Passage. As the eponymous 2003 U.S. government report put it: teens are *"Hardwired to Connect."* If we don't give them proper healthy challenges, they will find improper, unhealthy ones, succumbing to temptations and connecting to the wrong people.

The question isn't so much: "What's wrong with teenagers?" it's more like: "How have we failed young people?" How have our educational institutions, our religious institutions failed young people? How has our society, more generally failed? How does our way of parenting fail our young people? **Bill Plotkin**

The reasons why the ROP listed above are dysfunctional are largely self-evident. ROP are designed to *promote* the wellbeing of humans, not destroy it. Those listed above are not *positively transformative* ROP. Nonetheless, it's worthwhile to hearken back to what we know about the structure of ROP for comparison's sake. With the possible exceptions of fraternity and sports team hazing and gang-banging, none of the behaviors above contain elements of ritual Separation and Return. They're solely about Ordeal, pushing the body into new, unsafe areas of action. These Ordeals are about thrills and dominance, not about reaching for the depths of the human soul.

You could make a case for fraternity and sports team hazing and gang-banging as serving community, at least as defined by those eponymous groups. But when community is defined with a pernicious ideology of Us vs. Them, "You're either with us or against us," that is not pro-social. These initiations are not inclusive. They don't include the greater human community. That is not wholesome. Yes, ROP initiate young people into a clan or lowercase "c" community. But at the same time ROP must awaken them to recognize their place in the greater, capital "C" Community of All Beings.

Perhaps the key, differentiating element is there are no Elders present. There is no mentorship. Children cannot initiate children into adulthood. Peers cannot initiate peers. These ROP do not carry the cultural wisdom of even the lowercase community. They do not carry the sacred insights into why Rites of Passage are essential for the health, well-being and preservation of that one community. Elders are the guardians of safety and meaning, ensuring that each risk taken during the Ordeal is appropriate, contained and maximized to offer the greatest possible return to the psyche. The Elders guarantee that the Initiates direct their efforts toward their own wellbeing and the goodness of all, not just toward those in community. The form that any Elder's role takes can be varied. But part of that service means saying, "Don't do that. It's not productive. Let me show you some alternatives…" That would nix fraternity hazing and gang-banging. Lastly, these ROP do not illuminate each individual's unique gifts, much less encourage them to manifest them fully.

> *It's essential to the Elders that young people become initiated into their deeper soul identity. And the Elders understand that for a young person to do that they have to lose their attachment, lose their faith in the adolescent persona, their social presence, their way of getting around as a social being – that identity they had just finished honing over several years. Then suddenly there's this crisis for the young person, where essentially the Elder is saying: "Now it is time to forget, or to loosen your attachment, to begin to move away from that way of being in the world that you just so beautifully crafted, and achieved success with."*
> **Bill Plotkin**

I have an alert set up in my browser to receive notifications whenever the words "Rite of Passage" and "film" are newly published together online. Almost invariably, the films I get notified about are stories involving teens doing activities similar to those in the lists above or below. I'm regularly notified about all the new films featuring dysfunctional teen initiations along with all the inconsequential ceremonies that don't do much. I almost never receive notifications about a film highlighting truly transformational ROP.

Often, what we regularly refer to as a "rite of passage" is neither healthy nor unhealthy, neither positive or negative. It is of neutral value. These are processes that contain the potential to become part of healthy Rites of Passage but they don't carry any transformative impact because they're not conceived of and implemented in this way. These processes can be thought of as neutral in every way, even morally. Here is a partial list:

- Getting a high school or college diploma
- Taking a "gap year"
- Getting a driver's license
- Having a first boyfriend or girlfriend
- Losing one's virginity
- Having a first drink
- Getting a first job or paycheck
- Turning 15, 18, or 21
- Getting tattoos or piercings
- Voting for the first time

We must distinguish what are effective ROP from those we might refer to as ROP, but are ineffective or incomplete. Unless acts like these are consecrated by a collection of Elders by means of significant rituals, unless they carry profound transformational impact for the youths involved, they will not initiate young people into Mature Adulthood. The old adolescent self will not die to make way for the new Mature Adult. It takes the collective will of the community to make it so. Though many of these activities take place in the average adolescent's life at some point, it doesn't necessarily mean they have acquired some essential new psychic or emotional skill set that will advance them toward adulthood. They need more.

> *The question then is, do we actually consecrate those markers? Do we celebrate those markers? Do we prepare our young people so that as they are moving from one stage to the next, that they understand that for every privilege there is a corresponding responsibility? In absence of that, the day a child gets a driver's license is the day they steal their mom's car; the day they are old enough to buy alcohol is the day they get drunk....and on and on and on....* **Chike Nwoffiah**

Even longstanding religious ceremonies - Bar and Bat Mitzvah, Catholic Confirmation, Quinceañera - originally designed as ROP, are often no longer effective in contemporary society. When I was 13, following a Bar Mitzvah, it was common among my Jewish friends to ask only one question: "What'd you get?" Cash, a car, college funds, paid vacations. These were common gifts a young person received for completing the ceremony. Nobody asked, "Do you really feel like a man now? Are you actually more mature? What have you truly learned about life?" Sadly, Quinceañera, Catholic confirmation, and Debutante Balls are, all too often, hardly any different. These once potent rituals can easily become empty ceremonies. The limitless reach of the marketplace, of consumer society, has infected and neutralized many of these once perfectly wonderful ROP. Transformational impact on the young person has been replaced with goods and services. Many parents' greatest aim is solely to impress family and friends with elaborate dinners and parties. (This is perhaps most evident with weddings in India, where lavish parties sometimes bankrupt the bride's family.) As for the young people themselves, their psyches may not be changed but their wardrobe and bank account may be.

It's time that we as a society stop using the term 'rite of passage' for events that are not proper, transformational, truly initiatory Rites of Passage. At best, they are merely ceremonies. Ceremonies do not transform or initiate. That's the preserve of rituals. Ceremonies are largely empty procedures that are designed to reinforce the status quo. They reinforce hierarchies and preserve power structures. Nowhere is this truer than with weddings. For hundreds of years, marriage as an institution has existed largely as a means to protect, bequeath and enhance titles and property, until recently almost exclusively through male lineage. If ROP does not serve the spiritual growth of the individual and benefit the community as a whole, it is not a proper ROP.

Rituals, on the other hand, are transformative procedures that are designed to upend the status quo. They eliminate hierarchies and restore even playing fields, making everyone equal and similarly empowered to contribute to community. Ceremonies reinforce the ego and are largely pleasant affairs. Rituals directly attack or deconstruct the ego. They can be challenging and difficult affairs, even unpleasant. No one likes to be taken down a few notches to be reintroduced to their humility.

There's an old distinction between fixed ceremony and radical ritual. In a fixed ceremony, the steps are clear and the outcome is predictable. In a radical ritual, only some of the steps are clear and the outcome is completely unpredictable. **Michael Meade**

The two terms are almost opposites. Ceremony goes by the book, follows a set pattern, is rigid in structure and makes no allowances for changes in the moment. Ritual is flexible in structure. Even though it follows a pre-set pattern, it need not strictly adhere to it. It is open to the spontaneous; it is creative and responsive to the realities of the moment. While ceremony strengthens and sustains *institutions*, ritual, though based on knowledge handed down through time, is crafted by *individuals*, sometimes in a group, sometimes acting alone. Its purpose is to subvert the old and invent a new status quo.

Rites of Passage are built on rituals. The word is embedded in the term. Think of "Rituals of Passage," or "Passage Rituals." They are not cookie cutter events. In order to be effective, they must adapt and flow with the uncertainties of the unique circumstances. It could be the weather. It could be that a key participant is late or can't come. Perhaps a participant suddenly is taken ill. It could be that the matches won't light and the fire won't burn. And unlike ceremony, the results, in terms of impact on any given individual, are unknown. There is no guarantee that any individual will transform from one stage of being to the next.[5]

---

[5] But having made this point, you will nonetheless experience multiple instances in this book where the terms ritual and ceremony are used interchangeably. Though the distinction is important to Michael Meade and to me, it is not necessarily important to many of the other wonderful teachers of ROP you will hear in this book. You will encounter moments when the two are used as synonyms, as they commonly are in everyday speech. Please be forbearing.

It must be said that smaller, everyday celebrations of life are not somehow harmful or "bad." Birthdays, anniversaries, Valentine's Day, Memorial Day(s), Christmas, Hanukkah, Ramadan and Kwanzaa celebrations are in no way detrimental to human growth and well-being. They can advance it wonderfully. They help us mark time, to acknowledge the passing of the seasons and the years. They remind us of our connection to the Source, however it's defined – to God, to community, to the family of humanity, to Mother Earth, to the nurturance we receive from those most near and dear to us, and to the all-important sacrifices others have made for us. They remind us to pause and celebrate life.

It's just that, as presently practiced, they are all too often missed opportunities for driving growth and change deeper into the psyche. All too often they are soulless, pro forma ceremonies, empty and insufficient. We are poised and capable of so much more.

Helpfully, Bill Plotkin separates teen Rites of Passage into two groups: puberty and late adolescence, with the acquisition of different skill sets defining each. His fine book *Nature and the Human Soul* elaborates on these differences. It's worth pausing to consider what they are, because their distinction will inform some of this writing.

But first, we must usefully define "ego" – that term so commonly used but rarely explained. Freud originally defined the ego as the self-awareness tool that allows us to express our primal or animalistic impulses (the "Id") in a manner suitable to the real world. Today, we think of ego as our fundamental sense of self, the view of myself that I have as an individual. Ego is the sum of what I tell myself to be true about the history of my interactions with the world. In our contemporary world, the term carries a negative connotation, as in "egotistical" or "egocentric." In actuality, it's both positive and negative, a necessity and a hindrance.

For young people to transition successfully from childhood through puberty the formation, growth and stabilization of the ego is a necessity. That's what we mean by individuation. "I distinguish my thoughts, words and deeds from the world outside. I know my boundary." Young teens must develop a strong sense of self and have confidence in that self. Much of that self-definition derives from bonding with peers. It's essential that a youngster feel a part of a team and have that sense of peer belonging to help define and strengthen the ego. The greatest measure of success for a teen accomplishing this transition is how well defined and assured that emerging sense of self becomes.

The ROP for late adolescents is somewhat the opposite. That ego which has been expanded on and refined throughout the teen years must now be deconstructed to accomplish initiation into young adulthood. Plotkin calls this "soul initiation." That ever more rigid sense of self must be exposed for the chimera that it is because in actuality there is no immutable, eternal self. All the stories that we build up about who we are and how the world treats us are just that – stories. Our sense of ourselves, that "me, me, me" sense of inviolability, must be supplanted with a deeply felt sense of interdependence – "us, us, us." We cannot survive without others and they are dependent on us. The strands of all lives are inextricably woven together. The Emperor of ego has no clothes. Plotkin argues that most people never make it past this Threshold at any age, much less by late adolescence. Understanding the distinction between the two stages is important since most of this chapter's (and this book's) subsequent emphasis on teens revolves around late adolescent ROP.

> *Initiation is essential for both genders. If there isn't an adequate initiation for the male gender it moves to violence. If there isn't an adequate initiation for a female it moves to victimization.* **Angeles Arrien**

Arrien's formulation of the need for initiation for both genders is simple, direct and powerful. That perpetrator/victim dynamic – men committing violence, often against women, and women being victimized – is all too common across cultures around the world. All too easily, men default to committing violence – a surrogate form of emotional release, a shadow expression of power – and women default to the role of victims. But it's important to remember it's not universal. Especially in these days of gender fluidity where many people switch genders or don't identify with either. So, leaving aside the non-binary folks for the moment, I would slightly amend Arrrien's statement and say "for most men" and "for most women."

For young women their first menstrual period is a huge initiation and yet it's often, in our culture, ignored and hidden and seen as something that is dirty and not to be talked about. And so, we literally take that initiation away from girls. For girls in indigenous cultures there were Elders who were there to talk about the skills that were needed for these girls to grow into women. They were taught the women's ways of that community and often it had to do with learning how to do weaving and there were other kinds of skills. But they were <u>taught</u>. And there was a moment of great celebration by the entire community, that this was no longer a girl; this was a woman and she now had new privileges and new responsibilities. And she had died to childhood and was born into adulthood. And that's a Rite of Passage. **Meredith Little**

When the girl goes into her menses that's her body saying we're now going through initiation. The women have to take her then. The boys don't have that overt sign so the boys are taken in a group. The boys begin as a group and the initiation teaches them that they are a unique individual. And the girls begin as a unique individual and get woven into the sisterhood and the group of the women. **Michael Meade**

I love the Michael Meade formulation above. He's certainly far more studied than I regarding world cultural practices. But I'm not so sure it applies to contemporary American culture in particular. Plotkin persuasively argues that initiating girls *and* boys into puberty is very much an initiation out of individuality into group. Yes, girls need a sense of sisterhood and identification with the Divine Feminine. But boys also need a sense of group identity, of working in unison with a team, of belonging to and appreciating something divine in Mature Masculinity.

In a lot of ways boys and girls experience similar things at this age. The hormonal changes are *huge*. Emotions are heightened and dramatic mood swings are common. Their tendency to act out increases dramatically. They both experience sexual interest, maybe for the first time. They physically grow, though girls tend to experience puberty sooner and grow faster. Voices drop, much more so in boys. They regularly experience cravings for more or different foods. Growth of body hair, sudden appearance of acne and more sweating are all common because they are physically becoming, and looking, more adult.

It is worth noting that girls are experiencing their first menstruation at younger and younger ages. Whether due to increased hormones and preservatives in foods or other environmental toxins, increased stress, more obesity, or less emotional stability with parents, the average age for first menstruation is now 12.5, down one full year from 100 years ago. It's not uncommon these days for girls as young as 7 or 8 to experience menarche. I find that shocking and painful.

How do we recognize a child's need for initiation? That it's their time? In the teen years, it's actually pretty easy to identify, especially with girls. That first menstruation is unmistakable. Yet, it's crazy to assume that a 10 or 11-year-old girl, much less a 7-year-old, somehow needs be initiated into adulthood. She certainly needs to fully understand not only what's occurring in her body, but also its implications. But along with those responsibilities she still has a right to her childhood.

For boys, it can be trickier, but not especially so. First of all, there are unmistakable biological signs. The scrotum drops somewhat. They might start having nocturnal emissions, more commonly known as wet dreams. Musky, darker smells become more interesting, whereas sweeter, more perfumed fragrances tend to appeal more to girls. Though all of these things should be noted and celebrated by alert parents and the opportunity should be seized to apprise the young man about his new rights and responsibilities, it doesn't necessarily indicate that initiation is now necessary.

Initiation for both boys and girls becomes necessary when they start dramatically "acting out." It's the time when Johnny starts beating up on his little sister or stealing money out of Mom's purse. It's the time when Susie suddenly loses interest in school and starts failing. It's the time when Tom grows listless and apathetic, when he stops listening to his parents and doing whatever he wants. It could be the time Heather starts doing drugs, maybe lots of drugs, or experimenting with sex before she's ready or in some unhealthy way. All these are key indicators that the child's time is NOW. She or he requires initiation. It's their way of telling their parent(s), however unconsciously, that their childish or pubescent self needs to die off so they can be reborn into something greater, some*one* greater, with more responsibility, more aliveness, more autonomy, with clearer, newer and different intentions. It's their way of saying "Life has lost its meaning for me. I need a new vision and a new purpose to understand and sustain my life."

Hopefully, the child already has a long-standing connection with one or more mentors. A capable mentor may be the first to spot the signs. He will also be the first to reassure the youngster that there's nothing wrong with him, that whatever he's feeling and experiencing is entirely appropriate and normal. That is key. Teens tend to think that there's something seriously wrong with them at this time. Since they don't seem to fit in, since the world itself seems inexplicable, stupid or just plain wrong, they worry that something in them might be broken. All that's really happening is that their bullshit detectors have reached new heights and their tolerance for inauthenticity has bottomed out. But if the adult powers around them only reinforce empty strictures, or worse, inauthenticity, lies and ill will, then the teen will start questioning his own moral compass and sanity. "Maybe *I'm* the crazy one!"

> *That fire [in youth] wants to burn. The biggest shame is when young people are told they're empowered and they're told their voice is wanted but then they experience that's in fact not true. That is even more*

harmful than saying, "No, here's your place!" They're told they have all this choice but then they see that they don't. What they're learning is that words and reality are not the same. And that's just crazy making.
Darcy Ottey

It's all about individuation. They must distinguish themselves from the world outside. "How am I similar to, and different from, my parents, my school, my friends, my neighbors, my government, my church, even my peers?" That outer world can suddenly seem wholly foreign. The youngster may be asking, "How did I get here? How did this happen?" Suddenly, he and the world outside can seem to be moving in entirely opposite directions. It's perplexing and terrifying. The truth is, these confusing thoughts are completely normal. Their genetic coding is fulfilling its mandate. The psycho-biological alarm clock has gone off. Now is their time.

I've been using the male pronoun above quite consciously. Girls are both the same and different. Girls may experience much of the same disaffection and may take to some of the same modalities of acting out as the boys. But they have one huge difference with boys: the physical changes they experience are far more dramatic due to menstruation. There is no mistaking that monthly process.

> *Initiation, in the end, has to do with the acceptance of pain. And women, at the time they're doing their first menstruations, have to go through a lot of pain, and they need to know that that pain has not been caused by anyone. It's a part of the whole process of becoming a woman. And they are so pleased by the prospect of becoming a grown woman and not remaining a girl forever, that they accept that pain, and they know it deep in their bones how important the pain is.* **Robert Bly**

You could say that the boys' yearning to be initiated is an unconscious imitation of the blood rite that girls experience naturally. Unconsciously, boys want to spill blood. There is often increased interest in fighting and battles and weapons and warfare. They want to seize and exercise power. They want to sacrifice their body to see what they're made of - how tough they can be. "How much punishment can I take?" The mystery of generating life has largely been given to girls. Boys crave a direct experience of it for themselves, one that biology alone does not afford them. Unconsciously, they may seek power commensurate with the tremendous power of the girls – their ability to bring forth life – by craving the power to bring forth death. That's why it's increasingly unsurprising that a small number of boys not afforded some healthy, contained introduction into these mysteries will enact versions of them they see on TV and in movies. They'll pick up real weapons and go on real killing sprees. They'll put their lives on the line and since they can't ritually and symbolically die to their childhood and experience the archetypal power of death, they'll cause the real deaths of others and die a real death themselves. Thank goodness it's not the norm, but there is a trend of this malevolent violence that is happening with increased frequency over the past 20 years, and it must be addressed.

Hawaiians and Polynesians were always circumcised. I thought that was a pretty good ritual to demonstrate the pain of coming into manhood. The circumcision happened when you were 11 or 12, not at two months on the table [like in Jewish culture]. It happened at a moment when you would clearly remember it. My grandfather said that was one of the principle reasons it was done that way. As the men held the boy by their thighs and arms, the kahu stands up and says, "We want you to remember this is why you never disrespect women. They endure this once a month.. This you're only going to have to endure once in your life." So, you get a clear sense of the pain. **Kalani Souza**

There is a really beautiful ritual in a certain tribe in Africa where after her initiation, the girl comes back to the village, and the women have made with her a belt of shells and beads, which she wears over her belly and abdomen. She is presented to the whole tribe covered in these beads, and the beads are connected to the entire tradition of the tribe – the bead memories, the shell memories. And it's like saying that she is noble in her belly and in her generative organs.

She stands before the tribe with one hand pressed to the earth and one hand held up. Someone explains that this hand anchors her into mother earth and this hand ties her into father sky, and this shows how she is protected by all of the old traditions. And the idea is for the whole tribe to understand – you have to respect this girl who now has become a woman and that it is up to her whether she keeps this girdle on or takes it off. And you better pay attention because she is tied into the world above and the world below.

Those things are missing in our culture and they're really important. When that's not seen, people don't see the value of that girl and they don't see the respect that has to be had for the feminine. So even those who are working mostly with boys, if that doesn't happen, the boys don't know how to respect the presence of the feminine. **Michael Meade**

It used to be a pretty big difference between the roles of men and women in early communities. In our world today, there's not such a difference in the roles. Men and women are now saying we are both capable of raising children and of being heads of corporations. That also is something that we need to address as guides. If the relationship between men and women is different and is changing, how do we prepare young men and women to be in the world? One of the beauties of having them go out together on a vision fast was not only to have their solo time but to come back and to hear each other's stories. They grew in understanding about what it meant to be a young man and a young woman and to honor those stories and to see how they were different from each other and how they were the same. I love that today we're asking that question even more deeply. Are there more ways that especially prepare them for womanhood and manhood that might look different from each other? And when do we bring them together? **Meredith Little**

If you're with boys and girls, women and men, and you say a certain word, it can have different meanings. When you separate the genders, you can get a more simplified understanding of what's being said and you can move along, and you can get to some depth. So, I think both separate experiences and joint experiences are important.

Especially if the point is eventually to have young men and young women who are able to express themselves and know that they are valuable and have some idea of what they are to do in this world, and what they have to give, then it seems to me that some of that will be accomplished separately and some of it will be accomplished together. **Michael Meade**

Women are just as volatile and just as dangerous in the neighborhood as boys are. It's more of a masculine kind of feminine pull. Because we carry both within the human body. You have some men who lean more towards the feminine side and some who lean more towards the masculine side. The same with women. There has to be parity because if we leave women out of this whole Rites of Passage process it's dangerous. I tell you, man, some of the home girls in the neighborhood are vicious. **Aqeela Sherrills**

I think if women are not well initiated into the healthy feminine then they move into imitating the masculine and that also leads to violence. It's underscored both ways. How can the healthy feminine rise without imitation of the masculine? And how can the healthy masculine rise to be able to create safety and protection without violence? Both are essential. **Angeles Arrien**

What happens with boys, if they aren't pulled into a meaningful process, they become outwardly very destructive. And so, everybody begins to pay attention to that because they form gangs, they get violent and they cause trouble. But I've been with an awful lot of girls who are destructive <u>inwardly</u>. Who are cutting themselves. Who are overeating. Who are depressive and hiding out. And that actually takes something away from culture too. It's just not as blatant. But there's a big loss there because I think it's natural to want to see the vibrancy and the beauty of girls as well as boys. And I think a healthy culture thrives on the exhibition, and the display, and the giving of that vitality and that beauty. And I think there is something really lost but it's more subtle. The boys are really going to stick it in everybody's face, typically. But the girls are actually losing something as well. And when the girls don't feel fully invited into life, they tend to hook up with boys that are going to be harmful to them, or destructive to them. **Michael Meade**

I've witnessed some of this inward destruction with girls first hand. I was filming a beautiful and talented teen girl in Colorado for a year or so. She was a cutter. She had scars up and down her arms and legs from lacerating herself. She had been terribly depressed for a few years and was on medication for much of her adolescence. She was also an out lesbian. Under certain, unhealthy circumstances this might be cause for much of her emotional distress. But I don't think it was with her. She had extraordinarily accepting parents and community. She also was a brilliant pianist and composer. Again, under certain circumstances, if she was not seen and encouraged to pursue her art that might logically cause distress. But again, that wasn't the case; her artistry was highly supported and her sexuality widely accepted. So, what was the source of her anguish?

    I think, like most teens, boys or girls, she didn't feel emotionally held. She didn't feel like her turbulent, questioning, (yet typical) teen anxieties had a home where they could be witnessed, acknowledged and loved. She didn't feel seen and understood in *all* of her fullness, including her torments, anxieties, depression and doubts. Though she had piano teachers and other adults she felt close to, she didn't have a mentor she could bear the entirety of her soul to. She also didn't have a mentor she could discuss LGBTQ issues with. When she ran into the limitations, hypocrisies and inauthenticity of adults, like all teens do, she turned that pain on herself. At 17, when she was able to experience Melissa Michael's ROP work called Surfing the Creative, she said that it, along with a nature-based ROP, helped save her life. Today they are a happy, well-adjusted trans person, living in a non-binary world.

> *With youth groups, when we've introduced Rites of Passage and some of the indigenous wisdom about what it looks like to be in adolescence - which is you're confused and it's not an easy time and it's full of painful feelings, and that's what's initiating you and this means something right is happening - they'll come up to us afterwards and say, "Oh my god, I can't tell you how relieved I am! What I'm feeling, what's happening in me, it means I'm moving toward adulthood. It means it's right!" It just takes that little tweak.* **Meredith Little**

Building resilience is a fundamental benefit of ROP. With "helicopter parenting," very few young people today face the kinds of everyday challenges that young people did as recently as one generation ago. Parents are so fearful of their child's well-being that they will rarely allow them the kinds of risks that they themselves might regularly have taken. When I was 10 or 11, I used to take my bicycle and ride from one end to the other of the two adjacent cities where I grew up in Champaign-Urbana, Illinois. I'd be gone exploring all day. I don't remember taking a sack lunch or even water. I just went. Though it was certainly considered a "safe" city and perhaps a safer time, there were still about 100,000 residents and the area covered as much as 25 square miles. My mother considered this admirable. No doubt she herself was consumed by going to school full time and raising a family as a single mother. But I don't recall her once expressing a fearful concern about me, let alone trying to reign me in.

We've medicalized and actually created diagnoses for healthy adolescents. Saying they're 'oppositionally defiant.' We've now discovered the adolescent actually has a different brain. They call it the adaptive brain. And in the initiatory process, the role of the emerging adult is to challenge adults, to say, "Hey, is smoking good? Smoking isn't good, is it?" It really took the young people challenging their parents to change the values. And so, we've actually medicalized the adolescent condition to disempower them from their natural role to challenge us and our values. And is it any wonder that we incarcerate more people than any other country in the world? **David Blumenkrantz**

Upper middle class and wealthy families in the U.S. seem intent on resolving every problem that children have. The teenage years are often referred to as "the driving years" for parents who ferry their children from one event to another. Couple that with three other social norms and it's no wonder that young people seem increasingly ill-equipped to handle the stresses of coming adulthood: 1) "Everybody gets an A," is the standard replacing healthy competition as the norm in schools, sports, social clubs, music lessons, etc. 2) Pathologizing and prescribing medication(s) for teen symptoms is 400% more likely today than it was 30 years ago. 3) Unless insurance companies expressly sanction activities, parents and other supervisors are unwilling to allow children to take risks because everyone is fearful of injury and litigation. Ultimately, too many adults seem unwilling to put young people to any real test so they can discover their own capacities. ROP are expressly designed to do that.

One of my friends sent her kid to a summer camp that I knew was a great summer camp for kids. He was a very urban, city boy, New York boy. Within two days he's like, "I want to come home, mom. I can't stand this. This is not me." She brought him home and I keep thinking, "He was one kid who really needed this." Never had anyone ever taught him to be in his body or to do anything physical. She could have sent him there and turned the phone off, right? Sometimes I think it's helpful for kids to get thrown into a situation they can't get out of and have to stick with. They're facing a world where we're all being thrown into situations that we aren't going to be able to get out of and we need to be able to cope with that. Often times, what kids need is exactly what their parents haven't been able to give them and they're gonna be most resistant to. **Starhawk**

As adolescence ends – if there is no effective initiation or mentorship – a sad thing happens. The fire of thinking, the flaring up of creativity, the bonfires of tenderness, all begin to go out. **Robert Bly**

It's bad enough that we all pay a price with the dysfunctional ways teens try to initiate themselves. But we also pay a huge price by denying them the opportunity to make powerful contributions to society. How many budding artists, mathematicians, engineers, designers, chefs and astronauts are we denying? They deserve the right to find themselves in their soul-chosen creative field. If we never awaken in them their draw to a given life path, or recognize and bless it when it naturally arises, they will never get the traction they need to inhabit their own life. Then the community(s) they are in will never receive the benefits they require from that particular individual's gifts. The community itself may not even recognize its own need. How sad is that? Everyone loses. Every person on the planet longs and deserves to be recognized in ways that are unique to them. But this desire is especially acute for teens.

Angeles Arrien taught me that the individuation cycle contains normal negation and abnormal negation. Normal negation, more commonplace, occurs when a teen decides to check out for themselves whether their inherited cultural, spiritual and familial values make sense and actually work for them. It's that time when young Catholics might ask themselves "Is there really a God? Is the Pope and the Church somehow closer to God than I am?" Or it can be as simple as, "If I don't brush my teeth every night will they really fall out?" "Is the world seriously adversely affected if I don't make my bed every day?" "Does chewing gum really make me look like a bum?" "If I masturbate will my hand fall off? Might I go blind?"

> *It doesn't matter which way you go with teenagers; they're going to choose the opposite. They just are clear that they don't want to be like you. And in their own way they're right to choose differently. Back in the day, I'm sure there were some sensible parents that managed to stay alongside their children all the way through their adolescence. But not too many.* **Jim Horton**

Abnormal negation means someone out and out rejects the conventional wisdom they've been taught and pursues the opposite. (As I understood her, Arrien doesn't mean "abnormal" in any pejorative sense. There's nothing *wrong* with "abnormal." It's simply less common.) Abnormal negation occurs when the teen swings to an opposite extreme. A young Christian decides to become a Devil worshipper. A Boy Scout decides to shoot heroin. An abstinent teen starts paying prostitutes for sex. A young farmer moves into an urban crack house. Many ROP will incorporate this understanding of youth needing to "sow their wild oats" into their very processes.

One of the most dramatic examples is "Rumspringa," the ritual that Amish and Mennonite communities utilize. Youths, ranging in age from 14 to 21, leave the community for up to two years to experience the world outside. They are given maximum freedom to do everything that is otherwise forbidden: have premarital sex, drink, do drugs, explore other religions, cultures and belief systems, stop working, travel, watch TV, use cellphones, computers and cars, even watch pornography. The beauty of this ROP is that, at least theoretically, Amish adults will never later wonder about the world outside and about any opportunities they might have missed. They won't wonder if they might have been happier with everything contemporary society offers. Statistics vary, but after this period of debauchery, 80-90% of the young people return to their communities and get baptized, taking vows of commitment to the Church and its values. Though there are no statistics to confirm or refute it, I suspect that this impressively high percentage is consistent with the numbers of youth successfully initiated by indigenous cultures throughout human history.

Whether we define our emerging selves through revolution or reform, outright rejection of the values and practices in which we were raised, or through re-calibration and adjustment, we find our way to a deeper sense of who we are, our own definition of freedom and our deepest realization of what we're here for.

> *Anybody that's doing anything to recognize and bless the unique, inherent qualities of young people, is probably doing some good. Because the general cultural atmosphere is to deny that. And that creates an unnecessary wound in young people. Young people don't feel welcome.*
>
> *And you can't feel welcome generally. I remember someone once saying to a whole group of young people, 'Boy, you are all so great!' And one girl raised her hand and said, "In which way am I great?" In other words, they don't want to know they're all great. They want to know 'did you see me?' So, anything that serves that function, I would imagine is doing something good.* **Michael Meade**

Blessings are a fundamental function of healthy society. It's built in to the whole process of ROP, primarily through Homecoming. Homecoming rituals are group exercises in blessing. The whole community turns up to witness and celebrate the transformation of the young person. But blessing needs to be reintroduced as a normal function of ongoing, everyday culture. Some people might argue, "Oh, we do that already with the "Everybody gets an A" standard mentioned above. "Every child is automatically recognized for her or his participation." NO! Every child needs to be seen for how she or he is *unique*. Children are not stupid. If they see that everyone gets a medal simply for showing up, they know those medals have no real significance. As Michael Meade notes, we can't give blanket commendations. They are empty of meaning. To some degree, blanket medal ceremonies function as the exact opposite to blessing rituals because they don't allow for individuals to be uniquely recognized.

It's been pointed out to me that the word "blessing" carries a Judeo-Christian connotation that can be offensive to non-Judeo-Christians and to non-believers. I respect that. What I advocate for in this book are *cultural* practices, not religious ones; practices that can be implemented throughout the entirety of the dominant culture and all its sub-cultures, including religions, but not to be necessarily *associated* with any particular religion. I know of no other word in English that carries the gravitas and potency of the word "blessing." I've tried all the synonyms: acknowledgment, approval, encouragement, praise. None come close to the power and effectiveness of "blessing."

> *During adolescence - your coaches, your mentors, your community leaders - these people are the ones who now provide your son or your daughter with the content that's necessary for them to make that transition into adulthood. At every developmental stage you have these matrices where each individual finds their energy, safety and possibility. At every stage each individual has these phases that they're going through: one that they've left, one that they're currently in in training and then another one that they're transitioning into. So, when we are working with adolescents our goal is to prepare them to move into their adulthood transition. We mentors are probably the best helpers for that child in this particular developmental stage because at this point, they want to show parents how independent of them they can be and want to be. They don't want to share with them information about what's going on in their relationship, they don't want to share with them information about finding a job or going to college because they don't think as parents we know that information. They're trying to move*

away from them. So that's why we're so important for those children at this particular age group because they still need adults. **Kwabena Terrence Shelton**

There are many ways for young people to actually prove that they have completed their journey into adulthood. The skills they've acquired that signify their maturity are relatively easy to verify. One of the most comprehensive references is a list of 40 Developmental Assets for youth as defined by the Search Institute. They are divided into two main categories: Internal and External Assets. Within these, they're broken down further into sub-categories like "Constructive Use of Time, Boundaries and Expectations, Commitment to Learning and Positive Values." I think this is one of the best lists assembled to objectively mark a youth's ascension to adulthood.

But there are many others. Most ROP and youth development experts - in fact, almost every group that works with young people - has devised its own list of key indicators of a youth's developmental success. Sometimes that list is synonymous with the community's list of key values and standards. Other times it's not. Regardless of whether the list is four, eight, twelve or 100 items long, the key is that each young person knows the standards she is expected to achieve and uphold, and that each community actually abides by those self-defined standards. Here are some of my favorite organizations with their lists. Note how each organization expresses its unique difference or flavor. To learn in more detail how these benchmarks are defined, please check out their individual websites.

Alchemy: From Dr. Anthony Mensah (**Adopted from* ***The Magical Child*** *by Joseph Pearce)*

1. Every person has a built-in capacity to succeed.
2. We are born with a driving intent to express this capacity.
3. All humans are one with nature.
4. Nature doesn't program from failure.
5. Each person is part of the cosmic whole.

6. When the intent of nature is not met with appropriate content, but with the intentions of an anxiety-driven parent or culture, the biological plan is wrecked.
7. Inappropriate content brings reaction instead of intellectual growth, and the child's ability to interact – use his/her intelligence – falls more and more behind, and more and more energy must go into compensation.
8. With the infusion of inappropriate content, the young person's intelligence is still out there in the previous passage, trying to make functional the intent of nature.
9. Rites of Passage in the child's education provide a meaningful response to the intent. The success of the biological plan hinges directly on the person – the infant, the child, the adolescent or the adult – being provided with the content proper for the intent of that person.
10. Consequently, all persons who experience this type of education will benefit from it.

Boys to Men:

1. Integrity
2. Responsibility
3. Accountability
4. Self-awareness
5. Authenticity
6. Resiliency
7. Empathy/Compassion
8. Inclusivity

Golden Bridge:

1. Embodiment

2. Respect
3. Lineage
4. Integrity
5. Authenticity
6. Collaboration
7. Beauty
8. Creativity
9. Conscious Human Development
10. Community
11. Global Consciousness
12. Lifelong Learning

Leap Now:

1. Integrity is the foundation of the curriculum

- Feeling your Feelings
- Telling the Truth
- Keeping your Agreements
- Expressing your Creative Voice

1. Personal Life Map
2. Understanding the World of Work and the Acquisition of Practical Skills
3. Cross-Cultural Exploration
4. Cultivation of the Body
5. Cultivation of the Mind
6. Developing Emotional Literacy
7. Social Skill Acquisition, Communication

Passage to Manhood/Peregrine Ministries:

1. Strength: The Courage of a Warrior

- The Value of Work, Adversity, & Challenge
- Rejecting Shame
- Pursuing Purity

1. Heart: The Compassion of a Lover

- Embracing Woundedness
- Honoring Women

1. Mind: The Conviction of a Mentor

- Building Character
- Building a Band of Brothers

1. Soul: The Confidence of a King

- God Rules; Jesus Saves
- Discovering Your Mission in Life

School of Lost Borders:

1. Nature-based.
2. Community spirit.
3. Co-ed ROP experiences for young men and women.
4. An experience with peers set in a circle with Elders and Elders-in-training.

Stepping Stones:

1. Helping youth develop a strong sense of self and solid internal compass.
2. Deepening our connection to nature.
3. Promoting authentic relationships.
4. Incorporating a Village-Model that includes youth, family and community.
5. Addressing key developmental tasks of childhood and adolescence through curriculum and practice.
6. Creating an intergenerational village of resources and support.

Lifeplan Institute/CA Mentor Foundation:

- Be thoughtful.
- Be honest.
- Care about others.
- Be connected to family.
- Save a little each month.
- Be generous with your positive spirit.
- Make a difference—and believe you can make a difference.
- Learn from the speed bumps.

In its own way, each list provides a standard of accountability for any given youth's transition into adulthood. There are infinite ways those measurement standards can be parsed and it is worth noting that the more clearly defined these standards are, the more clearly the youth will understand what's expected of them, giving them a greater chance of meeting these expectations and standards. What follows is my own personal list. Not every teen is going to learn all this, or learn each item to its intended depth. But for me, these are key lessons.

- Learn your **capacities**: Explore the depths of your physical, mental and emotional capacities.
- Learn **emotional intelligence:** how to handle your feelings. You must learn not to repress them! Feeling emotions equals strength, energy and freedom!
- Construct and reinforce **ego** for younger teens. Builds a healthy sense of self complete with self-empowerment and confidence. Engenders an "I can do this!" attitude.
- Later, the deconstruction of **ego** for older teens. Transition from "Me, me, me…" to "Us, us, us…" Become a part of the fabric of the web of life and learn your place in the cosmos. Identify with "Big Self," not "small self," what Jack Kornfield calls "the body of fear."
- Find your **mission:** learn what your particular purpose might be, what unique gifts you have, what your medicine is.
- Engage in **service**: It's about community, not just the self. True happiness comes from putting your talents at the service of others.
- Learn **tribe:** strong bonding with peers, sharing similar experiences.
- Welcome **inter-independence:** you must learn to rely on yourself but you must also rely on and support your peers. Your ROP comrades are your battle buddies. They can, if you let them, become "lifetime battle buddies."

The children that I've interacted with here in in Hawaii, I can tell they've been initiated to one degree or another, and that's not all of them but a few. Because they have a sense of their role in the community, how they can be helpful. Not just that they need to be helpful but how they can be. How to be respectful of their Elders without giving away their autonomy. It's a very rare thing to see. And that's because it doesn't happen very often in the mainland United States where I'm from. But also, it's a difficult thing to recognize if you don't know what you're looking for. One of the problems culturally with the West and its interaction with Rites of Passage is we don't even know what people who have gone through them look like. ***Chris Schaeffer***

The proof of initiation is in the body. Each individual's physical manifestation of change will be different. Nonetheless, for each there should be a marked difference in their body before and after. There should be more vitality. Their eyes should sparkle and glow with some new awareness. There might be more excitement in their voice and gestures. They might be calmer. Either way, they should be more at home within themselves, exuding more confidence and ease. If it was present before, anxiety should disappear, replaced by clarity and composure. There should be more smiles, more laughter, more joy.

But it's not enough for us to notice these changes, to call them out and say, "You've changed. You've been initiated." It's up to the Initiates themselves. They are the ones who get to make that determination. They have to express bodily, and ideally verbally too, "I'm a different person. I feel changed. I am no longer_____. Now, I am _____. I feel like a new woman. I feel like a new man. I feel reborn." If they don't feel like this in their body, in their bones, and express it in some form, then it's safe to say they haven't been initiated. For whatever reason, the transformation has not yet occurred.

It's interesting how the English language creates a separation between the words "right" and "responsibility." Colloquially, they're used almost as opposites. The word "right" tends to carry a positive connotation, like receiving a treat. Certainly the "Bill of Rights" in the U.S. Constitution and "Human Rights" are phrases that create positive associations. Meanwhile, "responsibility" tends to carry a more negative association. It's at least weightier, like a burden. Perhaps it's only a feature of Western culture that creates this great divide between these two notions that are both fundamental to the passage of teens into adults.

At Pacific Quest, the second phase of the program is called kuleana, which is the Hawaiian word for responsibility. That's usually how it's translated. But I recently learned that it's both the Hawaiian word for "responsibility" and the word for "right." It's the same word in the

Hawaiian language, which makes a lot of sense. With every right comes a responsibility. And every responsibility gives you rights and privileges.
Darcy Ottey

This is an example of what kuleana means to me. "It is my kuleana to teach my children and grandchildren their native culture and the values and beliefs of our family." If I internalize this statement and agree that as a makua and kupuna (parent and grandparent), my responsibility is to teach my children and grandchildren the culture, values and beliefs of our family, it becomes a goal, a mission, a duty. But, if I add the additional meaning of PRIVILEGE to this statement, the perspective changes to: "How honored am I to be able to have this responsibility of having children and grandchildren to share my knowledge, stories and thoughts." This additional meaning to the word allows one to truly think about what they are doing, how they are doing it, and to express a gratitude that is sometimes lacking in taking on a responsibility. When given a task or responsibility, adjust your perspective to include privilege, then the task will take on a new meaning and that is KULEANA. **Searle Wailana Grace** *and* **Diane Kamaolipua**

It starts with the transformation of the individual. Then it ripples out and impacts the immediate family. Then it ripples out and impacts the school or workplace. It ripples out and impacts the neighbors, the places of play and the places of worship. The effects of positive change are literally immeasurable. It's commonplace to say "the youth are our future." They are more. They are our past and our present too, and they impact everything.

As their flesh once labored to bring forth flesh
   So the minds of the elders labor,
   With like passion,
   To bring forth a mind.

INITIATING TEENS

By rites of initiation
  They would accomplish
  The metamorphosis of matter into man,
  The evolution of a mind for meaning in the animal
  Which is the issue of their flesh

By this
  they would ensure that the race endure
  As a race of men
  The rites of this second birth
  Into the metaphysical cosmos,
  Everywhere mime the conditions of
  The first physical birth

The novice is
  Purified of the past,
  Relieved of possessions,
  Made innocent,
  Placed nascent in the womb solitude...

The matter,
  Which is man himself,
  And the myth of a race,
  Are joined.

His solitary meditation
  Is a gestation
  And, in the end,
  A man emerges by ordeal,
  To be newly named, newly rejoiced in.

Maya Deren (1952)

What You Need To Do *Now*

Seize every opportunity to Bless Teens:

- Celebrate their physical changes: shaving, periods, first bra, deepening voices and physical growth.
- Celebrate their emotional changes. It's normal for them to be more withdrawn, want more privacy and be more introspective. Tell them you see it and it's OK. Tell them the truth about how much spending less time with them may be a hard transition for *you* to make but that you fully endorse these steps they're taking to enter adulthood.
- Bless them when they *help out*, when they *volunteer*, when they *share their feelings*.
- Call out and name the actual thing(s) that you've observed them doing. "I see how hard you tried to fix your bike and, even though you didn't succeed, I honor your effort." "Thank you for being patient with your sister." "I'm proud of how you took responsibility for Mr. Smith's broken window." "Thank you for helping your brother with his homework…" "Even though you didn't score many points you played great on defense." "I love you." "I see you." "I see the goodness in you."
- One, just one blessing can make a difference! THEY MAY NOT SHOW IT, but they'll hear it AND NEVER FORGET! But remember, it must be sincere! Teens know when they're being bullshitted.
- Find mentors for your teens: an aunt or uncle, a neighbor, a coach or teacher. Ask them to spend at least one afternoon a month with your youngsters. Pay them if you must. But make sure it's someone they already feel drawn to and are comfortable with.
- Go to YouthPassageways.org. Review multiple options with your teens to see what they're most drawn to and sign them up for a ROP experience.
- Bring the ideas of Whole Person Development into the work you do with youth at the individual, family and community levels. For instance, bring cultural or identity exploration into one-on-one direct care. Or use

mentorship to frame your organization's community outreach. What can your direct care staff learn from the demographic you're serving? What skills can you harness to empower them in their work with you?
- Facilitate internships where students receive academic credit for doing service learning. Consider partnering with a local community college or university so college age students (perhaps juniors) mentor high school students through community work, service learning, etc.
- Use role definition and redefinition to build rapport with the youths you have served. Renaming is a common feature of ROP. A new nickname or sacred talismanic name can be an incredibly powerful tool. Develop something personalized to an individual that carries with it an acknowledgement of trust and expectation. Explore how individualization - deepening a youth's understanding of his/her roles - can intensify their investment in your mutual activities. You might also try this with coworkers, colleagues, and others. I myself took on a new "spirit name" when I completed my MKP NWTA. That name has evolved and changed over the years to reflect my latest "growth edge" - what it is I most need to maintain diligence around. Of late, it's "Vigilant Lion." It reminds me to check my blood sugar 24/7 and maintain vigilance around what I eat to effectively manage my diabetes. It also reminds me that I must be ferocious in my commitment to staying awake, so I don't lapse back into default habits of neuroses and ill will. Using that name in public MKP ceremonies and occasionally in my email signature recalls me to that promise.
- Seek out local or national programs that specialize in mentorship or Rites of Passage to see how the ideas of Whole Person Development can translate into your organization. This might mean working in tandem with a wilderness or mentorship program, or seeking consultation on council practices. This is where a wide variety of variance and individualization will come into play. The cross-pollination of knowledge and services will benefit both your organization and the community you serve.
- Invite one or more youths to sit on your board of directors and/or

steering committee. This initiative has met with incredible success in Expeditionary Learning schools across the nation. Youth representation in decision-making processes empowers them to take ownership of their education's overall direction. Having a "seat at the table" can often be the very thing that thrusts a youth into ownership of his/her maturity. I have done this with some success on my Warrior Films non-profit board.
- Empower youths and interns to teach weekly classes in meditation, re-centering, digital detox or movement. Alternately, they can simply hold space for others to practice on their own.

3

The Mature Masculine (and How It Serves Women!)

Boys need a place to be themselves and to be in the fullness of themselves in an appropriate way inside the community they're part of, and be allowed to express themselves. They're gonna do it inside the culture in community or outside of it. If it's outside it's more likely to be dangerous.

If we don't learn to channel all of these powerful masculine energies that are hardwired in our bodies, we have the potential to become destructive in a lot of forms. Some boys become destructive by joining gangs, some become destructive by going to college and running Enron. There's no difference here. It's about the appropriateness of boys brought into manhood no matter where they come from. **Jim Mitchell**

Men are made, not born. **Frederick Marx**

What would you do if someone told you your son would never become a man? That your nephew would never experience maturity? That your cousin or grandson would never feel from the inside the beating heart of what it really means to be an adult male?

Well, it's happening right now, in our country, today. Millions of boys – black, white, Asian, Latino, rich and poor boys, good boys – smart, sensitive, and loving boys, vulnerable and open boys, are not fully growing up, are not accomplishing the transition from adolescence to adulthood. Without initiation and mentorship, these boys will never know what is sacred about their own masculinity. They'll never know their own unique mission in life; they'll never know what it is to serve family and community rather than their own self; they'll never know their place in the order of things, the depths of their own greatness or the true limits of their own reach and they'll never know what an empowering gift their own feelings can be – how they can learn to master them through acceptance; how their tears, their shame, their anger and fear can ignite the fires of passion and can actually set them free.

This was less true in Western society before the Industrial Age. Boys raised on farms or learning crafts were apprenticed by their fathers and other men. While they were taught practical and professional skills, they were also taught by men what it is to be a man, what civilized behavior is – the rights and responsibilities of adulthood, the kuleana. Once men started moving off their farms and out of their shops and studios to work in factories, that ancient system broke down. Couple that with the destruction of indigenous cultures across the planet by colonialism and imperialism and there now remain few organic links through the chain of time to the practices and wisdom of the past.

My close friend Tom Pitner and his friend Jim Warner designed a ROP program for boys in 2000. They called it "Becoming a Man - A One-Year Rite of Passage Program for Adolescent Boys." They wrote an incredibly useful manual on how they did it. I would have re-published it here in the appendix were it not 67 pages long. Get yourself a copy.[6] You will find it enormously helpful in constructing similar programs for boys you know. They begin the handbook with these remonstrations, presumably to help

---

[6] https://www.oncourseinternational.com/wp-content/uploads/2021/02/Becoming-a-Man-Summary.pdf

recruit men as mentors. If ever there were phrasing to make literal what Joseph Campbell termed "The Call to Adventure," starting a man on his "Hero's Journey," this is it!

> *British Antarctic explorer Sir Ernest Shackleton placed this advertisement in London newspapers in 1900 in preparation for the National Antarctic Expedition (which subsequently failed to reach the South Pole). Shackleton later said of the call for volunteers that: "It seemed as though all the men in Great Britain were determined to accompany me, the response was so overwhelming."*
>
> **MEN WANTED FOR HAZARDOUS JOURNEY**
> *Small wages. Bitter cold. Long months of complete darkness. Constant danger. Safe return doubtful.*
> *Honor and recognition in case of success.*

Both boys and girls, men and women, need initiation and mentorship. But I believe boys and men need it more. Especially in these times. [Generalizing alert! I will now make sweeping statements about men and women, even more than before. I get how risky this is given our present cultural climate, where any statement made can and will be interpreted in zero sum terms, as exclusionary or detrimental in particular to women. Please note that I am in no way saying these statements apply literally to *all* men or *all* women. These distinctions certainly do not apply in every circumstance. Nonetheless, I think making them can be helpful. You don't have to read *Men are from Mars, Women are from Venus* to understand that.]

Men are primarily the ones in positions of power in countries around the world, in governments, corporations and institutions of all types. The vast majority are of course uninitiated. Though living out their suspended adolescence in "adulthood" may be no more statistically common than women, the repercussions of their dysfunctions are far greater. They are the ones who are mostly to blame for the slew of problems presently facing the globe: climate change, extreme wealth inequality, warfare, violence of all kinds, asserting dominance over others. Given all the residual harmful effects of male dominant culture perpetrated by (and on!) men and boys, this chapter's emphasis on what males in particular need to become fully mature seems appropriate.

> *I was working with a group of young boys. I was working with them through goal setting. "Where do you want to be in five years? Where do you want to be in ten years?" And a young boy wouldn't do that assignment. He wouldn't do the exercise. I didn't want to put him on the spot so later on I pushed him and said, "Hey man, what's up?" He said, "Brother Chike, no, I don't want to do that." I said, "Come on, what's going on?" He kind of looked at me and said, "Nah, I'll be dead, you know, I don't want to do that." And he just walked off. As I was driving home I suddenly found myself literally shaking. I had to pull over. Mind you, I had been in the U.S. barely three years. I was shaking. The gravity of what he said hit me. Not only was it what he said but the way he said it. He could have just said, "Oh, I'm just gonna go get a drink of water." It was so cavalier. It was so certain. And it was just okay and that was life. And we're talking where would you be in just five years. I couldn't wrap my mind around that. I just couldn't. I was completely crippled by that experience. I remember getting on the phone with my father and saying, "My life has no meaning if I'm operating in circles such as this." I was confused.*
>
> *That was the beginning of this journey to what we call a Rites of Passage program. And two, three years later this Oriki Theater Rites of Passage program was born. What came out of that conversation with my father, and the series that followed it... he was basically saying, "Create a space for that young boy and he will live to tell his own story." I said, "How can I create a space for this boy?" It wasn't just about going back to him to lecture him, "No, you're not going to die! No, you're going to do <u>this</u>...! No, no, no..." That was not what my father would*

say. He would say, "Create a space. Create a space." And that kept gnawing at me. As I went back to my father and we kept talking about this, all of the sudden it began to make sense - what "create a space" was supposed to look like or mean. And I never forgot that. **Chike Nwoffiah**

If you're thinking, "Oh, that's clearly a low income, inner city boy of color that Chike is talking about." It may well be. He works largely with African-American teens in East Palo Alto, CA. But stop right there if you think that higher income, white suburban boys don't face their own dramatic coming of age challenges. Theirs just come in different forms. It may not be death by gun violence. Theirs tend to come with greater likelihood of alcohol and drug addiction, greater likelihood of suicide, greater likelihood of committing armed violence on a massive scale, greater likelihood of dying while drinking and driving. Rich white boys are category leaders in a number of scales of dysfunction. They may be well educated but they are no wiser than any other boys in avoiding the pitfalls of their unconscious drive to be initiated.

That's the complacency I often face when addressing largely well to do, largely white communities. "Oh, that's an issue for *them*. We don't have those problems in *our* community. *Our* kids come from good homes." Dream on! Many parents are fooled by the unconscious protection that privilege affords. Money and skin color and social status might protect some boys from facing certain kinds of self-destruction, but not others. The statistics don't lie. Privilege is not a dysfunction deterrent.

I filmed a case in point. In my TV mini-series *Boys to Men?*, Spencer was a fine Jewish boy who was Bar Mitzvahed at 13. Bright, funny, sensitive, affectionate, and caring, he had a lot going for him. He came from a "good home" in a "good community." Both his parents were regularly present – his father was even working at home – and both were thoughtful and loving caretakers. His largely white New Jersey suburb had good public schools and was considered relatively safe. There was only one problem. As a 15 year old, Spencer was obsessed with the idea of going into his school armed with semi-automatic weapons to shoot and kill his teachers, administrators and fellow classmates. Not long after I started filming his year-long story, I started to think of him as the prototype Columbine killer.

Fortunately, Spencer, as far as I know, never committed acts of actual violence; he did eventually transition into adulthood. But his story is nonetheless exemplary. He had seizures from the time he was a small boy. His physical limitations kept him from participating in sports with his peers. When I met him at 15, he was somewhat overweight and "schlubby," not physically coordinated or adept. Despite the fact that, like many boys his age, he was into violent video games and the World Wrestling Federation, due to his physical limitations he was largely ignored, humiliated or outright bullied by male peers most of his young life. He was largely ignored by girls or was too inhibited to approach them. He was a seething cauldron of resentment and rage.

I started filming his story about a month before he underwent brain surgery. Modern medicine has attributed certain kinds of seizures to abnormalities in the hippocampus and has had tremendous success by simply removing it. The family understandably hoped the surgery would be a game changer. They fully expected that after his surgery Spencer would eventually assume a life of physical normalcy for an average teen. And that's what happened. Eventually his seizures stopped and he was able for the first time to pursue many previously forbidden physical activities. But the accompanying windfall of emotional and psychological shifts did not materialize. Spencer still fantasized repeatedly about violence and revenge on all those who judged, excluded and humiliated him.

Receiving some adept mentorship and a real ROP could have made all the difference. Spencer needed rituals of new physical challenge. An alert mentor might have insisted that Spencer accompany him on a backpacking trip. Spencer needed to experience being away from home, away from monitoring machines and away from Mom in wholly new and significant ways (Separation). He needed to experience his new human body in ways that would test and prove its new capacities and resilience (Ordeal). He needed a chance to bond with a man, or men, in ways that had been previously forbidden – out in nature, under open skies, without the comforts and confinements of home – in order to begin to recognize his own deeper nature and see himself as a true male peer. He needed to return home and be celebrated and honored by his family and community as a man among men (Homecoming). This ROP might have accomplished what no successful surgery ever could. He needed the symbolic death of his old identity as "a boy with seizures" and a rebirth as "a young man capable of anything." I hope Spencer eventually found his life's true calling.

It's arguably more important for men to have a sense of mission or purpose in life because they're more dangerous without it. Men have a strong built-in desire to want to serve someone or something, to know that their life has meaning and is of positive purpose. This is no less true of women of course, but it is fair to say that historically much of that sense of purpose for women came through child rearing and service to the family. There's a longing in men to feel part of a team or a group outside the family, to work together with others to realize a common purpose. A man's gaze tends to be outward, toward making an impact, toward how he can provide for his family, yes, but also for his community. He tends to want to effect change in the greater world. This is a large part of how a man gauges his own power. Obviously, this drive can take very positive or very negative forms. But the drive itself is very much inherent in the nature of men.

Very few people understand this anymore. Many missionless, purposeless men in their own bitterness, depression and addictions - due to drugs, alcohol, sex, work, food or TV - have given up on themselves. At some deep unconscious level, they know what they're missing in life, how they themselves were never taught by other men how to be a man, how to reach for and find fulfillment in life, how to understand and utilize emotions effectively, what spiritual connection and contentment feels like and where to find meaning. No one was there for them so why should they be there for someone else? How could they be?

> *I thought working 80 or 90 hours a week was the appropriate way to prove that I was a functioning man in society and I damn nearly killed myself doing that. I had four massive bleeding ulcers from that behavior and that still wasn't enough to wake me up and say, "Stop that." We as men, because we have this phenomenal capacity to focus on whatever it is we're doing, whether it's destructive or not, we can completely ignore all the signs saying, "That's inappropriate behavior. Stop it! Do something different!" So we continue down those paths, a lot of times, until we burn out, we self-destruct, we crash and burn, and then, maybe, finally, we wake up, after our third marriage has blown up, after our kids look at us and don't know us, after we look across the table and see our partner, our wives, and we recognize we're complete strangers to them. It takes that kind of stuff sometimes for men to wake up. Initiation helps to wake them up sooner so they don't have to go down those paths to begin with. So, they start channeling their energy in appropriate ways to begin with.* **Jim Mitchell**

Men who were never mentored, never initiated, never brought to know their mission, end up delivering all sorts of negative messages to younger men: "Don't follow your dream!" "Take what you can get!" "Happiness is not important." "Settle for the money!" "Grow up; get real; resign yourself…" "Get a real job." "Don't take risks!" The truth is many older men are simply threatened by the exuberance, vitality, dreams, love, innocence and happiness of younger men because it reminds them of what they've lost, how they themselves settled for so much less, how they ended up feeling pointless and futile. Fortunately, these older men still have a little boy in them somewhere who knows and remembers those early dreams. No matter how old they are, it's never too late for them to experience ROP, to be mentored, to find some joy and fulfillment in life. But those little boys are usually buried alive under mountains of passion-killing directives. They have to be dug out of the rubble.

That innocent little boy, that "golden child," represents the purity and goodness that all of us enter this world with. It's the "God within," our

THE MATURE MASCULINE (AND HOW IT SERVES WOMEN!)

"Buddha nature," our "essential goodness." We are born with that wholeness and sense of oneness. It may be a matter of years or it may only be a matter of seconds before that innocence is met with some rude awakening. Pure innocence is not sustainable even in the best of families and the happiest of circumstances.

It's usually in later years, although not much later, when that Golden Child starts being handed some of life's hard lessons. Betrayals and hypocrisies in the adult world start to appear, maybe regularly. Even though the wounding we take on is painful, it's not a bad thing to receive it because we can't function effectively in the world with naiveté. Robert Bly, one of the godfathers of the "Men's Movement," has spoken about the Naïve Male needing his comeuppance. Without proper mentoring, that older, wounded boy usually starts to develop his own shadow strategies for getting what he wants. He starts to become driven largely by his unconscious fears and appetites. As he gets older, those strategies can become his dominant mode of interacting with the world. They may remain, becoming more pervasive throughout his lifetime, the driving force of much of his destructive, "adult" behavior.

> "The Mature Masculine must be reclaimed by the modern world. Its virtual absence from technologically advanced societies has resulted in one of the more serious moral crises ever to face Western civilization... In our world, genocide is barely noticed. Rape is used as an instrument of both pathological male self-expression and ethnic war... Violence is becoming the preferred solution to interpersonal disputes. In all this, we see evidence that Mature Masculinity, in its fullness, has all but been forgotten, and that 'Boy Psychology' is prevalent." **Robert Moore & Douglas Gillette, *King Warrior Magician Lover***

In 2008, I was asked to give a presentation to about a thousand U.S. Army Non-Commissioned Officers in Washington, D.C. They had flown in from around the world to attend a weekend of presentations on ending sexual harassment and abuse. The Army's stated goal was to end it within ten years. They failed. Miserably.

But I don't fault them for trying. I was scheduled as the first speaker. After all the welcoming speeches by officials and politicians, we were running half an hour late. By the time I came to the podium, I was told to reduce my presentation from 30 minutes to ten.

I wanted to show clips from my *Boys to Men?* series which clearly illustrate ways in which masculinity formation takes place in teen boys. I wanted to explore how those issues play out in adult men and can impact them in relation to sexual harassment and abuse.

I couldn't do any of that in ten minutes. Instead, I said I wanted to address the men in the room directly. (Though the conference organizers were women, the audience looked to me to be about 98% men.) I basically told them that until they could feel their own feelings the likelihood was extremely small that they could ever relate to or understand the feelings of sexual abuse victims. I walked off to a smattering of polite applause and was not invited back to a similar gathering the following year.

I might as well have told the men that until you live on Mars, you'll never understand Earth. Suppression of feelings is one of the key lessons every soldier is taught in boot camp. During battle time deployment, it is certainly true that feeling feelings can get one killed. Circumstances of life and death demand that soldiers make the best, most rational decisions they can in the moment. Though intuition can be extremely valuable at those times, succumbing to accompanying emotions of fear, anger, sadness and shame can be life threatening. Training takes over and normal mental processes are overridden by programmed autonomic patterns. But what's an invaluable MO in wartime can itself become a killer in peacetime.

The problem is human emotions are not faucets that can be switched on and off at will. Once men and boys are trained by parents, peers, schools, workplaces or the military to hide, repress and deny emotions, they don't come back with ease and facility when needed. With them switched off, we will remain unconscious of what makes us most human. This doesn't mean those feelings no longer exist. They're just driven underground where the danger of the truths they represent can be repressed. Then, when feelings arise in others, just like in ourselves, we insist they be choked down, often with insults and judgments: "Don't be a pussy. Suck it up. Stop acting like a baby. Be a man!"

The latter judgment points toward part of the military problem. Women aren't "man enough" to suck it up when they come forward with their stories of sexual harassment and abuse. That's their "problem." If they were "man enough," their pain would be treated like all pains in the military – something to be ignored and dealt with privately. The military is not institutionally or culturally equipped to deal with the pains that victims of sexual abuse and harassment experience. The documentary *The Invisible War* makes this painfully clear.

Still, my presentation didn't fall entirely on deaf ears. Women responded. During the evening reception, one woman told me privately she had been waiting her entire life to hear a man say what I said. Other women also came up and thanked me. I don't recall speaking to a single man.

As I've said, my own journey on the path to the Mature Masculine began when I was nine. After my father's sudden death, there followed many years in which my dad's name was never spoken in our house. I drove all my grief, confusion and fear underground and never once had a conversation with my siblings or mother about my dad. Silence became the norm. Though the term didn't exist for another 15 years, I basically grew up with post-traumatic stress. Whenever my peers asked about my dad, I simply said he was dead. That ended the conversation. It was only a matter of time before those painful feelings I had repressed surged to the surface and I acted out.

The one and only time I ever hit a woman was when I was 18. My girlfriend and I were in Jamaica. I was masking my fright at this strange new world behind bravado. The Third World we called it then – low income people of color with ways foreign to me. I needed intimacy and wanted reassurance, but I wasn't conscious of it and didn't know how to ask for it. When my girlfriend was her usual social self at a party one night, talking with numerous other men, my frustration and jealousy boiled over into rage. I called her outside, started to yell at her and ended up hitting her on the shoulder with my fist. I was like many men who enact their inability to express feelings and emotional needs by acting out in violence. It's a common male shadow strategy. We were already drifting apart anyway, so once we got back to the States, we had the good sense to break up.

I believe a lot of domestic violence would disappear if men were taught emotional intelligence from an early age. No one showed up to teach me. If only I had a mentor as a teen, things might have been different. Of course, most men don't have mentors and are not taught emotional intelligence. But that incident told me something was wrong. I didn't know what to do or how to do it, but somewhere inside I knew I needed to work on myself. The irony with my girlfriend was that we only grew closer after we broke up. She became my best friend.

I didn't realize it at the time but I was drawn to the company of women and gay men. I unconsciously felt my emotions were safe with them, and I could risk being vulnerable. I unconsciously steered away from strong Type A males who were just like me, driving most of their emotions deep underground. My father certainly modeled that behavior for me before he died. I ended up projecting my father's and my own emotionally repressed behavior onto other men. I also judged "strong men" as arrogant and full of themselves, just like my dad – self-appointed leaders seeking obeisance. This pattern emerged in my teens and continued into my 30s: reject "strong" men and draw near to women, gay men and "softer" straight men.

Robert Bly says American men are the walking wounded, unconsciously seeking their father's blessing. That was certainly true for me. As a filmmaker, I sought approval and recognition through my work, thinking it might somehow fill that void. Certainly, a great deal of my artistic life has been spent analyzing "father issues." That was also a fair summation of most of the men I knew. The evidence of that father wounding and of all those sons' unconscious seeking is too great to recount here. Suffice it to say that too many men are suspended adolescents, ruled by their fears and unconscious appetites, still trying to prove something to Daddy. Unfortunately, given the immeasurable extent of horrible consequences, those men largely run the world. Conversely, it's worth noting that female-led countries have fared much better in their Covid-19 infection and mortality rates than male-led ones.

By the time I entered college at 17, I considered myself a feminist. I was raised by a feminist mother and, to a lesser degree of influence, a feminist older sister. Feminism, gender equality, and fairness all made implicit sense to me, along with all other forms of social justice – race, religion, sexual orientation, class. But even so, in lessons I learned during adolescence from my mom, like "You need to learn how to be a good husband to your wife," there was always an implicit if not overt tone of shaming. "You need to measure up. You need to succeed where millions of other men have failed. Otherwise, you will not be good enough. You will be a failure." Being a man made me suspect and insufficient.

So, I grew up suspicious and insecure about my gender. I was not proud of becoming a man. In my 20s it led to suspicions that I might be gay. If my film mentor and some of my friends were gay, perhaps I was too? I felt no physical attraction to men. But I chased myself in endless mental circles wondering if I was denying something to myself. I drove myself so crazy with worry over relationships that I once thought maybe if I just cut off my penis all will be well.

Though my mother and sister would have been horrified at the notion, they planted some of the seeds. They never missed an opportunity to recount parts of the endless list of male crimes against women and girls, against humanity in general – the crimes of patriarchy. Were these statements accurate? Yes. Was it important for me to be aware of my male privilege? Yes. But was I somehow personally to blame for these earlier crimes? No. Was it my responsibility to carry shame on behalf of all men? No. Yet I was brought to feel it was my shame to carry by virtue of being born male. Along with the mental confusion, this instilled in me some resentment and fear around women. When they criticized my behavior, it felt controlling. I didn't want to be controlled; I wanted to be inspired to be the best man I could be. I didn't want to be shamed into being a better man. I wanted to learn what is noble and good about being a man. That meant having Mature Masculinity modeled for me by emotionally open, psychically strong, virtuous men. Thanks to "men's work," this was something I finally experienced in my 40s.

But that was later. Back in my college days, I read Susan Brownmiller. "[Rape] is nothing more or less than a conscious process of intimidation by which all men keep all women in a state of fear." I also read numerous other feminists. Partly due to this education in feminism, partly due to the admonitions of my mother and sister and partly due to my natural shyness around attractive women, I never would engage in any behavior around women that could be misconstrued as offensive. I would never say anything complementary about a woman's appearance unless or until I got to know her very well – not clothes, not hair, not eyes, certainly not body shape, nothing. I would almost never touch a woman unless she touched me first or she explicitly invited me to. I would never open a door for a woman for fear of signaling some incapacity on her part. I would never offer to pay for something like a meal or coffee for fear of reinforcing economic inequities or setting up unwelcome concerns about unspoken expectations of repayment. Even when having sex with long established lovers, I would never assert strong "top" behaviors unless I explicitly received encouragement or permission.

Fortunately, I had enough sense to start therapy in my early thirties. I started to realize how I was transferring my controlling mother on to other women, that my fears of offending them were mental projections. I started to understand the deep pain I carried due to my unconscious wounds. My therapist helped me understand that my fear of secretly being gay was simply a metaphor for my repressed feelings. I displaced the fear of all that unexpressed pain with the fear of "my secret," of "really being gay." I wasn't gay. I just had to turn and face a lot of hurt that I didn't want to accept about myself. It wasn't my sexual orientation I needed to bring out of the closet, it was my emotions.

I was nearing 40 when I started "men's work" and learned about emotional intelligence. I only then discovered, as a more confident heterosexual man, how to give and get love from other men. What led me there was purely intuitive. My brother had done The ManKind Project's flagship workshop -

the New Warrior Training Adventure (NWTA) - and called to recommend it to me. I sensed that I could benefit from being among these men. Secretly, unconsciously, I had desired it for all the many years since my dad died. I was ready.

There was a period in my early 20s when I had an inexplicable desire to join the military. That urge made absolutely no sense to me, yet there it was. My family was pacifist. I demonstrated against the Vietnam war starting when I was ten, first with my mother and later with my friends. Militarism was anathema to me. I was a perfect example of abnormal negation.

I unconsciously recognized my need for initiation. I never could have articulated these issues then but I wanted to be taught how to be a man. I wanted to learn toughness. I wanted to experience the distinct stages of Severance, Ordeal and Return. I wanted to learn how to become an equal with Type A men[7].

I never joined the military. It was the NWTA that taught me even the toughest men are precious and tender at their core and, when approached in non-threatening ways, will often share their own rich emotional life. I learned that being vulnerable not only shows courage, it opens the door to others and makes deep relationships possible. I learned that my heart was my great gift to the world, not just my intellect. I learned that my own silence was toxic. For my survival and well-being, I needed to articulate my feelings. My life was never the same.

I also learned how to take pride in being a man. In fact, there is something sacred about being a man. I no longer feel personal shame about the crimes of patriarchy. I recognize how I perceive and react to the world very differently from women and that's OK. I have acquired strong awareness and facility with my emotions and delight in their skillful application.

---

[7] In the absence of other broadly sanctioned opportunities for initiation, men in particular are drawn to the military. The military has tremendous recruitment success partly because their advertising appeals to the semi-conscious need by recruits for initiation. "Be all you can be." "Looking for a few good men." Though they certainly deliver partway on that promise - teaching subservience to the collective, living for mission, the tenuousness of human life and the importance of service - they just as certainly do not fully deliver on it.

As for my relations with women, I've since lessened my fear of causing offense and my willingness to carry shame and have changed some earlier behaviors. Times have also changed. I now view it as socially acceptable to offer to pay for meals or movies or to open doors. But I still default to steering clear of any topic in conversation, like compliments, that could be taken the wrong way. I used to think I was inept at flirting. Now I recognize that I simply don't engage in it, occasionally because of intimidation, but mostly for fear of offending or harassing. It's important to me now to take pride in my masculinity and use it for good in the world.

Certainly, ending sexual harassment and abuse is a fundamental part of Mature Masculinity. But the point is that we as men should not be shamed into doing the right thing. It is not effective. No amount of finger wagging is ever going to motivate a man. It's not very effective on teen boys either. We must be blessed and inspired to speak out and take action because we know in our hearts it is right. We must learn, through ROP and mentorship, that service to the feminine is the ultimate and most fulfilling form of service. Assuming leadership of our own lives demands nothing less.

> *When teens, especially boys, aren't blessed to take an appropriate place in the community, then the community begins to do without their leadership in future generations. And it also begins a process where, since they're not allowed to take their place in a positive way, they're going to take their place inappropriately. So now you've got the current generation that is at war with the next one because it's showing up in inappropriate ways. And that conflict is destructive in and of itself.*
> **Jim Mitchell**

When men are not blessed and "seen," they cannot break the cycle of dysfunction they were raised in. When the Elders don't bless the youngers, there is no generativity. The seeds of youth empowerment and growth are not watered. So, the next generation becomes like the last. And the cycle continues.

Nonetheless, I see hopeful changes in the societal landscape. Take sports, for example. As a lifetime devotee, both as a player and spectator, I have come to appreciate the ways that sports coaching has shifted over the years. The old school, perhaps typified best by famed Green Bay Packers coach Vince Lombardi, thrived on military strategy, tactics and approach. It was imperative not just to beat an opponent. You sought to crush him, to destroy not only his ability to execute but his motivation to fight on. It was war. All or nothing. Or as Lombardi put it, "Winning isn't everything. It's the only thing." Training was approached like military Boot Camp.

Every athlete knows they have to make enormous and regular sacrifices in order to compete at the highest levels. It's difficult for strength and conditioning coaches to know what stress is sufficient to condition the body, and what is pushing too hard. But in addition to an often-herculean physical regimen, military model coaches regularly belittle and even humiliate players, abusing them verbally and emotionally like a Marines drill instructor. The most recent negative example of this comes from University of Maryland head football coach D.J. Durkin who was fired after 19 year old player Jordan McNair died of heatstroke following the first workout of summer. That workout included ten 110-yard sprints in 80-degree temperatures. The teen complained of dehydration but was urged, some say abusively, to work harder. When he was later checked into the hospital, his body temperature was 106 degrees.

The same dysfunctions that define what has been called "Toxic Masculinity" are standard for this paradigm of coaching. All the military humiliations discussed earlier apply here too: "Don't be a pussy. Suck it up. Stop acting like a baby. Be a man!"

Phil Jackson, the winningest coach in NBA history - of the Chicago Bulls and LA Lakers - was, at least to my awareness, one of the first coaches to instill a different ethic. Perhaps due to his coming of age in the 1960s or perhaps due to his interest in Native American practices, Jackson tried to instill his players with a sense of collective mission or purpose. Built into that collective mission were personal goals for each player that not only reflected their basketball aspirations, but their growth and achievement as men. He seemed to be saying, "If we're not becoming better human beings in the pursuit of basketball excellence, what is the point?" He understood that happier, more mature and evolved players made his job of jelling them into a cohesive unit easier and made the players themselves more successful. He tried to instill a sense of the sacred into the long journey of an NBA season, making each season something of a ROP. "What are you learning? How are you growing?" he was saying, often literally. For road trips and Christmas gifts he used to give each of his players a different book that he hoped might benefit their growth as men and to expand their awareness of themselves and the world.

Our film *Hoop Dreams* hinted at some of these cultural differences in coaching. Gene Pingatore, the coach of St. Joseph's High School, symbolized for me the outgoing military model of coaching. His style was based partly on the infamous coach Bobby Knight, who he idolized. Luther Bedford, coach of Chicago's Marshall High School Boys' Team, while certainly no direct opposite, was different in style and approach.

The moment that best exemplifies this difference occurs during the boys' senior year. Coach Pingatore admonishes his team to be silent on the coming bus ride and to think about the ballgame. He sits stone-faced at the front of the bus. In a direct edit that we call a match cut, we instantly shift the view to the Marshall bus where the kids are loud and raucous. While Bedford sits up front in the bus looking typically world weary, Arthur sits in the back playing cards with his pals. Though Bedford, like Pingatore, would yell at the players and directly and repeatedly point out their mistakes, he certainly embodied a more laid-back approach. But his wasn't a product of any New Age philosophy or studied methodology. His more relaxed demeanor was born of hard trial. He knew too well that the challenges his players faced every time they walked outside the school door – at home, on the streets, in the job market - were greater than he could possibly overcome. He recognized that the players needed to have fun and blow off steam. They didn't just need playing time on the court, they needed bona fide playtime – to be kids again, to let loose. He provided them with a refuge from the world outside, a sanctuary where the little kid in each of them could romp.

ROP and mentorship, when properly delivered, whether through sports or other means, tend to include awareness of and respect for the feminine. One essential component of Mature Masculinity, if not the most important, is to serve the Divine Feminine. This is no less true of gay men, whose expressions of service to the feminine may show up in service to their partner, other men or women friends, clients, and co-workers, or to themselves. "We Serve and Protect" is a slogan that should not be limited to the police.

When men are depressed, especially when accompanied by unemployment, it's often because they're not serving the feminine. They're not "being a man." They feel inadequate. They feel like they're not measuring up to their role as provider. They're not competent caretakers and breadwinners for those they love. They blame themselves when their children don't receive the quality living conditions, clothes and gifts that their peers do, even more so when they can't get them proper medical care or when those children go hungry. There are studies showing that men tend to respond to a baby's cry with more distress than women. When the children are unhappy, much less unfed or uncared for, men feel like failures. Maybe this stress is innate from as far back as when men were hunters and gatherers. In any case, I believe this sense of failure to be both cultural and genetic, both nature and nurture. But we must understand that when men feel useless, they are dangerous.

Faced with feelings of impotence, men tend to implode or explode. Implosion looks like depression, apathy, self-medicating, suicide, or addiction to sex, alcohol, drugs, TV, sleep or food. This is only a short list. Most of the world already knows what explosion looks like. Violence. Violence against women, children, or other men. Men feeling impotent is a huge contributor to domestic violence.

A man judging himself as an inadequate caretaker can show up at other times. When a man's partner has been attacked, sexually assaulted or harassed, the impotence felt by the male can lead to implosion and drive couples to eventually separate. A man will all too often blame himself for not preventing the violence. Even when a man himself is the perpetrator of attacks on women or children, he can commit additional acts of psychic or emotional violence on himself. He often knows, somewhere in his conscience, that his job is opposite. (Which is not to let perpetrators off the hook. They're always responsible for the violence they commit. It's to point out that the antecedents can be complex.) Their job is to serve and protect the Feminine. Not because they're the "weaker sex," but because they're the guarantors of generativity.

To discuss everything that comprises Mature Masculinity and why it's so needed requires a separate book. But let's highlight some key points. Some of these we've already touched on, and most of these are similar to, if not actual duplicates of the benefits of teen initiation listed at the end of Chapter Two.

- **Accountability and integrity.** I believe a man, in his heart of hearts, wants to be seen as a man of honor. He wants to know that he can be counted on to fulfill his commitments, that his word is his bond. Until a man learns how to make agreements with himself and others that he can keep, and learns how to live in integrity by renegotiating those agreements as needed, he cannot be counted upon. Upholding agreements is the pillar to making relationships work and is paramount to social cohesion. The military teaches this, but shockingly few other mainstream institutions emphasize it. Many take it as a given, but very few actually teach it.
- **Emotional intelligence.** This is especially important for men today. Dominant Western culture still teaches men to repress their feelings. Men must be encouraged to feel their feelings, starting with being able to identify what they are and where they live in the body. It's fine for a man to control his emotions. In fact, being able to control emotions is ideal. But there is a big difference between controlling emotions and repressing them. A man must learn to skillfully identify when, where and how to express them. Until a man can claim full awareness of them and appropriate expression of them, conscious control of them will mean nothing.
- **Mission.** A man without a mission is a sailor without a compass.
- **Service.** "Who, or what, do you serve?" is a question every man needs

- **Brotherhood**. Capitalism has taught men how to live in competition with each other. Most men feel like they have to compete with other men for scarce resources: property, jobs, money, material goods and women. Men need to learn how to live in cooperation with each other. ROP teaches this.
- **Help**. Men need to learn how to ask for help. So much of how we are brought up, and likely some of our genetic coding, is to be self-reliant. But that self-reliance can quickly lead to isolation. I call isolation "The Male Disease." Men need to be able to reach out to other men for support, to reach past the fear and shame that can entomb them.
- **Living in harmony and balance with the feminine**. One to one masculine/feminine relationship is Ground Zero for peace in the world. Without peace and tranquility in oneself, in one's primary relationship, in one's home, there can be no peace in the greater world. I was gratified that, for many years, people who entered the home Tracy and I made together often spontaneously commented on the serenity and calm they felt. Though we certainly had our challenges, our fights and our own shadows to contend with, we succeeded in creating a harmonious and tranquil home.

In Chapter Eight, I talk in detail about a ROP experience I had out in the mountains of the Eastern Sierra. Let me mention one aspect of it here. I had a profound vision of the Divine Feminine. On the final night, as I stayed awake and prayed, staring into the vast night sky, unpolluted by city lights, smog or even clouds, I saw the entire firmament as a female dancer – legs spread wide in a great leap forward, arms parallel, all pointing to the north and the east. She was the icon of artistry and force. But also of Eros because her crotch was exposed at the midpoint – a dark clump of galaxies and deep space. She was creation itself, ready to be served and loved, and yes, penetrated, to bring forth all that exists.

The entire subsequent year came to be about service to that Divine Feminine in the form of my wife. That was the last year of her life and

I spent much of it tending to her. I did everything I could think of to make her last days as pain free and happy as I could, pumping every ounce of love into her I had in me. This was my Rite of Passage into Eldership. I had much to learn about putting my own needs aside in order to stand wholly in service to her. Grief brought me to my knees again and again. I was humbled.

Eros was served too. The proof of that came in the days after her death. What started as a way for me to stay in connection with her, to serve the memory of our time together, quickly became a book. *At Death Do Us Part*, published three years ago, is the first fruit of that coupling. This book is the second. Now, much to my amazement and surprise, I think of myself not only as a filmmaker but as a writer of books. It all stems from that desire to make love with that dancer in the sky.

Men serving the Divine Feminine, who have not buried alive their little boys, who still receive nurturing from their Elders, who have kept alive the flame of innocence, passion and love in the face of enormous challenges – not least of which is a dominant culture that stultifies humanity, demanding that all answers be found solely in consumerism – those men are heroes. Just being alive, truly alive to a world of service, possibility and adventure, and yes, to suffering and sorrow too, in a modern world that increasingly resembles The Matrix, makes you a hero.

But say you're doing more than that. Say you're teaching yourself and others about what you missed out on, seeking and finding ways to get yourself initiated, getting and giving mentorship, truly coming to be all you can be. Let's say you're reaching down a generation or two and extending your hand to younger people, or to groups of younger people. That's even more impressive. Then you're a Hero's Hero.

Those men who stand in service to the Divine Feminine, and stand in service to the next generation by mentoring and initiating teen boys, are some of the real heroes of our world today. These are no small challenges given that most adult men living today were not themselves initiated or mentored. They have no idea what to do, how to do it or why it's essential. There aren't enough of these good men, but there are many. At the back of this book you'll find my personal list of The Ten Best Mentorship Practices along with my list of the Desired Qualities of a Mentor. You'll also find listed some of the men, women and organizations working hard today to bring back initiation and mentorship to teen boys in our time. You'll find them along with their weblinks. Dive in and rejoice.

What You Need To Do *Now*

- Get yourself a free copy of Tom Pitner and Jim Warner's "Becoming a Man - A One-Year Rite of Passage Program for Adolescent Boys." https://www.oncourseinternational.com/wp-content/uploads/2021/02
- /Becoming-a-Man-Summary.pdf
- If you're a man, get yourself into a men's support group. If you're a woman, invite the men you love to do the same. But do it without telling them they're somehow wrong; do it without shaming them. There are many men's support groups besides MKP's I-groups.
- Take a workshop or a training exclusively designed for men like MKP.org or Noble Man.
- If you're in LA, join the Men's Community of LA. Colorado has Men's Leadership Alliance. Minnesota has a thriving community of men meeting for almost 40 years. Atlanta has "100 Black Men." Look around, there are similar supportive communities of men everywhere.
- Pick up books by some of these authors: Jed Diamond, David Deida, Stephen Johnson, Robert Moore, Doug Gillette, Robert Bly, John Lee, Bill Kauth, Richard Rohr, Richard Heckler, Sam Keen, Bret Stephenson, David Gilmore, William Pollack. All of them offer a wealth of knowledge on Mature Masculinity.

4

Mentorship and Eldership

Our society doesn't often offer mentorship for young people, someone who really will stand with them and walk through this time. To me it's indicative of the lack of Elders being honored in our culture. **Meredith Little**

I think of mentoring as "practice eldering." That you begin to practice being an Elder by being involved in the lives of others, by trying to foster depth and meaning and new values in those other lives. **Michael Meade**

At adolescence, the higher self dials into the human being. Guidance starts. It says look for truth in the world because it's not a given. You only learn by being close to people who are living out that truth. That's the mentorship process. **Orland Bishop**

If the deep conflicts of youth are ignored and left unresolved, the new adults will be unable to solve deep conflicts in the culture. If the adults feel they were not nourished, their Elders will be ignored and forgotten. **Michael Meade**

Links in the chain of human time are now broken. In most contemporary Western societies, the elderly and the young largely exist only in ghettoes of their peers. The elderly in the U.S., if they can afford it, retire to Arizona or Florida where they often inhabit gated retirement communities with similar retirees. Many of these communities expressly limit or prohibit the presence of young people. A lot of these retirees live like suspended adolescents, pursuing leisure activities full time – golfing and tennis are popular – and do little or nothing to pass on the knowledge and life experience they may have accumulated. It's a wasted resource of immense proportions. And those seniors are the lucky ones. Most of the aged are secluded in nursing or retirement homes in their towns of origin, again cut off and excluded from daily interaction with the young.

> *The intergenerational transfer of knowledge becomes critical for capacity building in a community, for adaptation, for the resiliency index. Remove the connectivity between the Elders and the children and you have undermined the structure of your village. With the creation of the childcare industry and the senior and elder care industry, we have in fact intentionally undermined the capacity for families to pass on their knowledge intergenerationally. In fact, in modern society, we've actually made a bold move towards the "nuclear" family, which doesn't include the extended family. And from a traditional perspective, one could say that that might in fact be undermining our capacity for sustained resilience over time.* **Kalani Souza**

Part of restoring the sacred to everyday life must include our sense of Time. ROP help to position us in time. We can see ourselves as part of a lineage. We can recognize, to a palpable degree, where it is we have come from and where it is we are going, in this life and to a degree, beyond.

For most people, if experienced at all, this sense is limited to their immediate families. They may recognize their parents, grandparents and great-grandparents and the ethnic or cultural or religious history they descended from. They may also recognize that "their name will live on" through the existence of their children, grandchildren and great-grandchildren. This is wholesome and meaningful. But there is something beyond the mere facts of lineage that needs to be called out and named. It's not enough for me to say, "My father was German, my mother Russian, and both come from a long line of Jewish ancestors." It's important for me to know and learn what that means. What is it to be German? What is it to be Russian? What is it to be Jewish? And equally important, what is it to be a refugee called or forced to leave one's home and come to a distant unknown land called the USA? Each of these questions drives inquiry back in time. In an ideal world, that inquiry is sated by stories. The stories that we hear from Elders are the means by which we learn the warp and weave of our particular strand of time.

The elderly, by and large, are not invited into schools where they might find avid and appreciative listeners to the stories from their past. Preschools, after-school groups, church groups, summer camps, private tutoring services - none of these institutions promote interaction across generations. None of them make productive use of the vastly underutilized resource of the elderly.

The same is true for inviting the presence of young people into the company of elders. Young people are all too often afforded little to no meaningful interaction with elders other than brief trips to visit grandparents. Young people are often not welcome in communities of the aged. In subtle or overt ways, they are told they are "too noisy, too undisciplined, too rambunctious…" In short, they are children. So, they are kept separate.

So, what happens? The young do not get a deep sense of connection to the ancestral lineage they're a part of. They receive neither the wisdom, the love nor the history. They don't receive the calming waters to cool and soothe the heat with which they so vibrantly burn. They don't become intimately familiar with their own roots – their own families, neighborhoods, cultures, seasonal and geographic history. They don't experience the realities of aging, or see a tangible vision of their own future and get a taste of where life might lead them. They also don't experience firsthand the quirks of character, with all the accompanying peculiarities, of being older, which is the very stuff that makes people unique and memorable. I remember my mom saying to me when she was about 78, "I don't care anymore what people think. I'm too old to not just be myself." That is one of the great gifts of Eldership. Seniors typically reveal who they are with great abandon. They're a wonderful model for children, especially teens, who can be too fearful or inhibited to express their true selves.

The inverse is true for the elderly. They don't get spiritually nourished by the young. They don't receive needed bursts of enthusiasm and energy, energy that can provide indispensable stimulation and excitement bringing forth new ideas and enhancing the will to live. They don't receive the unfiltered spontaneous wisdom and love of the young. They lose out on the recognition and profundity of witnessing genetic and cultural coding in action. They lose that foretaste of the future, of seeing how their own genes and cultural memes might play out in coming years. They may never catch even a glimpse of the shape of the beads in that imminent human chain to come. There is no generativity.

A first priority in bringing the sacred back to the everyday has to be rejoining the communities of Elders with the youngers. One of the most common and productive fields in which to do that is ROP. Initiation rituals restore an integrated, meaningful sense of time and place for Initiates. No younger should depart for ROP without receiving the blessing of an Elder. No younger should engage in ROP without the guidance and support of an Elder. No younger should ever return from ROP and experience a Homecoming without the blessings and acknowledgment of Elders.

Similarly, no Elder should ever miss out on the opportunity to support and witness a younger person's ROP journey. Doing so will only reduce the fountain of nourishment for their own life.

Elders and youngers are two halves of one whole. Elders provide mentorship. Youngers are the mentees. But age alone does not secure one a position in this equation. Too many "elders" are not fit for mentorship because they're still self-obsessed. Youngers can and should mentor peers and those younger still. There's no reason why college seniors shouldn't mentor college freshmen, and college freshmen mentor high school seniors, and so on, down the line to grammar school students.

We need to create systems of tiered mentorship, creating mentoring relationships through the whole of the normal life span, whether inside institutions or out. As Michael Meade reminds us, "Mentoring is practice eldership."

How mentorship creates wholeness in community is one of my takeaways from Meade's version of the Borneo Half-boy story. It takes a younger and an Elder dancing together in the sacred circle of community to make the community whole. Without it, there is no fullness, no completion, no joy. Without them dancing together, the village forgets how to dance.

Most leaders I meet - whether of corporations, non-profits, community groups, social service agencies, schools or government - do not comprehend the sustaining dynamics of their own leadership. I usually ask them "Who are you mentoring?" Most of them have ready answers and are actively mentoring a few individuals. But when I ask them about succession, what plans they have made to qualify and train their replacements, most come up short. Most have yet to give it much consideration. They're too consumed by running everything. In most cases for them, steering requires 24/7 attention. This is shortsighted. They are not building generativity into their thinking and arrangements. They're not training their mentees, much less acknowledging and encouraging them, to assume command of their operations. They're in denial. They're not fully accepting the reality that they may drop dead tomorrow – and if they're truly working 24/7, with all the accompanying stressors, dropping dead of heart attack or stroke is all too common – and that once gone, the institutions, the networks, the relationships, the knowledge they've built and sustained, all too often will die with them. Most of these leaders haven't yet have named, much less trained, their successors.

That's bad enough. But then I ask them a second question. "Who is mentoring *you*?" For most, this question is anathema. Though they rarely say this, all too often their attitude is "I'm the leader! I'm the one in charge, making the decisions. I don't need a mentor!" They tend to think that, though they might have peer groups that can support and help sustain them, they are beyond the need for mentorship themselves. They tend to think of mentorship in hierarchical terms, that a mentor might be like a new boss they don't need or want since "the buck stops" with them. This is shadow. It's the standalone shadow that I find most commonly in men. "I can do it all myself. I don't need anyone else." Some will immediately call to mind mentors who helped them on their road to leadership and do so gratefully. This is good. None of us exist in a vacuum of our own self-creation, even though that's often what we think, especially the more successful we become. Naming and acknowledging our forebears is essential. But it's only a starting point.

Why do most leaders stop seeking mentorship when they realize a certain position of age or authority? It's tempting to say "hubris" and leave it at that. Hubris *and* grandiosity, perhaps. They think they've grown and learned enough to become uniquely qualified to handle all the personal and professional challenges they might ever face.

But what about when your board fires you even though you're the company founder? What about when a higher-up forces you into retirement after 30 years of service? How about when a corporate raider launches a hostile takeover? What about when constituents vote you out of office or your doctor says you have brain cancer and have one year to live? What about when your husband says he's leaving and he's taking the children and the business with him?

It's not just an age issue. It's not just things that only happen to us in our later years. Though the preponderance of these hypothetical events will occur in later years they're by no means dependent on age or longevity. Normal life spans have their statistical tendencies but there are no universal playbooks. You could be 30, a multi-millionaire, and have your competitors buy out the company you founded, like many Silicon Valley entrepreneurs these days. Where do you turn then? Who will support you to turn with confidence and clarity toward the next phase of your life?

Part of what these leaders miss is the importance of modeling what they hope their own co-workers, employees, constituents, clients, students and even customers, will do. Any leader in her right mind wants those followers to mentor and to be mentored. She understands the importance of compassionate, hands-on guidance and how this improves skill acquisition and operations. But there aren't many employees who are going to take a boss seriously if she doesn't practice what she preaches. Conversely, having a boss demonstrate the humility and wisdom to actively acknowledge mentors will deeply inspire and motivate those same employees. That's what real 21st century leadership accomplishes. The historical *command and control* model of leadership is dying. The future of leadership is *inspire and collaborate*.

I've been speaking of leaders in the classic sense – as the heads of institutions. Ultimately, I mean it in the most universal sense. *All* people are leaders of their own lives. In order to assume and maintain proper understanding and control of our own lives, *we all need mentorship throughout the entirety of our lives*.

By not maintaining relationships with active mentors, we deprive ourselves of care. Among other things, mentors provide safe outlets to express feelings, at the very least allowing mentees to let off steam. Otherwise, leaders create conditions that allow those feelings to steep and fester, creating energetic blockages and perhaps, eventually disability and disease. I know of leaders who were veritable saints, doing tremendous good in the world, taking care of multitudes, yet they died young because they simply refused to take care of themselves.

> *You can have different forms of mentoring. There is a form that I call survival mentoring, where what happens is, and I think mostly with young people, they are struggling so hard that you just have to go and help them survive. And you do whatever is necessary. You bring whatever resources are necessary. You provide protection and support. And sometimes that doesn't involve anything that is terribly initiatory. Just make sure they stay alive.*
>
> *Then I've seen forms of mentoring which stay a little bit general.*

We're helping them with their life skills. We're helping them with their ethics. We're helping them with their awareness of themselves. It's not aimed at getting to the full depth and the awakening of the self, of the soul. That's the third form - the attempt to really involve in the initiatory awakening of what they came here to do; what they came to life to do. In its depth, I think mentoring is about the spirit inside both the mentor and the student.

The old idea of learning was considered a sacred activity. The root meaning of the word learning is "to sing over." And I think there's a singing over the souls of the young that mentors get involved with. And so, I like the kind of mentoring that is involved with initiation. And I think if genuine mentoring is going on, the young people will have initiatory experiences. **Michael Meade**

The first and second forms of mentorship are well illustrated in the anecdote below, which also makes clear how mentorship and initiation are complementary and mutually essential.

I had the sweetest moment with one young man. He was getting ready to go home and he and I went upstairs. He'd never used a washing machine. And he learned about stripping his bed, etc. He felt so empowered he couldn't wait to go home and tell his mom, "I know how to do my own laundry now." For a lot of these kids that's not a big deal. But for this young man that's like a ticket to being a responsible member of his family. It was one of my favorite moments of the summer. ROP can't all happen while on the mountains. Some of it can happen. We certainly teach a lot around values, a lot around self-care and a lot about right relationship with each other. But some of these practical things come over time, come with the mentoring, come with the ongoing education.
Melissa Michaels

My primary interest for this book is the third form, mentoring the soul -

helping mentees tease out the deepest meaning and understanding of their life experiences, helping them live a most fulfilled and happy life. God bless those men and women out there who do first stage mentoring – helping young people secure all the practicalities they need to be safe and sustain life. And the same goes for second stage mentoring, helping mentees acquire life skills, ethics and self-awareness. There are multitudes of people who can and do mentor young people in their business or profession to be better doctors, carpenters, accountants, salesmen, teachers, businesspeople, etc. Whole self-help libraries exist offering job and career guidance. We need only determine what path we want to take and we can plot out the skills needed to acquire proficiency. But the kind of soul mentorship that Meade talks about is a precursor. That is to say, you can't follow the path you want to take until you know what that path is. Soul mentorship helps you identify that path. So, the three stages that Meade identifies are not necessarily sequential.

> *Mentorship and initiation are two sides of the same coin. You cannot have mentorship without initiation and you cannot have initiation, a successful initiation, without mentorship or stewardship. And what's really true about initiation, it has a beginning, it has a midpoint and it has an end, as every Threshold does.* **Angeles Arrien**

Three stages in initiation, three stages in mentoring. We have to do all three phases well: beginning, middle and end. The Initiate needs to be in a working relationship with a mentor before, during and after any ROP. Before, in order to prepare the Initiate and make sure she's ready. During, to serve as a touchstone to remind the Initiate of her preparation and to remind her the mentor will be there on the other side. After is arguably most important. Nothing is more crucial than having the mentor there to help the Initiate integrate her new learning into everyday life. Without that, the Initiate is at risk of simply having a peak experience, a "high" no more lasting than a drug experience, without understanding the necessity of building those lessons into the myriad practicalities that will construct her future.

Angeles Arrien pointed out to me how Western culture, especially the USA, does great beginnings; we're visionaries. We easily start new projects and try to implement new dreams. We love meeting new people and starting new relationships. But we do terrible middles. We tend to be superficial in relationships, unwilling to take them beyond the surface level. We hit vulnerable places, often refusing to open to our feelings, much less share them with authenticity. We also push back against accountability; we don't want to accept that our words and actions must be in alignment. We talk a good game; we're great salesmen, but we often don't follow through. We also do terrible endings – there's no closure, there's no demonstration of skill level, of mastery. We're good at recognizing the MVPs and All Stars of sports and the arts, the celebrities of mainstream culture, but not so much the MVPs of everyday life. Yes, there are talent shows, music competitions, beauty and cooking contests. But outside of immediate family, who even recognizes these winners anymore? Community-wide affirmation rituals are a dying art.

Take the 4H club. Who in popular culture even knows any more what they do? Who knows that they provide awards and recognition to young farmers and those practicing the "domestic arts"? Since every county in the U.S. has a 4H agent, who even knows that they offer ROP and mentorship to every teen in the country?[8] They certainly qualify as everyday heroes. But where else do we provide ritual events that recognize each unique individual for being the MVP of their own life, for crossing yet another threshold on their Hero's Journey?

It is essential that mentees be provided with public opportunities to display their talents. If we're not given positive platforms to display our skills, we will do it through shadow. We will unconsciously do whatever we can in order to achieve recognition – "acting out," seizing the limelight, doing anything we can to be seen. We will become unduly demonstrative,

---

[8] A program designed, written, and implemented by my friend Larry Hobbs.

manifesting, as Arrien has pointed out, the derivative words "demon" or "monster." All three terms contain the same root word: "-mon-" which translates from Latin as "warn."

There are some who argue that initiation needs to happen before mentorship is really needed. That without initiation, mentorship will not really take hold. The Initiate will not be "born into" an understanding of his or her fundamental *need* for mentorship without the Passage Ritual. Others, myself included, say initiation should happen only after mentorship has been well established and the Initiate has already acquired some life skills. This idea is consistent with what I've written above; I say before, during and after is ideal. But in my typical agnosticism, my both/and approach, I say yes to both formulations. Under the right circumstances, it's possible to initiate someone and have them acquire a mentor later. That approach can work. Remember, there are no rules. This is art, not science.

Initiation is the beginning of the journey into a different way of being for a young man or a young woman. Mentoring is the part where, after we've opened the door into a new way of approaching life, a new set of core values that we want to build our lives around as appropriate men or women, we ask "how do we hold on to that?"

We as humans have a phenomenal capacity to resist change. Part of being able to hold on to that new way of being is to have appropriate allies that we can lean into. That's where mentors come in. Do I have somebody that I can go to when it's really hard to hold on to this value of being an accountable man?

When I don't want to have integrity, when I really want to punch somebody out or I want to pick up some wallet that's got money coming out of it and take the money and throw the wallet away, who do I lean into when I'm challenged by my old ways? Who do I lean into when the parts of me that don't want to live at my highest and best come in? When I want to just settle for something? When I want to tell myself, "It's too hard. It's too hard to learn to play the guitar even though I love it. I don't want to discipline myself to do it." Who do I lean into for mentoring?

Mentors provide a backstop. Their job is not to tell me what to do. Their job is to keep me in the challenge and keep me at choice. Basically, it's about what's at risk if I do something and what's at risk if I don't?

If someone wants to go down an inappropriate path, the question we ask is: "Are you willing to pay the price?" Our job is not to stop them. "You're 15 years old. You're going to do what you want to do." What we do is challenge them. "Are you willing to pay the price if you keep engaging in that behavior with your mom or dad? And what do you imagine the price is?"

If we can help him get to what the price will clearly be if he continues inappropriateness, then he's at the choice point of saying, "Maybe I don't want to pay that price. Maybe I do want to hold on to something different." That's what the mentor does. They kind of work around the boy. When he tries to go down any unconscious paths, they stand in front of him and they keep bringing back the consciousness, and then step back and say, "What do you want to do?"

"Now that you're clear about the price you'll pay, now that you're clear about what happens if you do that and what happens if you don't, do you want to go down that road still? Choose. You've got to choose." The mentor can't make the choices or the young men and women won't develop their own capacity to make choices, to look at things from that same approach of conscious versus unconscious, being accountable for the choice versus "Somebody else made me do it. My friends made me do it." That kind of thing. If mentoring moves into being bossy, trying to control the young boy, trying to tell him how to do it, he won't respond to that.

It's a tough job. Not everybody makes a good mentor. And yet, without that, the journey that started when the boy got initiated is probably at risk because, when you think about it, wherever the initiation happens, the Initiate has more familiarity with his old patterns than what these new ones from initiation are teaching him.

Some of those old patterns are not helpful. They're inappropriate and may be destructive. But they're familiar. They feel safe even though they're not. Without a pull to draw me toward the new ones, it's highly likely some of those old patterns will try to reemerge and start running my life again. The mentor is there to go, "Time out. Let's take a look at this." **Jim Mitchell**

A mentor is somebody who's made his or her way through the transition. Somebody who's walked that same dark path from childhood into adulthood through adolescence, and can shine a light back on the path. That's an absolutely essential component. Young people can't initiate themselves because nobody's lighting that path for them. So, they stay put. **Darcy Ottey**

It was that sense that there is somebody there who will listen, who really cares, and who has experienced enough to see, really see that young person and what their yearning is and what their way is and what their gifts are, and show up for them. And help them with their self-exploration, help them ask the kinds of questions that help a young person to become reflective, as is happening at that age anyway. And help guide them toward self-understanding and what they really like, and help them develop their own values. And all of that being in preparation for a time that comes when the mentor and the others around them know, okay, now this young person, it's time for them to be put into the Threshold phase. They are ready to have the initiation itself happen. And then for those same mentors to be there on the other side. **Meredith Little**

Mentoring comes from the tradition of the mind. What does the mind need from someone who knows? It's not just their own knowledge alone, but the lived story. In every kind of knowledge is a subtle feeling of truth. If you've lived it, that truth resonates with the inner longing of another human being. So, this is what's transferred in mentorship. The longing connects with the lived truth of what happened in a person's life. And the individual follows that truth. **Orland Bishop**

Mentors must always work with whatever arises in the Initiate's life. Life itself will open the doorway to abundant lessons. Alert mentors often need do little but contain the Initiate during her times of trial and help her tease out the valuable teachings embedded in the experience.

It's like cooking, which is one of the images that used to be used in the South Sea Islands - the person is being cooked. And so, I've heard people, modern people, say well, I'm initiating myself. Well that goes against the whole idea because if I do it myself, I'm either going to have the temperature way too high or way too low. But if someone else is regulating the heat, they also have to know how hot it can go and how much a person can take, and so I think that makes it really difficult to just try it. So, what I've been doing is trying to find circumstances or notice circumstances where somebody is already in something initiatory. They are in such hot water, that now you could bring the understanding to them, rather than bring them in and try to create the right kind of hot water. **Michael Meade**

For about six months, I was filming a Latino man in East Oakland. When I met him at age 18, Miguel already had a wonderful mentor. We filmed them together and we filmed him experiencing a modern day ROP with Melissa Michael's powerful Golden Bridge program in Colorado. Prior to all that, when he was 11, on a street corner right in front of him, one of his friends shot and killed his best friend.

The water was hot. Boiling. What he needed then, but didn't have, was a mentor. He needed someone who could hold him through the course of healing, to help him process the trauma – all the anger, grief, shock and fear. He needed an Elder, a teacher, a coach, an uncle, a neighbor... *someone* to step up and be a mentor, then and there, and say to him, "Now you're going through a Rite of Passage. You didn't ask for this. In many ways, you're too young. But here it is. The universe has thrust this upon you and now death is here. You have lost your best friend. Even worse, you have seen another friend kill him. It is now your task to make sense of what does not make sense. I will be here with you. You will have to go through dark and unwanted emotions – anger, sadness, fear, maybe even shame. There is no way around them; you must go through them. I will be here to hold you. But I promise you this. If you go through them fully, and continue to ask yourself all the hard and often unanswerable questions, you will come out of this with some gift, some new understanding of your life, some piece of gold that will serve you and those around you. It will serve you well, *for the rest of your life.* I promise."

That's mentorship. That's how mentors work with the challenges that life thrusts upon us. That's how, given proper support, each of us learns to process the horror and heartbreak that is our common human inheritance.

Mentorship is essential when the water is hot and the Initiate is already being cooked. But it's also essential when it's not. When life doesn't provide immediate fodder for mentorship through dramatic circumstance, there are two basic directions mentoring can take: 1) Work with the Initiate's historical wounds, eventually getting the Initiate to recognize that each wound contains a gift. 2) Work with their natural proclivities and passions - be it math, football, piano, carpentry, engineering, design, medicine, baking, chemistry, physics, or skateboarding - getting the mentee to tease out how and why the activity(s) is fulfilling. Joseph Campbell called it "following your bliss." Doing what makes us happy in the short term is essential to securing a long-term foundation for happiness in our life, even if what we eventually do looks nothing like where we started.

No single path is exclusive of any other. Maybe there will be two or three paths. Mentors can and should be flexible, able to work with and nurture all paths of development simultaneously, alternately or in succession. Follow them all and see where they lead. I tell mentees regularly that nothing may stick. But that's not what matters. What matters is they follow it until some other door, opportunity or attraction opens. Then they must follow that. These are the ways that life itself, or the universe or God, guides us to where we need to go.

The same is no less true for making the wrong turns or the wrong decisions. One mentor taught me many years ago that when I'm stuck, sometimes it's important to make a decision, any decision. Just choose. In the choosing, the universe typically has ways of accepting or rejecting that choice. If sudden, new opportunities emerge that are consistent with that choice, great. You know you've made the right decision. But if inordinate difficulties and roadblocks suddenly appear, or worse, disaster strikes, you may well have made the wrong choice. Also, great! You can simply return to the fork in the road and go the other way.

I was taught a similar decision making mechanism utilizing a simple coin toss. It's a straightforward exercise. Label Choice A on one side of the coin and Choice B on the other. Flip the coin. See the result. Then ask yourself a simple question: How does this choice land in my body? What do I feel? With a skillful mentor you will ferret out the correct choice quickly. The answer is in your body, not in your head. Here are just a few of the possibilities: If I feel joy that's usually the right choice. But if I merely feel pleasure, like "Oh, easy. I can get stress-free wins that way," then it may not be the right choice. If I feel simple fear that's often a good sign. That means the next stage of my growth might lie in that new challenge. But if I feel overwhelming dread then likely that is not the way to go. I may be having unconscious premonitions of disaster. Similarly, if I simply feel sadness, that could also indicate the correct choice. It could mean I have to let go of some old behavior or attachment. That could be good for my growth. But if I feel a deep, fundamental grief, that I'm giving up some essential part of my being, then maybe that's not the right choice.

These are rudimentary examples offered purely as guideposts. The real truth always lies in the individual, in the *body* of the individual. If that first scenario fails somehow to lead to a conclusive answer, then simply posit the opposite. Repeat the exercise and say the other side of the coin came up. How do I feel now? The point is that the feeling body allows us to arrive at what is fundamentally true for the individual by overriding the usually knotted thinking brain.

> *The idea is that people don't enter the world empty. Everybody enters with something already in their soul. Every child that comes is valuable because they already have a gift; they already have something to give. Tribal cultures - not to idealize them because they had their own problems - did have the understanding that each person came to give gifts. And the idea of a culture was to make gift givers, not to create consumers. The exact opposite of the modern idea that everybody is empty and has to consume.*
>
> *That might seem like a simple statement but that's a serious argument in Western culture because Christianity, early on through the Catholic Church, came up with the idea of the "tabula rasa," which means "the table scraped clean." And the idea was that the soul entered the world clean, and then life and how the individuals are treated determined their nature. And that goes against all the old traditions, which said that everybody has an inner nature or a second nature that already has characteristics that will determine that person's longings and that person's values. I love that idea. I think it's way more important.*
> **Michael Meade**

When I work with mentees, I have a particular structure that I follow. It's worked well for years and has plenty of room for adaptation. I meet with them monthly for an hour. Since most of my mentees do not live nearby we usually meet on the phone, though we can meet online to see each other as needed. I let them know I'm also available between calls when tough stuff arises. I do like to see them in the flesh at least once a year. If they're MKP men, I aim to staff at least one weekend training with them yearly so I can see them up close. I like to observe them in leadership roles and interacting with others. If they're not MKP men, then I like to see them in their chosen professional capacity, ideally in public. As I write this, I have an LA actor mentee I'm hoping to see on stage soon.

When it comes to missing meetings, I'm strict. As long as my mentee is accountable (and if he doesn't volunteer, I'll insist!), then missing one meeting is permissible. Not two. Every action has consequences, intended and unintended. Miss two meetings with me without prior notice and we're done. I have too much else to do. Life of course always intervenes with schedules and meetings need to be moved. As long as each of us gives the other at least 24 hours notice, we reschedule and I'm good.

I commit to working with them for a two-year span. At the end of each year we do a review session when we each speak to what's working and not working in the relationship. If mutually desired, we then renew our commitment. I also ask each mentee to write down their personal and professional goals for each coming year. That becomes the standard of accountability we use to measure progress.

Two years is not a lot of time. 24 phone meetings, a weekend together, maybe a couple face-to-face meetings. Relative to lifetime commitments that mentors commonly made in pre-modern times, and some still make today, it's very little. Though I usually extend the term another two years if asked, I feel that two years is sufficient for the mentee to learn what it is I have to offer. I feel that it's healthy for mentees to move on to other mentors since everybody has different strengths and weaknesses. I don't want mentees to inherit my blind spots.

In keeping with the "giveaway," the spirit of service, I never charge a fee. This is my lifetime default. This is how traditional societies commonly operated. Most indigenous people consider it a karmic crime to accept goods, services or cash in return for services rendered. Their economies were largely based on gift giving and barter and maintained maximum equilibrium where no one had too much or too little. But we live in the modern world where money is our most commonly accepted means of exchange.

Like most people, I have my own money shadows. I have to remain awake and vigilant to reap the abundance the world offers to me in support. If I don't, I'll succumb to my own timidity and darkness: "Who am I to ask for money? I don't deserve it." Or, "The world is out to get me. Fuck 'em all. I'll do everything myself." When it comes to sharing my books and movies with individuals, it seems both easier and more generous to simply give them away. It feels petty to ask for $15 or $20. So, I challenge myself to insist on the money.

I don't like being a salesman, much less selling myself (another shadow of mine). I don't like to negotiate on my own behalf. That shadow used to show up regularly in my dealings with clients and customers. I remember one time concluding a phone call and being very excited about a new partnership opportunity. When I got off the phone, I went to the kitchen to share the news with my wife. She was happy for me, but then she deadpanned, "Did you explain to them that you don't work for money?" Ouch! What's even more telling is I have no memory whatsoever of who the call was with or what it was about. Yet I'll never forget what Tracy said afterward.

She tutored me in working harder to protect my own financial interest. I now tell mentees up front that when our time together ends, we will have a conversation about how they can support my work. What I seek from them, as I do any contributor to my work, is mission alignment. What about my work appeals? What aspect do they most want to support? What can they do that's of value to me that also excites them? As a working artist always in need of support, there's nothing wrong with me having this conversation and asking for something in return. They can donate money or frequent flier miles to my non-profit. They can volunteer time and talent in their area of expertise. They can connect me with their contacts who could prove helpful as supporters. Together, we explore ways they can contribute as we transition our collaboration to new ground. In this world of inter-independence, I too have to earn my keep. It would be a dereliction of duty not to.

It's also a mechanism for continuing to keep mentees in my life as friends. We have a shared, deep history which would be a shame to discard. I do the same thing with my DocuMentoring Studio. When the stars align, I get to hire my favorite, most motivated students to work for me long after they've graduated from my film program. I instituted this practice with my mentees a few years ago, having seen far too many earlier ones disappear from my life forever. From the perspective of a strict zero-sum equation, I've probably done more in service than I've ever received from mentees in return. But I feel good about it. I was happy to be of useful service to those earlier mentees and now I'm happy to ask the new ones for something in return.

But I don't look at it as a zero-sum equation. Working with mentees has helped my character development and grown me as a man, not least in the method of support I described above. Mentoring others has also brought clarity to many of the practices I've written about in this book. It has made me a better listener and support resource. It's helped illuminate for me one of my great gifts: building, maintaining and deepening relationships. This leads to one of the golden rules of mentorship. The mentor needs to learn and grow from the relationship as much as the mentee or something is wrong.

> *If I look at a Rite of Passage event, the whole thing has mentoring potential. In the days following the event, there's so much gold in there for me - what I've been taught and what I've been shown about myself - from every moment of that event. If I choose to sort of see it in that way. The way I've been regarded or seen by young men can tell me a lot about the truth of who I am.* **Adge Tucker**

I discuss all the issues above with mentees in advance. Then we lay the whole thing out in black and white and agree to the terms like a business contract. That is important. Making clear agreements is the starting point for living in integrity in the world. Without it, accountability has no foothold. Though no written agreement is ironclad, and most need revising at some point, handshake agreements are even worse. They're recipes for he said, she said disputes and are grossly inadequate.

Our actual monthly meetings are very simple. We take as long as we need to check in with each other. We share our latest challenges and victories, in all areas of our lives, with an emphasis on feelings. I, as mentor, need to be just as willing to authentically share everything that's going on for me, however dark the feelings. Sometimes the thread of our work together follows what has come up regarding me and my challenges, some questions, concerns or interests the mentee has about my life and history. But most of the time I follow the mentee's check in and explore what's up for him. The key is that the mentee decides where he wants to go and how he wants to spend our time together. Often there is some emotional work he needs to do to better understand how his historical wounds are playing out in his present life in the form of destructive behaviors, shadows or simple unhappiness. Sometimes I get him to think through what the repercussions will be on either side of a choice he needs to make. I usually give in to my storytelling instincts during a session and share at least one suitable tale from my own history.

The way I work with those who mentor me is largely the same. Though each mentor has his own idiosyncrasies, I adapt. What is noteworthy about my mentors, who I'll lovingly characterize as "old-timers," is how informal our meetings tend to be. We don't need formality. We don't need time to "drop in." We get right to the heart of matters without any pretense or build-up. "My wife is dying. I feel tremendous fear and grief about it. I need to do a piece of work around it in order to remain fully present and available to her." I believe I spoke those very words to my mentor on one or more occasions. Very clear, very direct, very simple, very deep. This is what I, in turn, model with my mentees.

I tend to think that mentors and mentees are best paired when of the same gender. (Though, again, I see this not as some kind of rule. It's a convention I've seen most viable.) There's nobody better to teach a girl how to navigate the world as a woman than a woman, regardless of either's sexual orientation. The same holds true for men. Though a straight man myself, my greatest film mentor in college and after, Ron Epple, was a gay man.

One of my lifetime sadnesses was that he died before he got to witness my greatest career success with *Hoop Dreams*. While I was making my rounds at the festivals and awards, I would have relished the opportunity to publicly acknowledge all he taught me in my formative years. I did the next best thing and dedicated my next film *The Unspoken* to his memory. Though saddled with plenty of his own shadows in the form of addictions, he was a brilliant, funny, good-hearted man who I miss to this day.

I've been blessed to have a number of truly extraordinary men mentor me. Certainly, the celebrated Hollywood writer, director and actor Harold Ramis was my most famous mentor. Harold was incredibly skilled and I loved him deeply. To honor his memory, I felt called to write a commemorative blog when I learned of his death in 2014. You can find it in Appendix V. I included it to show how mentorship can play out in an uncertain world. It also serves to remind how important it is to remember and honor the mentor.

In the back of this book there is a document called The Ten Best Practices of Mentorship. It is a simple bullet-pointed list I have written, culled from a lifetime of lessons. I won't go through and restate every quality on the list. I'll just point out two that I've already alluded to: 1) the mentor must be challenged and fed alongside the mentee; 2) mentees talk 80% of the time and mentors 20%.

> *We need to listen to our young people. We need to sit down with them and say, "You seem unhappy, what's going on?" And not try to take it away, not try to take the pain away, not try to tell them, "Oh let me tell you what to do," but to really listen to them. And if we do that, often that averts them from having to do something bad in order to get attention, in order to be listened to. They have a lot to say that we need to hear. And until we stop what we're doing and really start listening to them they're going to get our attention any way they can, and in our culture that's usually by being bad.* **Meredith Little**

It's very hard to genuinely recognize and bless the qualities of another if the person doing the blessing hasn't found the blessings in themselves. And so the act of doing it for the benefit of someone else does polish one's own gifts and reminds us that we have a welcome in the world as well. That's another value of mentoring. **Michael Meade**

Anyone who gets to be an Elder is also a healer, woman or man. Anyone who lives long enough to extract the knowledge from his or her own life is automatically a healer. In alchemy the idea was the "opus", the work of a whole life. In working with the young person, I like to imagine what we're doing now may be temporary, but hopefully seeing something that can work in their whole life. And we won't even be around to see it. We won't even be there. **Michael Meade**

The key aspect of being a good mentor is actually having some knowledge or some experience or some wisdom to pass on so that you actually have some earned authority, that you have paid your dues. You've lived your life; you've put the work in so that you actually really do have something you can pass on. Secondly, I think your mentee has to be willing to invest some authority, to accept that somebody else actually does maybe know more than they do, somebody else might actually have some wisdom that they don't yet have, and be willing to accept that. Third, I think mutual respect is part of it. That you respect each other. You respect the person you're mentoring; you are caring about them; you're really thinking about them and really thinking about how to create an experience that can actually benefit them, can help them to grow. Fourth, you have to be able to critique your students. But you can learn to do it in ways that build self-esteem and are supportive rather than tearing somebody down. **Starhawk**

The amazing community organizer Aqeela Sherrills - one of the architects of the historic LA gang truce between the Bloods and the Crips in 1992 - was mentored by the famed football player and actor Jim Brown. He understands how he would not be the man he is today were it not for Jim.

> *Jim challenged me in a way that that no man has ever challenged me. I'm an avid reader. I study a lot. So, I had a pristine philosophy when I met Jim. And Jim just shattered it. POW! His style of mentorship was to throw you in the fire and let you burn and then kind of advise you as he's turning you over. Just brutal. He's verbally and psychologically abusive. Definitely. These are the wounds that he's lived with and this is how he came to be the man that he is. So, this is the way he teaches. So, it's imperative that as his mentee, you have to figure out how to not take those things personally or they will destroy you. That's how spirit is. Spirit is brutal on you.* **Aqeela Sherrills**

Spirit *is* brutal. In my interview with him, Aqeela later spoke about how after years of working alongside Jim and running many of his community-based operations, Jim betrayed him. Aqeela swears by the power of this "necessary betrayal," that moment when the mentor signals the relationship is over and the mentee is on his own.

> *We had our necessary betrayal. The betrayal is necessary because it's similar to this whole idea of the mama bird and the baby bird. When the baby bird gets old enough, the mama bird pushes the baby out of the nest. So, either it flies or it hits the ground and dies. At some point the baby bird has to be able to find and make its own way. This betrayal is necessary. It's an initiation as well because you have to analyze and do that deep inquiry about what brought you to that particular place.*
> **Aqeela Sherrills**

I respect Aqeela's point of view. However, I don't believe that a dramatic betrayal of the mentee by the mentor is necessary or desirable. More likely, it will occur "organically," without great drama, with amicable parting and be initiated as much or more by the mentee.

I certainly don't betray my mentees, at least not consciously. Our relationship is not unlimited. I suppose that could be construed as betrayal. If so, at least they understand its limitations going into the relationship, that it's of limited duration and I'm not available indefinitely. They know in advance to expect "abandonment" when it comes.

But the key word above is "consciously." After a period of time, it's only logical for the mentee to become aware of the *unconscious* limitations of the mentor. The "betrayal" then usually comes when the mentee learns about some of the mentor's shadows. She sees her limitations and blind spots and starts to realize that the mentor's actions and values are no longer completely in line with her own. In an ideal world, that becomes the time when the mentee herself chooses to separate from the mentor. The betrayal may be deeply felt by the mentee but the separation is nonetheless initiated by her. Too many mentees stay enamored with their mentors and separate only after prolonged disillusionment, if ever. That's when it becomes incumbent on the mentor to recognize the pattern and kick the bird out of the nest. Though it can be done amicably, I believe.

> *There's a program for [the Seattle organization] Rite of Passage Journeys called the Solo Crossing. This program is really about stepping into adulthood. And one of the things that we ask the students to do is to find a mentor in their home community who they're going to share that they're going on this experience with, who's gonna drop them off on the first day of the program, and then who's going to be the person to pick them up. For the younger youth, it's the parents that play that role. But still recognizing that as folks are stepping into adulthood, they're moving into different relationships with their parents. Through that we're trying to help the young person be able to reach out to other adults in their lives. A lot of them don't want to do it. "I don't know who to*

> *ask." And so, we're helping them on the front end to determine who to ask, knowing that there's going to be a caring adult in their home community who's heard their story, who understands what they've gone through when they return. It's not ideal. But it's a step towards what we're trying to build as a community.* **Darcy Ottey**

It can be difficult for young people to find mentors. It both is and isn't a young person's task. It is their task to recognize alignment, to see something in an Elder that calls to them. "I want some of what *he* has!" "When I grow up, I want to be like *her*." They need to see responsible adulthood embodied and practiced. That mysterious pull to what another person models is the foundation for connection.

But it isn't their task to find available adults. That is an adult's responsibility. That is our task. We need to step up and make ourselves available to others, especially to youngers. Too many mentoring organizations bemoan the scarcity of adults willing to be mentors. No doubt this is partly a function of our increasingly economically stressed society – too many adults are completely consumed simply in earning enough money to keep food on the table. Some mentoring organizations recognize this and have resorted to paying mentors. If that system works, great. But plenty of adults – and let's be honest here, they're mostly men – are unwilling to make time available under any circumstance. They're unconscious or uncaring, not only to the needs of youngers, but to how they themselves can be served in the bargain.

Chike Nwoffiah, through his organization Oriki Theater, has solved this problem. Oriki Theater provides ongoing mentorship and ROP services to African-American teen boys in East Palo Alto. Chike reached out to his Alpha Phi Alpha college fraternity, the Eta Sigma Lambda Chapter at San Jose State University, and got them on board. Now incoming freshmen understand that through the course of their four-year college education, as part of their pledge to the fraternity, they will be mentoring a high schooler. Beautiful.

I want to end with this story from Michael Meade. It's a stunning illustration of the mysterious power of mentoring.

I was doing a workshop for people about mentoring and a woman told this story. I'm a storyteller so I can't guarantee that I'm telling exactly what she told. It probably has been embellished in my mind. I like to tell it because of the quality of showing up. And it has some of the humility that's required. And it has some of the unknown that intrigues me.

So…a woman takes a job with a mentoring program and she is assigned to someone. She has to go to the house of this girl. She goes and knocks on the door for her first mentoring meeting; it's supposed to be one hour a week. No one answers the door, but she senses someone in there. So she waits around. No one ever answers the door, so she leaves. She comes back the next week and puts in her hour. Knocks on the door. She thinks someone is there. They don't come. She stays. So, week after week, she visits. She begins to call it "mentoring the door," where she just knocks and hangs out by the door. And then the period for which she agreed to do it is over and that's the end of it and she moves on. Several years later, she gets a letter from the girl. It says, "I was on the other side of the door. And now I'm in college and I want you to know that I was so depressed and I was in such pain that I couldn't open the door. I couldn't bear to be seen. But every week I waited for you to show up and knock on the door. And I want you to know that I'm in college now and doing well. The fact that you came and stood outside the door is probably what kept me alive." **Michael Meade**

What You Need To Do *Now*

- Go out and get at least one mentor for yourself. Let yourself be guided by a simple criterion: "I want some of what she has, what he has." Structure your request around simple requirements, ie., "I only need one hour of your time each month."
- Find a local mentoring organization that fits your availability and sign up.
- Let your neighbors, relatives and friends know that you're available to help mentor a child.

- Make a point of taking young people you know (whether children of friends, neighbors or relatives) out for a nature walk or activity as often as you can, ideally once a month. Take them to Homecoming Celebrations for organizations you admire.
- Make sure your kids have regularly scheduled interactions with their grandparents and other extended family members.
- Volunteer at your church, school or local community group to ensure that kids continue to have regular interactions with those in other age groups, like taking them on field trips to Senior Homes.
- Designate one or more people in your workplace to be your heirs, to take over your job responsibilities, even if far down the road.

5

Bringing the Sacred Back to the Everyday

...healing through ceremony in community is a foreign concept in most of today's culture. Most of our modern-day, non-indigenous group ceremonies are centered around ball games, vacations, holidays, feasts and celebrations with minimal intention or sacredness. We need intention; it is the intentional part of our ceremonies that harnesses energy and creates the possibility for healing and happiness. The healing power comes from a shared sense of the sacred. **Anita Sanchez**, ***Four Sacred Gifts***

Making Every Moment Sacred. That's been a lifelong goal of mine. But I didn't know it until I attended a Vision Fast ceremony high in the Eastern Sierra Mountains in Aug. 2015. Until then it was an unconscious wish. But it's as true now as ever, and in fact it has been since I was a teenager.

Due to my father's sudden and inexplicable death at the age of 41, I was driven, at only nine years old, to try to understand the meaning of life and death. How can death come so unexpectedly? In the wake of inevitable, perhaps sudden or random death, what does life actually mean? Is it merely a

BRINGING THE SACRED BACK TO THE EVERYDAY

grand exercise in absurdity? If we're all subject to strange arbitrary cessation, what is it that can make life worth living, worth cherishing, feeling that life is sacred?

I unconsciously searched for ways to understand it all. Judeo-Christian practices, which I never studied but nonetheless absorbed through the dominant culture, struck me as inadequate superstition. I developed a dynamic of outward silence and internal chatter about death that continued for many years. It contributed to my readings into Eastern spirituality in my teens. When I was 14, I picked Alan Watts' *The Book* off my parents' shelf. Five years later I read Ram Dass' *Be Here Now*. Those guides and other books about Eastern philosophy provided means for me to think about all the big questions, including my father's death. They helped point me in the direction of understanding. Was it really possible that life could simultaneously encompass both transience and grace?

Seeing irregular, dramatic moments in my life as sacred was never a problem – events like my wedding, holding my mother's hand and looking into her eyes as she died, taking trips to Zanskar and Dharamsala to make a film, meeting the Dalai Lama, seeing a buffalo show up at the founding of the All Nations Gathering Center in 2015 in Pine Ridge, SD, treading lightly on the Sphinx while making *Saving the Sphinx*, visiting the Bahai temple in Delhi, shooting the men's basketball high school state championship in Champaign's Assembly Hall, even having my friend Walt teach me how to drive a stick shift in high school. The list of events I experienced as sacred is long.

My challenge has always been to see the sacred in the everyday, the quotidian - washing the dishes, putting out the garbage, standing in line at the post office, dealing with customer service on the phone, picking up my wife from the BART station, going to the dentist, even getting a speeding ticket.

When we are conscious of our mytho-poetic identity, or as David Whyte puts it, when we're conscious of the truth at the center of the image we were born with, we are able to be in conversation with it, with our consciousness. Our contact with our muse, with our deep creativity is that much greater, and it flows that much more fully. **Bill Plotkin**

The first anniversary meeting of the All Nations Gathering Center in 2016 in Pine Ridge was a stunning example of how to make every moment sacred. For the brief 24 hours most of us were together, every moment was woven into ritual and recognized as sacred. No moment was left out, whether eating breakfast and saying a prayer over the food, calling in the grandfathers and grandmothers to open the meeting, having every single person - young, old and in-between - check in with what's present for them so we could honor their feelings. This was a *business* meeting! But business as it's conducted in the cultural mix of Lakota and MKP ways.

One of the key items of business was selecting new administrative staff to support the ongoing work of the Center. Roger Dobitz stepped up to claim the critical role of principal administrator. His job was to lay out the path ahead and begin the implementation of the grand dreams of Becky and Dallas Chief Eagle.

The process of selecting him was done ceremonially. The call was put out to the whole circle - about 40 of us in total. Roger heard the call. He knew it was his time and stepped into the circle. We all recognized he was the right choice because we saw his emotional reaction. We were present to the outpouring of his heart and stayed with his tears until he was fully enrolled. Dallas and Becky stepped into the circle to express their support for him. Other men and women lined up behind him, symbolizing their commitment to follow his lead. Roger addressed his fears and concerns. Verbal pledges of care and encouragement came from those standing in support. Mechanisms were put in place to deal with future arising issues. It was all done in a ritual way with great feeling.

And so it went. Other people who stepped forward were enrolled and ritually welcomed into other support roles. In this way much of the afternoon passed. Plans were made, roles were allocated and the first glimmerings of institutional structure came into being. It was practical; it was productive; it was efficient. AND it was sacred, conducted with great power and feeling.

If only processes and procedures like this could be replicated on a grander scale. They certainly exist already in institutions like MKP, Youth Passageways and the 13 Indigenous Grandmothers. But what if school boards were run this way? Neighborhood watch committees? Parent Teacher Organizations? City councils? Local businesses? Sports clubs and teams? What about corporations? Inter-governmental bodies like the U.N.? Choosing a president?! If every moment were treated as sacred, the quality of our leaders would never be in question. The process itself would root out the unqualified.

Rites of Passage contribute to this approach to life. We have lost the sense of the sacred in everyday life - what it is that makes human life such a rare and precious offering. We are neglecting every opportunity to drive deep into their psyche every human being's understanding of their own life – its value and meaning. Everyday ceremonies help us do this. Perhaps the key benefit would be how it would improve the quality of our personal lives, how it would make us happier and more fulfilled.

And now to contradict myself… Perhaps the hard but simple truth is that, in a strict sense, every moment and every space *cannot* be made sacred. Otherwise how are we to distinguish rituals from the mundane? How are we to draw markers in time that bring us to a heightened awareness, to say, "Now we are separating from Chronos and entering Kairos"? You can't turn a light on unless it sometimes turns off.

In the world of dualities we inhabit in the everyday, the so-called relative world, we must become skilled and equipped to call out and name the times and places when we transition into another way of being. Robert Moore was careful to make this distinction, to delineate "sacred space" from "profane" or everyday space. This is important. ROP must take place in "sacred space" that is carefully set apart from the everyday.

Mircea Eliade thought that tears of grief erupting in everyday profane space were required for sacred spaces to appear and make regeneration possible. Those tears will occur on their own in normal life. But if community does not cohere enough to support a person in walking confidently into and through those tears to see what's on the other side, they will shrink and recoil from them. Sometimes we have to invite those tears through ritual in order to move someone to the other side.

But the sacred/profane dichotomy is easily resolved once we abandon either/or thinking and recognize instead a dialectical process. The seeming contradiction is resolved in synthesis. The two opposites become one and are both contained within the non-dual. We return to the world of the absolute, the world big enough to encompass all the dualities, the One. The world that holds light and dark, day and night, off and on, life and death, man and woman, as parts of the same whole. In that world the profane is just as sacred as what's commonly called "sacred." In that world doing the dishes is just as exalted as crying out to God on a Vision Quest. Going for a bike ride is just as important as a high school graduation. And voila! We have looped back around to the notion that everything is indeed sacred.

One of the hallmarks of ROP is how it rejiggers our everyday concepts of space and time. One aspect of time I've already spoken of, transiting from Chronos to Kairos and back again. There are other aspects of time that need to be addressed.

Let's begin by first acknowledging that separating space and time at all is an artificial, intellectual construct - an abstraction. Space does not exist separate from time, and vice versa. Einstein taught us that. We also know that one single square meter of earth, wherever it is, will not remain the same indefinitely. All kinds of environmental and human activities will impact its form. In fact, there are many activities already occurring out of sight, below the ground, that may soon be impacting its future shape – the insects, worms, moles, rodents and the microbes in the soil, not to mention tree and plant roots. If that square meter is solid ice somewhere in the Arctic, changes might come slower but they will also come. (And, in fact, those changes are coming faster and faster.) All things change, perpetually and ceaselessly. No place is immutable and everlasting, including our planet and sun.

We know there is no literal, physical center to the universe. There is no single point around which everything else revolves. Even if we could locate the physical space from which the Big Bang occurred, it would not necessarily have meaningful bearing on the universe that presently exists.

Though most people know that our planet is not that center, there are people who act as if it were. Any educated person knows the universe of Copernicus is an illusion, yet we don't treat the planet with the recognition and respect that a temporal and fragile home deserves. Instead, many talk about colonizing Mars because of how much we have degraded our own planet.

Ritual space however, does have a center. When we come together to create ritual space, we choose a single object or place and designate it as the center - the axis mundi. For the time that we co-inhabit that ritual space, that named object or place becomes the symbolic center of all that occurs. It also serves as a physical reminder of the intention(s) that caused the gathering in the first place.

This concept is handed down to us from many different cultural traditions. Axis mundi is the Latin phrase. Merriam Webster defines it as "world axis: line or stem through the earth's center connecting its surface to the underworld and the heavens and around which the universe revolves." Figuratively, we can say it's the center of the world or universe. Typically, an object or geographic place is chosen to be a physical representation of the axis mundi. But any material object really functions as a metaphor. It is the symbolic crossroads of the four directions – east, west, south, north - along with the above and below, the heavens and the earth. It is sometimes referred to as the navel of the world. The form it usually takes is a literal or figurative mandala, although it can also be a staff, a stake, a rock, a tree, a park, some hills or a stretch of land many thousands of square miles. Whatever form it may take, once ritually consecrated, it serves as a reminder that says, in effect, "This is the center of all things." Wherever we find ourselves physically, axis mundi extends an invitation to remind us to always move from that place of center, to be grounded in that sense of wholeness, to know exactly where we're going.

As far as we know, we humans are the only creatures that have identity crises. It's hard to imagine a bear, or an elk, or an eagle or a caterpillar having an identity crisis. Waking up one morning and saying: "Well, I'm wondering if I'm being the true me. Maybe I was born an eagle, but I really should be a raven or a blue bird." **Bill Plotkin**

The individual human body can also express the symbol of axis mundi. This concept is consistent with the Kabbalah, Hinduism and Buddhism. Each of us represents that center, and there is nothing inconsistent with there being multiple "centers" because it's a symbol. Nonetheless, it's a powerful tool reminding us of wholeness. In each unique place and in every moment it regrounds us in the idea that NOW is a decisively meaningful time and place of integration and orientation.

If you're ever lost in a forest, the first thing to do is nothing. Stop and get your bearings. Find your axis mundi; remember that it is your own body. Observe what's going on around you. The trees are not lost, the bushes, the grass, the nearby stream. These are not metaphors. They are exactly where they need to be in order to facilitate their existence, to maximize nutrients from sun, water and soil. If you examine them closely, they will tell you where you are. Leaves will likely be tilted toward the south to maximize sun exposure (at least in the northern hemisphere). Roots will expand in the direction that maximizes their water absorption. If you know approximately what time it is and can see the sun, moon or stars, you can easily orient north, south, east and west. Even the stream will provide important information about elevation – if you want to go downhill, follow the flow of the water.

Most modern people today have no experience of center. Directional and navigational skills are in decline. Geomancy is somewhat of a lost art already, and geography may be next. My own sense of direction gets worse as I increasingly rely on GPS. Certainly, many people have no literal sense of axis mundi, or what we might call home. My late wife moved 13 times in the first eight years of her life. That deep sense of uprootedness followed her through her lifetime, making it an emotional and psychological challenge every time she had to move. This is the experience of many in our modern world. Even more sadly, many more of us have no *metaphorical* sense of home. We carry no internal coordinates with which to orient our way through life. There is no sense of ground zero that we carry in our bodies. Without "sacred space" there is no figurative terra firma on which to discard and burn all that has proven undesirable in our personality, our behavior, our beliefs and epistemology. No terra firma to discard and burn all that has proven unsustainable in a healthy, wholesome human life, in order for it to become the compost that generates a new way of being. Without sacred ground there is nowhere to stand for regeneration.

Now let's talk about time. Scientists' best guess these days is that the universe is about 14 billion years old. That is a long time. Our solar system is estimated to be about 4.5 billion years old, which is when our little planet was born. Human beings as a genus is 2-3 million years old. Our species, *Homo sapiens*, has been around for about 200,000 years. "Modern humans," about 50,000 years.

That's not very long. That is, at most, 2,500 generations. For more than half of those generations, human beings had no written language to record events. They relied on pictograms or verbal storytelling to pass down information. Most of the events we teach in school as "human history" date back only about 5,000 years – a mere 250 generations, an incredibly brief span of time that should make us feel pretty intimately connected with every other human being alive on the planet today.

For most of those very few generations, cultural traditions like initiation were passed down from Elders to youngers in an unbroken chain from generation to generation. They were what connected each of us to the past, not only to our great-great-great-great-great-grandfathers and grandmothers but to the knowledge of our people, whoever those people were, embedded in legends and myths, that made human life intelligible and tolerable. Without these stories and practices, we assume ourselves to be autonomous players on a world stage without a script, acting out lives that have no coherence, experiencing life as chaos, inexplicable and without inherent meaning. Basically, how many people in the modern world experience things today. We have lost that connective tissue to our ancestors. Initiation restores these links in the human chain that are broken and re-situates each human life in a chain going backward and forward in time. It restores generativity.

> *We have uninitiated people in our politics, in our places of importance. And being uninitiated, their value system that they try to force onto our communities and our cultures isn't connected with what's really important. And so we're saying, where are the initiated politicians and leaders and teachers? Because the experience of being dropped alone and severed from the [status quo] cultural story, and severed from the [status quo] cultural values and messages, and just given to ourself and to the land... it uncovers health. It uncovers what really makes a difference.*
> **Meredith Little**

Only two things are required to create what is commonly referred to as "sacred space": Intention and Attention. Intention is easy – why am I called to be here? What do I want to accomplish? What are my ideal outcomes? It's essential to be absolutely clear what those things are. Without a clear terminus in mind we will never know when we have arrived. We must also call out loud and name those intentions, whether it be to a small group of people, a lover, an auditorium full of participants, a cat or a vista of open land surrounding us with no human witnesses present. Most people call this prayer. We need to make clear declarations to let the universe know what it is we want. It can't respond if it doesn't know.

In the late 90s, when I was breaking up with a long-time lover and moving from Chicago to northern California, I was challenged to make a list of all the qualities I sought in a future life partner. The bullet-pointed list ran a full page, maybe longer. I don't know for sure because, sadly, I lost it. But I remember it being lengthy. Before losing it once and for all, I misplaced it. And so, it happened that one day, 1-2 years into my relationship with my wife Tracy, I rediscovered it. I was thunderstruck. There in a single, itemized, comprehensive catalog, listed in black and white, were all the qualities she possessed. Until that moment, I did not realize I actually had succeeded in manifesting the ideal woman partner that I sought five years before. I already knew Tracy to be remarkable. I had been adamant about wanting to marry her. But what I had completely forgotten was that I had pre-visualized her. Through a simple ritual, I had, to some mysterious degree, called her into my life. Intentions are powerful. So, it's important to set them with great care. Remember the old joke: "I always said I wanted to be someone… But I realize now I should've been more specific." Don't be "someone," choose with great care exactly who you want to be.

> *What I have witnessed again and again is that healing almost always occurs in the company of others who are keenly focused on a sacred intention of care and support where healing is wanted. The members of this community call on their connection to each other and all their relations. They acknowledge spirit in their own cultural tradition; they may call on the elements of water, earth, air, fire or light. They employ ritual and practice that speaks to them, such as talking circle, dance or meditation. The teachings of my Elders always show up in the most basic values of people's life-giving relationships to each other. When people are relating to each other through goodwill, honesty and caring, then the healing energy of relationship naturally takes over and positive things happen.* **Anita Sanchez, *Four Sacred Gifts***

Attention is just as important as intention. Without attention it's simply impossible to know what is going on anytime or anywhere. (Sometimes it's hard even with it!) If we don't know what's going on, with some depth and clarity, we'll never know with any assurance what an appropriate response should be. And because everything changes all the time, even setting great intentions will never guarantee that we will proceed directly or smoothly to our intended outcome. All kinds of unforeseen events will occur, perhaps many of them unwelcome. It's incumbent on us to adapt and respond accordingly.

Zen is the best practice I know to develop the habit of paying attention. We practice staying awake and alert to everything that is happening inside and outside the body through meticulous and relentless discipline. Most people call it meditation. When thoughts seize our attention and take us away from the present moment, we reground ourselves in the breath. This is similar to many different forms of "mindfulness" practice. It really doesn't matter which form you adopt. The key is to have the discipline to do it with great regularity so it becomes a reflex to stop and consider "What is actually going on here?" before taking any reflexive action. Lately, I prefer the term "concentration practice" to "meditation" because it really is about concentration - concentrating fully on all that is happening in the moment. "Meditation" and "mindfulness" can sound dreamily insubstantial to me, misleading people into thinking that all they have to do is sit down and space out. It's quite the opposite. If we're inattentive, we might miss the importance of seemingly small events that arise. It takes a lot of practice to learn to control our minds rather than have our minds control us.

Tracy and I got married in August of 2003, adjacent to the outdoor flower garden at Green Gulch Zen Center in Marin, CA. At the start of the ceremony we were visited by a few dragonflies. A few minutes later, in the middle of welcoming statements and introductions, the numbers increased to a relative swarm, all circling around our heads. The presiding Zen priest paused for a moment and watched, as did we all. Then he said, "It is not inauspicious when dragonflies do not appear at weddings." He paused and smiled. "But it can be auspicious when they do." He chuckled, as did many of us. Then we all watched some more.

He hadn't missed a beat. ("Ah, this is here now!") There wasn't much that needed to be said and certainly nothing to be done. Just make room for the unexpected arrival of all these dragonflies. It was mysterious and wonderful. Only later did I bother to check and discover that according to the website dragonfly-site.com, *The dragonfly, in almost every part of the world, symbolizes change and change in the perspective of self-realization; the kind of change that has its source in mental and emotional maturity and the understanding of the deeper meaning of life.* Dragonflies had arrived; we paid attention; we were blessed.

Ritual is a wonderful practice for attention. It cannot and should not proceed without absolute awareness of all that is present in the moment. Remember, it is vastly different from ceremony, which proceeds largely according to a predetermined plan. Ritual necessarily incorporates the unforeseen with spontaneous attentiveness and good humor. We may not fully appreciate conditions that at first blush might be intrusive, or worse, unfavorable. As a practice for life in general, but especially during ritual, all that arises needs to be embraced and brought into the whole.

In 1977, when I arrived for my first ever visit to Pusan, Korea, I was grumpy because there was a storm and I had to lug my backpack through town all day in the rain. I happened upon a tourist agency. When I complained about the squall to the woman behind the counter, she politely explained to me that this was the first rain the city had received in many months, bringing with it great relief from a drought. Most city dwellers were delighted. I hadn't even noticed. Chastened, I made my way onward with a lighter heart and sunnier spirit, making every moment sacred.

What You Need To Do *Now*

- Design some simple rituals you can do at least once a week, maybe even each day, to bring the sacred back into your everyday life. Examples:

1. Lately I've taken to saying to myself "All is right and good with the world." In the time of Covid and worldwide economic, social and political disaster, it may seem outrageous or uncaring. But remember: though it's essential we set strong positive intentions for changing the world, we must let go of any attachment to outcome. Accepting reality itself, whatever form it takes, brings calm and equanimous mind. It's not about what happens to us that matters; it's about how we respond to what happens. I do this exercise with regularity, almost like a mantra, at

moments that have a neutral feeling tone, ie., nothing special happening, say, just cleaning the stove. But I also say it when I'm irritated or angry, when I've dropped a glass on the floor or cut my finger. Of course you should rewrite the words to suit yourself best. Whatever the words are, I recommend saying them aloud.

2. Light a candle or incense each morning and say, "I'm grateful for my life." This candle or incense can act as an axis mundi, bringing you back to gratitude when needed.
3. Go for a slow, mindful walk around your neighborhood, block or even living room! Pay attention to the little things you may have otherwise missed without this new attentiveness. Were there any tiny coincidences (the equivalents of dragonflies perhaps) that may be considered sacred to you?
4. Visit a new museum once a week. Pay close attention to each exhibit, and if one speaks to you, understand it may hold something special for you.
5. Schedule tea or lunch with a friend and tell them how much they mean to you. Be genuine, honest and thoughtful with this compliment. This not only brings the sacred into your life, it brings it into theirs, as well.
6. Gift-giving itself is a sacred ritual. Give a small gift or do an act of service for someone you care about. If it's a gift, choose it from items you already own. Let them know what personal meaning the item or service has for you. Let them know it may be for no special reason other than you're grateful they are in your life. Not only does it serve our own growth and deepen connection with others, it helps reorient our society away from consumerism and consumption.
7. Consider ritualizing the process by which you choose leaders, in any group or institution you belong to, to make room for feelings and the sacred. This also brings into the process the necessary intentions for these leaders to succeed in their new role.
8. Tracy and I used to do the "Candle Ceremony" every day. We met for as little as one minute, usually at the kitchen table, to light a candle, join hands, look into each other's eyes, and say something that we treasured

about the other. We learned this from Rich and Char Tosi's wonderful "Couples 1" workshop.

Remember, what is sacred to you may not be sacred to someone else, and vice versa. The point is to bring the sacred - whatever that may be, no matter how big or small - into our own lives, and when possible, into the lives of others. Of course, some sacred moments may be personal and best kept to oneself, but also ask yourself if the moment can or should be shared with someone else.

6

Parents

From the beginning, initiations have been seen as a time of severing from whatever mother or father there might be, and being given over to the Greater Mother, the Greater Father, and feeling our place in a world that is bigger than our family system. That, in many ways, also helps bring healing to some of the young people who come from split families. **Meredith Little**

From the moment a child is born, a parent's primary role is clear and sharply defined: keep the child safe from harm. In the entire animal kingdom, human babies and infants are some of the least capable creatures of fending for themselves. They need everything: food, clothing, shelter, protection in all its forms, and they need it literally spoon-fed, and for many months. Later, as toddlers and small children, they still require relentless parental oversight. When does the transition begin for them to become more independent? Childhood? Puberty? How is a parent to know when that time has arrived? How tricky is it in their teen years to define that moment of Threshold, of departure, separating adulthood from their long adolescent journey? How difficult is it to walk that razor's edge, for a parent still wanting to keep their children safe and healthy while also preparing them for their coming rights and responsibilities? And once arrived, what happens to the role of the parent?

> *Young people are, on one hand, over indulged and on the other hand, not really truly validated. They're constantly being told how wrong they are, how dumb they are, how stupid they are or what mistakes they've made. And on the other hand, a lot of times parents aren't really giving them the kind of boundaries and discipline and limits that they really need and crave. I think it's hard. I think it works really well with young people when they feel respected, when they feel like you see them, you see their possibilities, you see what they can become, you honor that, you are there to support that. And at the same time, you're not going to put up with bad behavior, you're going to set boundaries, clear boundaries, and hold those boundaries. Often times they'll test that but when you do hold them, I think they feel much more secure.* **Starhawk**

The best gift a parent can ever give a child is doing their own emotional and psychological work. If they haven't turned and faced and, to some degree, healed their own childhood trauma, they will likely perpetuate that trauma in their own children. We touched on this in Chapter Three. This is how generational trauma functions. Parents have to decide "never again." They must undertake serious self-growth work and/or work with a therapist. Until their inner child and inner teenager are recognized, healed and blessed, they will be incapable of recognizing, healing and blessing their own children and teens.

My mother modeled this for me. She did her own healing work and supported me in mine. Her therapist Sandra became my therapist. In order to help heal the wounds dating from my father's death that remained in the three of us children, my mother brought us back together as adults in one marathon session with Sandra. That's when I first met her - five years before beginning my own work with her. A few years after that, I did something similar. I asked my mother to join me and Sandra for a four hour session to root out some of the remaining ghosts from my past. She agreed and for that I sing her praises still today. It put our relationship on a whole new footing where it remained for the rest of her life.

Hopefully, most children become well practiced in experiencing a staircase of mounting challenges and in building new skill sets. In all the consternation and hand-wringing over teens, which is a typical part of parenting in this day and age, with all the pushback from youngsters who feel themselves unfairly victimized by what feels like arbitrary and authoritarian rule, parents intuitively understand that because, in a sense, they too are victims. Most likely, no one has taught these parents how to help steer their children through the multiple dark temptations that lure them away at every turn. No one has taught them when and how to let their children go. If they were lucky, they received from their own parents or other relatives some healthy modeling. But all too often parental modeling is insufficient if not plain awful. It's rare to find parents who were taught how to send their children across this Threshold from adolescence into adulthood. Their own struggles and conflicts - both internal and external - speak achingly to the overarching pattern of ingrained societal inactivity and ignorance that must be addressed and changed. Parents need help.

Parents must be taught to recognize the signs that youngsters make, signaling their need for change. We talked about this in Chapter Two. But recognition must lead to action. In conjunction with neighbors, aunties, uncles and grandparents, fellow community members of faith, coaches and counselors, whoever is available, parents must facilitate for their children a proper course of action into ROP. If a youngster is endangering themselves or others, overindulging in drugs or alcohol, skipping school and hanging out with gangs, committing regular serious crimes, with all urgency that youngster should be removed from his or her everyday surroundings and set on the course of ROP. If for some reason this isn't possible, then the youngster ideally should still be removed from the home and sent to live with other trusted adults – ones who, while watching over and safeguarding him or her, can also apply their own unique and different style of adult supervision. This relieves the mounting pressure between the youth and parent, acting as an escape valve to ameliorate tensions.

If some new form of living arrangement is not possible, then at the very least it's important for parents to thoughtfully and generously renegotiate cohabitation rules. To let out the leash, so to speak. The parent needs to make clear that she is giving the youngster more freedoms but at the clearly defined costs of more responsibilities. These behavioral parameters must be distinctly named and scrupulously defined. Curfews may be extended an hour or more. Perhaps light drinking will be allowed in the house. Sex with others might be permissible for the first time. Perhaps driving the car for longer periods or for longer distances.

But let's be clear. In these circumstances, it's also the parents who must take on new responsibilities. Parents must have thoughtful and detailed conversations with youngers, making it absolutely clear what safe sex looks like, what driving responsibly means and the potential dangers of alcohol. Each newly negotiated rule requires a mini-education in what those potential dangers are.

In my senior year of high school, I found myself in my bedroom one day introducing three of my classmates to marijuana. We were all having a raucous good time until I heard my mother's car pull in the driveway. We froze. When my mother walked into the house, I clearly heard my older sister exclaim, "Mom! Do you smell that?" My mother paused for a moment, then calmly said, "Well, I guess I would rather have him doing it at home than out on the street." That always impressed me as an extremely wise instance of parenting. And not just because it saved my ass!

The following poem is taken from my friend Diana Sterling's brilliant book *Parent as Coach*. It grew out of long and thoughtful conversations she had with her son as he was growing up. It is written from the perspective of a teen speaking to a parent.

If you RESPECT me, I will hear you.
If you LISTEN to me, I will feel understood.

> *If you UNDERSTAND me, I will feel appreciated.*
> *If you APPRECIATE me, I will know your support.*
> *If you SUPPORT me as I try new things, I will become responsible.*
> *When I am RESPONSIBLE, I will grow to be independent.*
> *In my INDEPENDENCE,*
> *I will respect you and love you all of my life.*

For both parents and youth, all rights come with new responsibilities. Kuleana – one and the same. And not necessarily only the immediate responsibilities for the commensurate activity, e.g., if the child is having sex in the house it is to be expected she will take appropriate responsible precautions to prevent pregnancy and STDs. If he wants to have more friends over more often, it is to be expected the bedroom will be cleaned more often as well. But there may also be entirely new "taxes levied." If she is taking the car for longer distances or on overnight trips, she must not only return the car cleaner than before with the gas tank full, but begin to perform regular maintenance checks for tire pressure and oil. If he is now allowed to sleep over at his friends' then perhaps he must be responsible now for doing all his own laundry.

There are limitless simple rituals parents can create to acknowledge and cement these rapid changes. If an allowance is being paid, then every week on "payday" the parent can do a simple exchange with the youngster before handing over the money. First order of business: "Are you in integrity with your commitments? If not, why not? What's getting in the way?" No excuses. Just out the shadows.

But the parent has to be scrupulously calm and even-handed. If the parent is triggered and cannot suspend his or her own judgments, it's best to interrupt the process and resume it later. As a parent, you have responsibilities too. No acting out of your own shadows! No fair making the young person account for things you yourself let slide.

Second order of business: "What, if anything, have you learned this week about yourself or the world?" Third order of business: Blessing. "I see and honor you for the woman you are becoming. This week you did all the studying necessary to prepare for your test and balanced that responsibility with completing your daily chores. I see you building resilience and adaptability." As a parent, just as with a mentor, one of your responsibilities is to see your child uniquely for who they are. If you stick to vague and general blessings, the teen won't feel blessed. Be specific in your blessings as a way for the teen to feel seen.

Working with the youngster to give away or throw out all the clothes, toys, books and other symbols of childhood can be another such ritual. Recognizing growth and achievement in sports, music, arts, dance, drama, wilderness training, farming, scouting or social club activities are great opportunities for small rituals. Most kids feel like their parents really only care about their grades. Applying simple rituals to other activities beside reviewing report cards underscores their importance too, and signals to the child that there is a rounded wholeness to who they are; they're not just a brain built to analyze and regurgitate facts, as the U.S. education policy "No Child Left Behind" seems to mandate.

So even though initiation should be left to the community - the aunties and uncles, the Elders - age appropriate ritual with the parents must be continued. Arguably, it becomes even more important. Dr. William Pollack has written persuasively about how critical a mother's love continues to be for boys in their teens. Even as they may be fussing and groaning over physical affection from mom, at some place deep within they still need it.

Can fathers initiate their own boys? I don't believe that's possible. I think the relationship of father and son can be a mentoring type of relationship. But the initiation piece, which is about how do I help him move away from who he is, move away from his current way of being, how do I help him have some sort of struggle where he finds the man he wants to be, and then how do I help him come back and bring that and live that way in society? No.

I think that fathers can participate in the third part, which is called

Homecoming. They can welcome him back as the new young man. But the work of the challenge especially needs to be around men who don't have the relationship that says, "I'm your dad," and that do have a relationship that says, "My job is to make sure that you go into your challenge and that you find yourself and that you pass or fail on your own."

My job here as the uncle, as the grandfather, as the Elder, is to create the space for you to do that. And you don't have to please me as dad, you don't have to get it right or wrong for me. You have to remember, in a father-son relationship, there are all these other dynamics that are always working. Boys, until dad dies - and for a lot of them, long afterwards, long after they're grown men and dad is dead - still have this longing for an appropriate dad, the love of dad, dad's blessing.

And so, if you bring all of that stuff into the initiation, it has a tendency to change its very focus, to taint it. That's why you seek men who don't have any of that. Their job is simply to initiate, not to father, in that moment.

It requires that the father trusts the Initiators and trusts that if something like death does happen, that's what had to happen. A father, taking his own son out to be initiated and then watching him come to harm, would be devastated. That separation is crucial.

Even how it's done today, when we work with boys, we still insist that the fathers - who may be on these trainings with us, but are in the background - they're away from the boy most of the time. It's so that we, the others, who don't know him can call the boy, challenge him on these places where he's learned to con dad, where he's learned to manipulate dad and get his way. We're not gonna fall for any of that.

We're going to keep putting him back at the choice point, keep asking him the questions of his challenge, keep inviting him to go deeper into his Ordeal, until he finds and discovers and rediscovers what he's looking for in becoming the man he wants to be. That's not the work of dad. Dad's work is to welcome him back as a new young man and to bless him and honor him, to see him in his fullness in that place. **Jim Mitchell**

Parents cannot initiate their own children. That's so important I'm going to say it again. Parents cannot initiate their own children.

I reflect on the Biblical story of Abraham, which I believe may be instructive regardless of whether you follow a Christian God, a non-Christian God or, like me, are not a believer at all. As you may recall, God demanded that Abraham sacrifice his own son Isaac in order to prove his obedience. Putting his own son to death to serve God? What kind of God might demand that? Fortunately, God, through an angel, rescinds the command. Yet I'm struck by how this parable can be seen as an initiation story. Perhaps God recognizes the need for Isaac to be initiated into manhood. Perhaps in addition to serving God, Abraham becomes a "Godly tool" to serve the growth of his son - a growth that can only take place after his childhood self is killed off in order to be reborn as an adult, an adult who understands his own primary purpose is to serve God. He becomes an adult when he knows that he cannot trust his own father, that he must only trust *The* Father. He must make decisions guided by the wisdom of the absolute, of the everlasting, not of the temporal, and he must make them of his own accord. It's an interesting hypothesis.

But I wonder if the exact opposite isn't also possible. Perhaps the story is a parable about why a father *cannot*, *should not*, *ever* be entrusted with the initiation of his son. He's serving his own agenda, not the boy's better welfare. He doesn't know that the angel will intervene so he's fully prepared to go through with it. Fathers *can* be crazy at times and wholly untrustworthy. It may well be incumbent on Isaac to stand up to his father and say, "No way." I've heard many stories from men who feel that the day they became a man was the day they stood in front of their father and said, "If you ever lay a hand on me or my mother again you will do it over my dead body. Never again!" So much of what determines a boy's ascension to manhood is his willingness to confront his father, in effect, transitioning from being a subordinate to being a peer.

That's partly why a functioning community needs to be there, to temper both the routine and the extreme behaviors of the parents. Returning to Michael Meade's metaphor, parents are likely to have the temperature too hot or too cold to properly cook the youngster. Most likely too cold since they will be far more protective of their kids, far less willing to put them to any dangerous Ordeal. Abraham, we could say, was much too hot.

The collective brain, especially when it includes the wisdom of Elders, is always more reliable than that of any individual. The collective brain knows that the youngster can take more of an Ordeal than the parent is willing to subject him to. And that same collective brain knows when the parent burns with too much passion, or worse, zealotry, and needs to step in to provide grounding normalcy. We can only mourn the fact that more members of Jim Jones' community of followers, including and especially the "elders," did not have the wherewithal to challenge his directives and stand up to save themselves and others from mass suicide. It may seem extreme to compare cult leaders like Jones to parents but it's worthwhile to remember that that is how many teens actually experience their parents.

> *One reason why it's good to have other people in the community to do the initiation and not your parents is that you and your parents, you have patterns, you have relationships, you have the things that they can do for you and can't do for you that all come out of who they are and who you are, and somebody else is just going to have a really different set of patterns and that can be really helpful. That sometimes can supply what's missing.* **Starhawk**

The journey of ROP for the youngster signals the time a different but parallel journey needs to begin for the parents. The popular conception of "empty nesters" already exists in our culture. There is a vague cultural recognition that when the children leave home, this is the beginning of a whole new phase in life for the parents. Friends and neighbors may comment and joke, but typically nothing much is done about it. That needs to change. Each parent must set out, ideally with the assistance of Elders, mentors and other community members, to construct their own rituals of death and rebirth.

Ready or not, they too must change. Their primary responsibilities have to shift. Their former roles must experience this symbolic death to be reborn into their new role. From primary caretakers they must transition into being peers - beloved, concerned peers, peers who will never stop worrying and wondering about their offspring, but peers nonetheless. This is no easy task.

We have a ceremony we call the father separation. It's an individuation process which takes place just before a boy goes off for his major ritual. His boyhood is about to end. A string connects the father and son with a fire in between them. All the men form a circle. It's very important that somebody stand alongside the father and somebody stand alongside the boy to act as facilitators. It always starts with the father. "Jim, standing across the fire from your son Jay, do you have some words to say to him at this time?" So, the father speaks whatever is in his heart – words of blessing, hurt, loss, love, fear. When he finishes the facilitator asks, "Are you done?" It's important; it's sensitive, because a father will stop when he gets choked up. You need to wait to make sure he doesn't have more to say, that he's complete. Then the other facilitator says, "Jay, standing across the fire from your father, do you have some words to say?" The son repeats the process and says what he needs to say.

Then the father's facilitator says, "Jim, are you ready now to lower the string into the fire and burn through it to signify the end of an important chapter in the life of your relationship with your son Jay?" And then the facilitator asks Jay the same thing. And then we bend down, everybody stands in the circle to witness, and we burn through the string. And then all the men pound their hearts, the folks put down their string, and we have a hug. It's that simple, but it's such a potent ritual. **Jim Horton**

Dr. Mark Schillinger is a colleague who founded an organization called Young Men's Ultimate Weekend in the San Francisco Bay Area. He was inspired by Brad Leslie, another colleague, who founded a similar organization ten years earlier in Vancouver, B.C. Both men have served teen boys magnificently over the years, helping initiate them into Mature Masculinity. Mark realized that parents need to be taught how to treat their sons differently when they return from their initiation weekends. The old patterns of command and control no longer work with the newly empowered teens. They need to be seen and recognized as young men. So, Dr. Schillinger instituted a parallel training weekend for parents. When the boys are off with the men learning how to be better men, Mark trains the parents in adjusting to their new role. Then, on Sunday when the boys are reunited with their parents, Mark conducts a Homecoming ritual. The parents are invited to call out the love they have for their sons, the differences they perceive in them and to name the ways things are now going to be different at home, the new rights and responsibilities the young men have. It's a beautiful process. But it works only because it meets the requirement that the parents receive training in a new way of interacting with their sons.

Women tend to experience this transition as a greater challenge than men. Despite recent socio-economic shifts, women still assume primary caretaking responsibilities in the home. The maternal instinct is so ingrained, so all-encompassing, it's difficult for many women to conceive of a new relationship with their young other than caretaking. For men, the shift can appear entirely consistent with their world view since they're more commonly given to thinking about career anyway, to having confidence in their role in the public arena. So it's less of a stretch for them to envision a child's new role outside the home. The same also holds true with single parents. Single fathers tend to weather this ROP with more acceptance and ease than single mothers. For women, the shift can require a whole new way of thinking about life, about their life's purpose.

That said, both women and men require rituals accentuating the changes. Now they need to ask themselves, "What is the rest of my life intended for?" Traditionally in the West, the age from young adulthood to middle age, let's say from 20-50, is about building a family and building a career. It's about learning the egolessness of raising children and the egoism of making one's mark in the world through work. Come late middle age, and certainly during Eldership, our priorities tend to and need to shift. They become more about legacy, about giving back. In a wholesome maturation cycle, the egoism of career and asset growth shifts to giving it all back, finding ways to disburse accumulated resources to maximize abundance in the greater world. "What are my grandchildren going to need to thrive? Who is going to pick up my work and carry it forward? How can I share the wealth, the assets I've accumulated, and put them to maximal good use in my community and in the greater world?"

> *What we call the adult midlife crisis is the second adolescence. Where the psyche gets disrupted by the question, "Have you lived from the source of your life?" Which is not the tradition, it's about what you've brought to transform and transmute tradition. So, if that's not integrated and collaborated with the soul, the disruption happens again and a second descent into the soul happens. And then the adult then has to come in and reaffirm the second stage of life. And many people have written about this second stage of life: Initiation and Rite of Passage.*
>
> *But by then, we have made a lot of enemies, so to speak, you know with life itself and people in life. And this is the critical part. I think the twelve-step model requires a lot of attention here. If we can do the self-analysis and say "you know I've been addicted to living without my soul, I've been addicted to the materialistic frameworks of life." Really the addiction is to try to live within the confines of one's own power and obsession with self-interest. Rather than learning how to share.*
> **Orland Bishop**

I've watched with interest how, nearing the end of their lives, some of the richest people in the world implement strategies for giving away their wealth. Bill Gates and Warren Buffet spring right to mind. Of course, those still mired in suspended adolescence will avoid philanthropy until their last breath. Jeff Bezos and Donald Trump fit this mold. Unwilling to face death, they might remain stuck in a fantasy of taking their money with them. Since wealth is the only means they know to ascertain their human value, they will extend every effort to make every last dime they can. How impoverished!

It's shocking how many wealthy and celebrated people do not make wills. This is irresponsible. Once we have assets of any note, we *all* need to make a will - the sooner the better. None of us knows when our time will come. A will can always be updated as circumstances change. By the time we hit our 70s we can know with some assurance it won't be too long. But legacy efforts need to start long before that. Among those with real wealth, not leaving a will usually guarantees a bequest of lawsuits and interpersonal battles among offspring and loved ones. What an inheritance! But it's not only the wealthy who refuse this responsibility. Unconsciously unwilling to turn and face their own death, mired in suspended adolescence, far too many people of lesser means leave their children a legacy of acrimony.

> *I come from a background where, even as I sit here right now, traditionally I'm really not sitting by myself. I am sitting here because my father, who is passed, is standing behind me propping me up and the spirit of my ancestors is with me. There's always that sense of the "we;" it's never about "me." In fact, back in the village, they used to tell us, "If a mat is on the floor, you don't just step on that mat." When you ask why, they say, "Because the spirits of the ancestors might already be sitting before you. You want to step on them?" So, you get these things put in your head. You begin to realize that there's more than just you playing out here so there's got to be a need to respect that. That's why we pour libation to the ancestors, to drink water, to drink wine, to eat... you welcome everybody, including those you see and those you don't see, and there's a sense that we are all journeying together.* **Chike Nwoffiah**

What You Need To Do *Now*

- Download our free Parents Guide at warriorfilms.org. You'll find numerous helpful and practical suggestions for what parents can do with kids every year starting from 6th grade until they graduate high school, roughly, from ages 12-18.
- Acknowledge your youth's contributions to the family, its functioning, and well-being, especially when those actions challenge their comfort zone.
- Acknowledge your youth for "pulling away" and for their challenges with impulse control. Let them know it's OK if they want more privacy, if they're less interested in family activities and more interested in peer activities, if they are drawn to new and different styles and expressions – in music, clothes, hair and body presentation, etc., even if they're "pushing back" – becoming more resistant, reactive, obtuse or secretive. Certainly don't reward them for being disrespectful or hurtful, but reassure them that given tremendous hormonal surges, losing control and being reactive are quite normal for their age. Reassure them that nothing's wrong, that the changes they're going through are entirely normal, and that with practice they can reduce their reactivity.
- Allow them to spend less time with the family. Encourage your youth to spend more time with their mentor and other trusted adults, especially those adults of the same gender as the teen. If they don't have a mentor, encourage them to seek one out with help from you or other adults.
- Invite your youth's friends over for dinner. Do your best to create a "safe space" for them to relax and feel free of judgment. The more comfortable your children's peers feel in your home the more likely they are to keep you informed about occurrences outside of it.
- Don't get locked into adversarial positions. If you and your youth come to a serious impasse, simply suggest the teen spend a few days with a trusted neighbor, family friend or relative until the situation cools down.
- Balance affirmation with discipline. We often remember when someone

tells us what we did wrong. If we don't hear what we did *right,* it can lead to friction, resentment and discouragement.
- Do your best to NOT expect the worst. Expecting the worst, especially when it's a pattern, can easily become a self-fulfilling prophecy. Give your youth trust [but not naiveté!] and you can strengthen your relationship. It will help them feel empowered to know they can learn from mistakes instead of repeating them.
- Move your focus away from the small things and onto the big things. Youth constantly try out new and different roles so they can better understand the ones they'd like to commit to. By paying more attention to how your youths *feel* and less on how they *look* you can keep them from shutting you out later when it matters most.
- Be proactive about expectations and discipline. Move away from confrontation and into contracts. The more clarity you share about expectations and consequences the easier it is for your young person to follow through.
- Share stories with your youth about the challenges *you* faced when you were their age: what you struggled with and how you got through it. Share about your common and completely natural need to be tested.
- Model the behavior you seek from your youth: if you want them to drink less, smoke less, drive more defensively, study more, etc., be sure you're modeling the same behavior yourself. Youth carefully observe what you do even more than what you say. They seek congruity. Share with them the ways that you learned how to become the man or woman you are today.
- Make honesty and transparency the gold standard. Even if in that honesty they say "Mom, I don't like you right now and I need you to leave me alone." There is a genuine difference for young people between *thinking* and actually *knowing* they can tell you anything. As a parent you will be tested. Repeatedly. Your job is to see your children for who they are, not for who you ideally want them to be. Again, you must do your own emotional and psychological work, keeping your own shadows in check. Try these as conversation starters. As always, check

in, sometimes repeatedly, about whether they're open to sharing.

1. If you had to give every human being one quality, what would it be and why?
2. Do you have any recurring dreams? Are you open to sharing them?
3. What is the meanest thing someone could say to you?
4. If you were invisible where would you go and what would you do?
5. If your life was made into a movie, who would play you? Why?
6. If you could have one superpower what would it be?
7. What is the most important quality for a friend to have?
8. If you could know one thing about the future, what would it be?
9. What does love mean to you?
10. What is the first thing you notice about a person?
11. What do you think is the biggest problem you will face in your lifetime? Why?
12. Describe the most beautiful thing you have ever seen.
13. If you could trade places with anyone in the world who would it be and why?

- Watch Warrior Film's *Rites of Passage: Mentoring the Future* with other parents. Share ideas about how you can implement Rites of Passage and engaged mentorship in your family's life.
- Watch the film at home and have a family discussion using the discussion prompts in the external resource section of the Parents guide.
- Have a neighborhood viewing and discussion in your home or at a nearby community center.
- Ask the YMCA, Boys and Girls Club, 4H, Outward Bound, or Big Brothers/Big Sisters in your community if they'd like to host a screening and discussion. All are great organizations doing related work. They might even bring staff and ideas of their own to bear.
- Establish open communication with your young people about the definition of "manhood," "womanhood," or "trans." Tie it to clear expectations around behavior and accountability.

- Form a parent's support circle with other parents of teens to provide mutual support. Tracy and I formed our own couple's support group like this. It aided not only parenting, but our relationship with each other.
- With your co-parent and/or outside parents, make preparations for the coming ebb and flow of your youth's decreased reliance on family and increased reliance on peer support. Develop creative ideas for meeting both challenges.
- Develop a weekly or monthly time for check-ins around the ideas of interdependence and overall well-being with your youth. Move away from "big talks" and more into consistent, open conversations. If that doesn't work, develop an openness to spontaneously deep dialogs. Teens often aren't comfortable with staged, big talks but can and will often drop into deep conversation at any given moment, especially when driving in the car.
- In addition to check-ins, engage in your youth's interests, specifically those residing in popular culture. For instance, discussing Rites of Passage in reference to the *The Hunger Games* or the *Divergent* book series. Whether it's a film, TV show, book or video game, these prompts can be valuable tools in fostering better relationships between you and your youth.
- Take inventory of the peers, mentors and Elders in your teen's life (and perhaps teachers and coaches). Who among them might be interested in joining you and your teen to have a dialog about heritage and traditions? Explore together the traditions in your own family and the different traditions in theirs. How are they similar and different? Initiation, coming of age, and Rites of Passage may or may not be overt parts of the conversation. Conversations like these not only deepen a young person's sense of self and belonging, they deepen and strengthen ties of community.

7

Community

What is the most important reason for Rites of Passage? Is it about the individual? Evolutionary biologists have agreed that the single most important unit of our species is not the individual, it is the community. Which means the purpose of rituals in general and Rites of Passage specifically were the survival of the community and the survival of the species. **David Blumenkrantz**

We all forget our purpose, for we go through the rigors of being born, then living as infants and toddlers. As we grow, we need to discover our gifts anew. The community exists to help individuals remember their purpose. **Sobonfu and Malidoma Some**

I'm forgetful. Especially with names. Dates I'm pretty good at, though I can be far off sometimes, especially with events of the last 3-5 years. One thing I'm not forgetful about is my purpose. I have the opposite problem. I may be so focused on the long term that I won't have equilibrium in the everyday. I'll judge that I'm off track, distracted by things that aren't in service to my mission. I'll lose patience for mundane things that deserve my care and attention, like cleaning the house, having a decent set of clothes to wear or giving my needy cat some love. I'll also question and begin to doubt my deeper purpose when I run into challenges and roadblocks with my work, asking, "If this is clearly what I'm here on the planet to do, why is it so goddamn difficult? Maybe I should be doing something else?" Though I note with gratitude it's quelled in recent years, I've had some version of that conversation in my head for at least 30 years.

In Chapter Two we looked at common life transitions for young people. There are many common life transitions for adults:

-Engagement and marriage
- Having a first child
- Buying a car or house
- First death of a close friend or family member
- Losing a long-held job, house or relationship
- Divorce
- Any of the above experienced by our kids
- Retirement
- Death of a spouse and/or parents
- Our own death

How many of these transitions help us clarify or redefine our life purpose? Where does each transition leave us on our Hero's Journey? How many of these transitions do we actually consecrate with ROP? Not many. Take just about any aspect of modern life and the same story applies.

As my wife was dying, we held a Life Honoring Celebration for her. At the end of my long introduction to the 40 or so people who were there, I shared this quote, *"A friend is someone who knows the song in your heart and can sing it back to you when you have forgotten the words."* Then, I continued with some encouragements: "I question and doubt my life song all the time. But this day is about Tracy. She's much better at it but even she forgets on occasion. So that's your job here today – to sing her life song back to her so she can remember the words. With authenticity and emotional vulnerability. Like our lives, like our deaths… please rest easy in the comfort of knowing that whatever arises is what's meant to be here."

COMMUNITY

"Singing our life songs back to each other…" That's as potent a thumbnail description of what friendship means of any I know. That's how people invested in our well-being reflect back to us their love and concern. That's the function of community. But along with the complementary stuff, we need people to say the tough stuff. "Whoa! Hold on brother! That's not the man I know." "That's not the man I know you want to be." "The man I know and love would do *this instead…*" If functional, our community holds up a fiercely uncompromising mirror for us to look into. It's hard to see ourselves fully and accurately. Thank goodness for the friends we have who are willing to help us do that. Adapting a popular aphorism from Shunryū Suzuki, community helps us learn what is absolutely perfect about us just as we are and what could use a little improvement.

> *One of the functions of initiation is to bring the young people fully into the community. And so that implies that you have a community, a community that understands the depth of the human psyche and the struggle to be meaningful in life. And so, one of the problems I notice in working with young people is even if we are able to assist them into getting to a deep place in themselves, what do we do with them afterwards? It's a serious problem because often there is no community to deliver them to. So, you wind up living with them or taking them home or trying to find a way to hold on to them.* **Michael Meade**

Many communities are broken or dysfunctional. Urban "development" and suburban sprawl destroyed many spatially contiguous communities. Other communities organized around schools, sports, hobbies and workplaces often become bureaucratized and eventually denuded of real interpersonal potency. Through hierarchical structures and soulless ceremonies, the possibility of deep human bonding and connection gets lost. Soulful sharing disappears. Meetings and ceremonies are not built to hold powerful emotions. Plus, there are no skilled "shadow watchers"[9] present to safeguard group intentions. Group gatherings rarely allow for the spontaneous creation of rituals of healing and wholeness.

> *We're in a chicken versus egg situation here. On the one hand you need an initiatory experience to go from being "me" to being prepared to be a part of a "we." On the other hand, the initiatory experience is very difficult to do unless there is a "we" into which you emerge.* **Chris Shaeffer**

> *The truth is that in our world today, communities are split. And we've grown up in a context that really doesn't have community... Following initiation, it's a big challenge for people to go back into a world that does not understand what they've done, will not honor what they've done, and think in some ways that they're threatening or crazy. How do we say, "That's what you're going back to?" There's no taking that challenge away.* **Meredith Little**

> *When somebody just has one day or a weekend, they might have an awakening experience of some kind and then they are transplanted from that incubator, from that context, back into the soil that doesn't sustain that seed and it can't really germinate and grow and flourish the way it otherwise could in community, in membership with other people.* **Christopher Kuntzsch**

> *The Elders, in order to initiate others, need to be in a common experience so they can know what the young person's experience has been. People*

---

[9] Shadow watchers are people who are willing and able to be present to make sure the group isn't acting out of shadow.

would go out on these wilderness events and the most common experience they had upon returning was negative. Their families, their neighbors, their brothers and sisters never had the experience. So, the young people always had a feeling of despondency and frustration upon returning because, while they had that experience of what could be transcendence, when they go home and try to explain it, their parents typically say "Ooh, you smell and you're dirty. Go up and take a shower." I've seen it happen for 30 years. Within a period of 24 and 48 hours the young people get into a state of despair that no one understands. **David Blumenkrantz**

When Initiates - young or old - taste some of the profundity of their own transformation from ROP, how can we in good conscience return them to families and communities that have little to no understanding of ROP? We risk completely disillusioning them or worse, driving them crazy or to suicide. That's why mentors are so absolutely fundamental. If the community is non-existent, or barely functional, at least mentors can watch over Initiates and make sure they understand they're not alone, to remind them there's nothing crazy or wrong with them. In functional society, ROP graduates would be universally honored, celebrated and reintegrated. Since that rarely happens, loyal mentors must maintain that lifeline.

It might be a while before there are culturally appropriate forms of initiation. As much as it's needed, it's very hard to do. And the people that I've seen, those who have tried it... Everybody has found it to be quite a difficult thing. What I like about initiation is the idea that there is a deep revelation of one's self to oneself. And to create the circumstances that allow that – because it takes a certain amount of emotional pressure for that to happen – is difficult and sometimes dangerous. And then you wind up with someone who needs a community to verify and sustain what they have just learned, and I find that difficult to do. How to create that? So, I know that we are in a period of struggling with that knowledge, and not readily finding forms.

I am working with, let's say, a traditional Native American tribe, which has a living initiatory tradition. They've been doing it. It hasn't been interrupted. It's been underground, but it's still going on. The problem they have is the young people won't come and do it because they don't trust the older people, because of what has happened within the tribe and within the families. So, they have a tradition, but it is not actually effective for the children they have. So, in that case what we have to do, from my opinion, is bring in some different approaches and different angles to create a bridge for the children of the tribe, the young people, to be willing to go in and get involved with the older people in the tribe again. There needs to be an intermediary step. You can't just take the tradition and lay it on them because they already feel wounded by the tribe. **Michael Meade**

Traditional ROP do require the sanctification of an individual's unique culture. Whatever culture we most identify with, whatever religion or spiritual tradition we consider ourselves part of (or apart from!), that too must be present in some form in a Rite of Passage. We must be initiated *into* something – and that something, the community or collective – must have some fundamental coherence and identity. And yes, even atheism or humanism can qualify as strong cultural identities alongside churches, synagogues, mosques and temples. The same goes for neighborhood or work-related associations, sports teams, or strong ethnic or social clubs. I feel hopeful, perhaps a bit more than Michael Meade, that some relatively simple cultural practices can and do help restore communities to wholeness.

Every time we run an event, [in Takaka, NZ] in a sense we are having to establish community. We're having to create this foster community whereas normally it would be an existing community that's just engaging in the work. But we're getting a disparate group of people together and we're having to bring them together - close enough so they can go to the depths the work requires. And that takes an enormous amount of role modeling and reassurance really, and vulnerability. **Adge Tucker**

We have an annual Kwanzaa celebration [in Akron, OH]. It's a citywide celebration and different community groups take control of the day and they host it at their venue. If it's people or young folks who have gone through an initiation and are transitioning then there is a way we introduce them to the community. If there are adults that have gone through an adult training, "Here they are... and here is what they're going to be working on in the coming months." So, we're utilizing that venue as a way to introduce them to the community. **Kwabena Terrence Shelton**

Healthy community can hold and contain the wild passion and fierce energy of youth without suppressing it. They can direct it to the places where it's most needed. They can recognize the value the young people are bringing and bless them into appropriate positions of authority to exercise it. These are some of the primary functions of community. Without them, the community not only won't cohere, it will not be able to sustain itself because it will cut out the heart of its own future.

In the U.S today, religious communities are some of the most functional. That shared, deep, soulful purpose unites parishioners into a meaningful collective. But even religious institutions typically allow only for "top-down" ceremony - services directed and controlled by the ministers, priests and roshis. For community to be truly effective, all members must be empowered to express their needs fully and forcefully. They have to know they have a clear stake in the process, in all processes. They have to understand the value of each human voice and what it can contribute to the collective. Ideally, no voice goes unexpressed. Every voice must at least be given room to speak. This is the norm in Quaker meetings and in the practices of "council."

The traditions of council practice are many, and whole libraries could be devoted to their collection. *The Way of Council* written by Jack Zimmerman and Virginia Coyle in 1996 is a good starting point for those interested in learning more. Akin to centuries-long practices among native peoples worldwide, the basic form is very simple. Everyone sits together in a circle. The talking stick is passed around the circle and everyone speaks in turn, saying whatever each person needs to. There may be an Elder who sets intentions by outlining particular themes or asking for input on one or more issues. But it doesn't have to be the case and anyone can say whatever is on his or her mind. Traditionally, there are no time limits, but those can be layered on if needed, allowing, say, five minutes for each person to speak.

Anyone can call a meeting. When a person is upset about something and needs to clear an issue with an individual or with the group, she can call a meeting. Whoever holds the talking stick speaks and says whatever she needs to. When finished, she puts the stick in the center and whoever feels called to speak picks it up next. In this way, by going back and forth, sometimes multiple times between two key individuals, they resolve their differences. If they can't do it on their own, Elders and others pick up the stick and offer what they can in the way of wisdom. Eventually the group mind is accessed and resolutions appear.

I saw a dramatic illustration of this during one of many MKP weekend staffings. The training was underway and it was not running smoothly. Men were missing their assignments and we were behind schedule. There seemed to be a breakdown in the system of mentorship and accountability; men were confused as to what they were supposed to be doing. Fear was rampant and men were angry.

Those of us not on task with participants sat together for a staff meeting. I don't recall the official weekend leaders even being in the room. Maybe one was. We began with a check-in. Directly and passionately, often volubly, many of the first 10-15 men expressed their anger, frustration and fear at the chaos they were experiencing. There was a lot of nodding and men holding up their hands to indicate, "I'm feeling that too."[10]

Halfway around the circle the transformation began. It was almost imperceptible at first. Men felt heard. They released the energy they were carrying. Subsequent men didn't need to vent. They, perhaps unconsciously, started focusing on what needed to happen. Each man still expressed his feelings and judgments, but the tenor of the check-ins shifted inexorably to solutions. I could feel the mood in the room shifting. There was less tension and more focus. The pressure had been released and men were calm. By the time the last man spoke there was even levity. Without designing or prescribing it, the group mind had asserted itself. There was a collective sense of what needed to be done without a single person assuming control, much less shouting orders. Each man asserted his individual authority and shared it with the collective. Every man was heard and every man understood what he needed to do next. I left the meeting in awe, dumbstruck at the beauty I had witnessed.

Council can be practiced in any group at any time for any purpose: prisons, community groups, workplaces, churches, schools, neighborhood associations, trade unions or government. It can be used for healing, teaching, learning and governing.

The first time I experienced it was in Southern Illinois in 1979. My best friend inherited an inactive farm from her grandfather and was doing her best to bring it back to life. We would attend summer gatherings with farmers from across the region once a month on a Sunday. Most of the participants were "back-to-the-landers," often hippies who had left urban communities to try their hand at rural and sustainable living. We congregated on someone's farm and everyone brought food to share.

100 or more of us sat together in a circle. A few words of welcome were usually shared by the hosts. Then the talking stick was passed. Some

---

[10] This is one of the fundamental verities I've learned about council practice. One person speaks for others. No matter how personal or idiosyncratic any given individual's feelings and judgments may seem to be, almost invariably there are others present who will feel the same way. Indicating this by signaling to each other with a hand raised also lets the speaker know he is not alone.

people would express pertinent info of use to the community - news about farmers markets, pooling resources for child and medical care, barn raisings, farm management and announcements of other gatherings. Others would address state of the world issues. Nuclear power plants were a big concern. Conditions of inmates like Leonard Peltier, housed nearby in Marion Federal Penitentiary, came up. Others would say a few words of blessing to the circle or hold the stick in silence for some moments before passing it. What anyone said was delightfully unknown until they said it. I especially loved hearing what was of concern to my friends and neighbors. Invariably, themes would emerge and people would respond to what got triggered in them by others. Those themes would be carried through and deepened. Akin to consensus, a kind of group mind emerged. Though energy shifts were rarely as pronounced and clear as what I experienced years later in that dramatic NWTA circle I mentioned above, the council always concluded with a sense of fullness and completion. Ease and satisfaction lingered afterward among the participants. The community had bonded.

> *Council encourages participants to communicate in ways that lead to a heightened sense of shared purpose. Council became a time, place and practice for healing, as well as a pathway for creating and sustaining community – a sense of connection with all of life. By fostering attentive listening and authentic spontaneous expression, the practice builds trust and nurtures relationships among participants, offering an alternative to the power dynamics that can arise from inequities of status, race, economic stature and other hierarchical structures. In the circle, everyone shares in the responsibility for guiding the process; thus, the emerging group spirit and the practice itself becomes the primary facilitating force, with servant leaders in supporting roles.* **Jack Zimmerman, Gigi Coyle, Marlow Hotchkiss, Leon Berg, and Lola Rae Long - *The Ojai Foundation Elder Council***

COMMUNITY

As Angeles Arrien pointed out, we're very good at beginnings in this culture. Take a look at births. We celebrate them commonly. We hold baby showers to honor and support mothers stepping into birth. After the child is born, it's also common for family, friends and neighbors to show up with meals and other forms of support. We're also pretty good at deaths. Funerals and memorial services are the cultural norm throughout society, regardless of religious or non-religious belief.

But dying? The process of moving *toward* death? Not so good. When one of us is dying, we're loath to admit it even to ourselves, much less to our loved ones. Most people will hide, repress and deny this simple truth from themselves and others until death is actually here. The medical system reinforces this blindness. It is designed with one aim: to prolong life at all costs. There's always one more test, one more treatment, one more drug that can be tried. It's a colossal lost opportunity. Few people in Western society get to experience this stage of life consciously, in all its richness and complexity. There's discomfort and pain, yes; there can be dread, shock, anger, grief and even horror. But there is also incredible opportunity for intimacy, love, clarity, insight and beauty, with as much or more depth than has been possible for a person's entire lifetime. Ask anyone who works with the dying. They'll tell you. It's common for many to say, "I didn't know it was possible to experience this kind of _____ [fill in the blank: love, ease, connection, fulfillment, satisfaction, awareness, simplicity, profundity, wisdom...]" In our age of secular belief in the religion of medicine it sounds almost sacrilegious to say, but the lucky ones in our society are those who can honestly and openly admit to themselves and their loved ones they're dying.

I'm a strong advocate of Life Honoring Celebrations. Since I wrote about it in some detail in my last book - how I originally got the idea and how I finally gained permission from my wife to host an event for her - I won't recount that here. I'll just say that it was a tremendously rich experience for all who participated, not least of course for Tracy and myself. Hers took place 12 days before she died.

The ritual is very simple to pull off. Start with a date and a location. Pick a near enough date so your beloved will still be strong enough, and a time of day that best works for her. Send out the invites, asking for RSVPs if you have space considerations. Make clear what the purpose is: to have people speak publicly of the difference the dying person made in their life. Make it clear that even though it's a Life Celebration, it's not a time for false bravado. All emotions are welcome.

This is the invitation I sent out for Tracy's:

> *You're invited to a celebration to honor the life of Tracy Seeley. She will be present. For those of you unfamiliar with her situation please click on her CaringBridge.org website. Details on the event are below.*
>
> *The purpose of this celebration is to let Tracy know how she's made a difference in your life and in the lives of others you may know. This sharing allows us to underscore how we are all connected, each a part of the other, and to celebrate that interconnection. Being together in this way also underscores with simplicity and ease how when we gather to speak our heart's truth and are witnessed by others, we deepen our understanding of the very meaning of life and invite grace into our lives.*
>
> *Ideally, every human being would have this opportunity before they die. Every human being deserves it. In our culture, though, fear and repression too often deny us this chance. So, come prepared to speak your heart's truth; step confidently into the simple reality of a loved one's passing. Use this process to begin your grieving process if that serves you, but also please come prepared too for a lot of laughter and light. This will not be a religious ceremony. All beliefs and non-beliefs are welcome.*
>
> *Following the sharing of words, we will share the blessing of food. Please bring a potluck item... Please, no gifts. Your presence is your gift to us.*
>
> *None of us can insist on the appearance of grace in this lifetime, but if we create ceremony with great intention and mindfulness, we can sometimes set the ground for grace to arrive and bless us all.*

COMMUNITY

Ubuntu,
   Frederick Marx
   (Tracy's husband)

When the event arrives, it's helpful to have chosen a facilitator or two. That way we - the beloved partners (or friends or relatives) - are free to experience everything ourselves and be fully present in support of the person dying. The facilitators can step in when needed to re-clarify the purpose, to stop people from going on too long, to encourage people who may be too shy to speak and to hold the event with sacred, loving intention.

Seat your beloved in comfort at the front of the room. Sit next to her and leave an open chair on the other side. Welcome and thank everyone for coming. Model the emotional vulnerability that you want everyone to freely express. If you're like me, chances are you'll be so moved that this won't be an issue. Recognize and introduce the facilitators. Then turn it over to them. When each person feels called to speak, they will be invited to sit next to the beloved at the front and speak their heart's truth about how dearly they hold them.

Personally, I think it's impractical at best and pointless at worst to sing somebody's praises after they have passed. Perhaps saying lovely things about them at funerals helps us mourn. Saying the same things to them while they're still alive may give us a jumpstart on that mourning. But why not use their dying as an opportunity to grow *ourselves*, to bring us into closer proximity with the reality of death, to face our fears and step willfully into our deepest hearts to speak the truth of what someone means to us? Why not tell them when they're alive? Why not let them see some of the difference they have made in the world around them? Even the most troubled and maligned person usually has positively impacted somebody. No matter how difficult anyone's life has been, they have usually created some ripples of positive change. And I believe that every person longs to know that, to *see* it - to know that our existence does not all come to naught in the end. We long to see that efforts large and small have impacts seen and unseen. It serves each of us to have tangible proof of this before we pass.

Life Honoring Celebrations should be every human's birthright. Thank goodness Tracy got to receive hers. Just in time.

What it did for her was rich. She got to experience some of the beautiful ways she changed friends' and colleagues' lives for the better, many completely unimagined. Without saying a single word about it, Tracy got to share her own grief at dying with her beloved community. Events like these make it possible for an individual's grief to be held by the collective. Individual mourning is neither realized nor complete until it is *witnessed*. We must be seen and acknowledged in the pain of our losses so it can flow freely through us and away. Once it's fully expressed, that pain will be held by others too. Life Honoring Celebrations bring mourning to the fore as a regular and significant part of everyday life, something to be wholeheartedly engaged in.

Sobonfu Somé used to tell a beautiful story about returning to her village in Burkina Faso after divorcing her husband. The villagers knew that her own grief would not find relief until her community of origin embraced and held it. In addition, they too needed to grieve. They were shocked and saddened at the separation of these two beloved leaders. They felt their own grief had no real outlet until her return because there was no public ritual to induce and contain it. So, the public grieving ceremony for Sobonfu served her and her people equally. It is as fundamental for the social cohesion of a community as it is to the emotional release of the individual.

Sobonfu also said, "Young people commit suicide because of the unexpressed grief of the adults." Those words ripped my heart. When young people see that their own parents and Elders – those who are supposed to guide, lead and model authenticity and have wisdom – themselves hide, repress and deny the depths of their own sorrow, then what is the point of life? If even the tears of disappointment, loss and betrayal that life inevitably serves up are not welcome, if there is no outlet for that most human of expressions, why go on? If life is truly this hopeless why not just end it?

I immediately thought of the situation on many Native reservations throughout the U.S. A few years ago, there was an epidemic of teen suicide. For all I know it continues today and we just don't hear about it. I immediately reached out to my friends Becky and Dallas Chief Eagle in Pine Ridge to see if I could help bring Sobonfu there for a public grief ritual. Maybe seeing their Elders cry at all the abuses they suffered might prevent some young native men and women from taking their own lives. Medical science has now established that generational trauma is genetic. Imagine how that inheritance might stop. Imagine what healing young Native people might experience from witnessing their Elders weep publicly at the innumerable historical injustices they experienced.

We should have nothing to fear from public grief. Unfortunately, all too often men in particular are shamed for being vulnerable and crying in public. In 2012, Barry Larkin was inducted into the Baseball Hall of Fame. He cried when he accepted his award. The media savaged him. "What kind of man is he?!" was the implication of many news stories. And his were tears of joy! It was brutal. Absorbing toxic lessons like public shaming contributes to sending men to early graves.

For many years, I somehow sensed that if I could ever cry in public it would be a major threshold for me - a coming out party. Years before I ever did "men's work," I learned the importance of releasing my feelings. But in practice I only felt confident crying alone or with my therapist. Though I might have cried every day for a year after my girlfriend left me in 1989, I was always careful to do it out of sight of others. One day, when a wave of grief hit me in the middle of teaching an ESL class, I felt forced to temporarily adjourn just so I could run to the bathroom and weep.

In January 1994, I finally cried in public while accepting the Audience Award for Best Documentary at the Sundance Film Festival for *Hoop Dreams*. I was proud of myself. In a way I absolutely had not prepared for, the eight long years of hardship and strife making the film, of little pay and long hours, of uncertainty and disillusionment, came bubbling up in me. I was actually feeling joyful, full of immense gratitude. But that was energetically entwined with the struggle and pain. I wept expressing my thanks. Finally, the rich interior life of my private emotions was finding its way into the social world.

Our cultural mores tell us that it's somehow inappropriate when we cry, that it somehow worsens things for others who are grief-stricken, that we're being selfish or offensive. Nothing could be further from the truth. Stepping into our own grief gives license to others to step into theirs. The more we are willing to bucket out our sadness when it arises, the more room and receptivity we create in our hearts for joy.

Seeing people cry in public binds communities together. Public rituals of grieving are even better. It is the glue that establishes trust. It allows people to know one another in depth, to learn to love one another and base their love on a rock-solid foundation of authenticity. In the modern world everyone wants to celebrate but so few are willing to mourn. That is truly sad.

We're very good at weddings but not so good at divorces. Think how much meaning and value a functional community could bring to families experiencing divorce. Ponder how simple rituals of separation could start acrimonious couples on the road to wholeness. How the burning of a string that symbolically connected them could begin to release the bonds that hold them and provide them with a fresh start. Simple statements from the two of them, once witnessed by all, could begin the process of healing by opening the wells of grief. Different community members could affirm their ongoing love and support for each of the partners, testifying to their willingness to not take sides.

Think how it could help the kids! They could be invited to make simple statements of grief, anger, betrayal or fear - whatever is present for them. It could do wonders for jumpstarting their healing. They could receive public expressions of support from others in their community who can help hold them through the Ordeal.

We celebrate when someone gets a new job but do little or nothing when they quit or are fired.[11] We celebrate when children are born, but what about when they leave home? We hold parties when a business opens, often

---

[11] Or when they face retirement. Think how necessary ROP are at that time to help someone shed a working identity from the last 30-50 years and be reborn into some new life purpose. The repercussions of people unprepared for this transition are all too well documented: depression and even suicide are all too common.

taking the first dollar in sales and framing it on the wall. That can be a beautiful ritual. But we potentially add to the owner's fear and shame, the sense of being an outcast, when we meet the reality of going out of business with silence. The implication is that it's on them; they did something wrong. Justified or not, "it's their fault." Who extends a sympathetic hand and says, "I feel your pain"? Who says, "We're going to invite all your friends here tonight and we're going to celebrate what you accomplished here. And yeah, we're going to grieve you moving on, too..." When people move into new homes we join in housewarming parties. What do we do to help those same people mourn when it's time for them to move out?

When I move into a new house or apartment, I like to walk through the empty rooms with a smudge stick of incense, sage, sweet grass or cedar. It's important to me to clear out the old energy and reset the space to zero. I do these little rituals, by myself if I'm living alone or with a housemate/partner, to welcome in a new time in a new place and to set intentions for a future of peacefulness and harmony.

Similarly, when moving away, I like to do rituals of closure. I'll usually smudge again, walking through the place recounting memories and thanking the space for "holding me." When I moved out of Chicago in 1998, I did a three-in-one goodbye ritual with the support of my men's circle: thanking my beautiful apartment, the city that I loved and my precious woman partner I could no longer live with. I wept tears of loss for them all. Afterward, I felt refreshed and ready to move on.

Shadow watchers also play key roles in effective communities. In institutions of old, functionaries like these used to be called ombudsmen. Their responsibility was the sensible and ethical functioning of the organization. If people had complaints or problems, they could find the ombudsman who would help resolve them. In our increasingly codified and controlled world, it's telling that these functionaries hardly exist. People have little to no recourse for places to go to resolve issues that fall outside the box. I'm gratified every time I actually get the answers I need from calling a computer help line. It seems increasingly rare. If only there were an option like "Press 3 if you're at your wit's end and feel there's nowhere left to turn..."

How communities come together and work to meet the challenges of young people defines who they are. In an ideal world, every community would have ombudspersons where young people could go for help to resolve disputes. Fortunately, some still do. They're called Elders. Those functional communities hopefully also have some form of council practice. All young people, regardless of their age, must command a seat in the circle and must be encouraged to share whatever they need to.

Teen initiation not only serves teens, it serves adults because it reminds them of their own purpose and their own gifts. It strengthens and restores the functionality of the community since adults have to work collectively to initiate teens. These adults have to be dedicated to one purpose and one purpose only – the growth and well-being of young people. By doing this, they publicly demonstrate service - "giving back" to their community. By sharing the gifts of mentoring and initiation - gifts they themselves once received from their ancestors (hopefully!) - with the next generation, they're "paying it forward." These cultural practices help the village cohere. If people are willing to come together to create healthy Rites of Passage for teens, it helps restore the fabric of broken communities. Everyone knows the African maxim "It takes a whole village to raise a child." But they usually don't know Michael Meade's deft inversion: *It takes the struggles of youth to raise a village.*

The MKP community has struggled for years with enrollment, first, getting men to join and secondly, retaining them as engaged members. Lately, I've simplified my own process for enrolling men into MKP. Standard logic used to tell me, "I should reach out to this guy because he really needs our work" as if it's incumbent on me to fix him. Though I believe most men clearly benefit from our work, it's not up to me to fix anybody. But there are many men I feel would benefit *us*, our MKP community, by sharing their differences, their wisdom and their life experience. Many are men of color, low-income men, young men and urban men. I long to be in deeper relationship with more of these men. They are the men I most learn from and enjoy. After first befriending them in other communities or other contexts, they are now the men I most regularly reach out to and invite to join MKP. Before I do it, I ask myself just one simple question: When the time comes to sit down together as brothers and break bread, who would I most enjoy sitting with?

> *Today we're a global world. The skills and the understandings that young people need to be initiated into to live in a global world are very different than they've ever been before. And so, as guides, we have to ask: how do we prepare them for their initiation, how do we help them to learn skills that are necessary for them today?*
>
> *How do we adapt to that? How do we cultivate and honor and nurture that we are a global community? What does that mean? They're not all gonna show up for us. And yet there's some need for us to keep looking. The yearning to feel connected to community is still a part of our nature. How do we satisfy that? Is it enough to create temporary communities or "artificial" quote "communities?" Or do we say that some of these communities, that are somewhat temporary, are not artificial? They're real. They are community and we can stand in for each other.*
>
> *Every young person should be sent out of the country to a different culture where they speak a different language. That's an essential part of any initiation today for a young person.* **Meredith Little**

We do live in a global village and it's important to recognize both the advantages and limitations. One advantage is that we can be instantly close to pretty much anyone in the world at any time. Though we can't touch each other physically, we can certainly touch each other metaphorically – touch each other's hearts, minds and souls. We can be extremely intimate and feel very close. We can fall in love. (We can also get very angry, get into fights and nourish hate.)

"Having the world at our doorstep" helps us learn to receive other cultures. We can't be in relationship with people from other cultures without being forced sooner or later to confront the new and different ways they do things. We are forced to expand our understanding of what it is to be human. A lot of people resist that. They don't want their way of doing things challenged. Much of the reactionary behavior taking political form throughout the world today is due in no small part to the feeling many people have that their way of doing things is under threat. They're reacting to the rapid pace of change and resisting the unwelcome awareness that their culture is not absolute.

Environmental change also forces us to approach issues on a global level. One country's policies have demonstrable impact on the environmental realities of others'. As in creation, so in solution. No one country or people can solve the problems alone. But certain countries like the U.S. can and should become global leaders in solving problems because we're a global leader in creating them. Institutions like the U.N., though notoriously slow and bureaucratic, should also lead in addressing these global challenges. It takes multilateral, cross-cultural, inter-organizational cooperation.

What we can't do in cyber land is look into someone's eyes, their real eyes, up close. We can't hold their hand, hug or kiss them. (Nor can we kick, bite, slug or scratch them. Though we can troll them!) I mention these examples of physical proximity because, at some point, physical encounters are the very stuff that makes deep human relationship possible. Unless you're physically close to someone, three of your five senses are inoperative. Crude as it may sound, you can't touch, smell or taste them. These too are features of what makes real human knowing possible. Functional community is based to some degree on human contact and direct interaction. Though cyber relationships and communities are rich in possibility, and the use of those terms "relationship" and "community" to describe them is wholly justified, their limitations must be recognized.

> *These kids who are primarily our grandchildren are that offspring and so they're more hyper and they're less attentive and they have TV and they don't know what rotary phones are. They grow with cell phones out of the womb... And they have technology that allows them to get access to information that we just never even dreamed of when we were*

their age. So, we're dealing with a different set of kids; we're dealing with a different set of parents. All of them don't have this structure of family to help them in their parenting and to help them in guiding their children through their various transitional developmental stages. And so the biological plan gets wrecked over and over and over again because there is no content that's appropriate to help them matriculate through those stages. **Kwabena Terrence Shelton**

I tend to define community in very existential terms. Wherever and whenever we find ourselves in the company of others we can, and I believe should, seek to define our time together as community. The word shouldn't be limited to its common associations with church, school, neighborhood, social club, political affiliation, social clique, sport, activity, or, of course, an online version. With communications as fast and as fluid as they are today, communities are no less so. They come and go, morph, grow, shrink and die in what can be as short as a few hours. Communities can spring out of single impactful events, like Coachella 2000, the "Arab Spring," disaffected Netflix customers, parents of children with autism or clients burned by therapists.

The source doesn't really matter. What matters is that people identify with each other and are invested in each other's well-being. In my email filing system, I have 18 sub-folders under "community." The communities I belong to include my Buddhist community (mostly Hollow Bones), my men's community (mostly MKP), fellow ROP practitioners, my neighborhood community (mostly "Next Door"), my athletic club, my business community (through my company Warrior Films), the filmmakers' community, my Veterans Writing Group, fellow high school alumni, various "thought leader" communities (SVN, Opportunity Collaboration, Renaissance Weekend), my late wife's University of San Francisco community and my artists community (mostly through Artists United). One of my great delights is mixing and matching members of different communities with each other, cross-pollinating and creating mutual support.

Arguably, the term "community" loses all meaning and all relevance, if used in so many different contexts with so many different people. But

I don't think so. There are commonalities among the people I befriend and enroll in my varied communities. Thoughtfulness, regard for others, intelligence, social concern, basic Mensch-like standards - there are many qualities common to all these different groups, whether friends, colleagues or neighbors. It's the qualities of the unique individuals that dictate the quality of the organization. Without those individuals I would never join, despite what Groucho Marx (no relation) famously said: "I don't want to belong to any club that would accept me as one of its members." I'm somewhat the opposite. I'll join any club that has people that I like that will have me.

Having the full range of ages - youngers, Elders, and those in-between - as participants in any community helps ensure its healthy functioning. Each age group needs to be seen and heard - to know its place is valued. Each age group can safeguard against the excesses and shortcomings of the others. Each age group has something valuable to contribute to the ongoing conversation of what makes for healthy, sustainable community.

> *It feels really important and it makes a more significant experience for young people if, during their initiation ceremony, the people who send them out and welcome them back and listen to the stories represent at least three generations. It tends to generate a much more significant impact on the young person. For youth groups when they return, we have the council of Elders, where each of their stories are listened to. The guides mirror back to them what they see about their way and their gifts and what happened to them. As part of that circle we invite their parents and significant others to come and be there and hear the story also. Often younger brothers and sisters will come. Or a grandparent. And that really makes a difference. Not only to be heard, to truly be heard by their parents and their siblings without judgment, but with celebration. In addition, that establishes the support for when they go back home. They have someone who understands.* **Meredith Little**

> *From a proto-Polynesian perspective, we tend to break our social grouping down into three generations: nā'ōpio, or the children, the makua, or the adult, child-bearing age group, and then the kupunas, or the Elder group. Knowing that the youngers, nā'ōpio, learn from the makua, the parent group, and the parent group learns from the Elders, or the kupuna group. But we also understand that kupunas learn from the children. So, it's cyclical, this awareness and this learning. And it is in that learning that the essential need for the initiatory experience is housed.* **Kalani Souza**

Angeles Arrien felt that the ideal number of people to create a Council of Support for initiates was 12. For her the number had archetypal as well as practical significance. These supporters needed to be available before, during and after initiation, and certainly need to be present for all key events like Homecoming. The 12 were ideally comprised of four of the best friends and closest peers, four of the dearest Elders and mentors, and four of the closest family members who were *not* parents or grandparents. Of course, if any weren't available in any one category, substitutions were fine.

Dr. Andrew Mecca has a similar concept for young people in his *Lifeplan* Guidebook published by the California Mentor Foundation. He recommends every youth establish his own personal Board of Directors, similar to a corporate entity. The sole purpose of this Board is to support the young person in realizing his or her dreams. In his *LifePlan* book, Mecca provides a worksheet and a roadmap to help youngsters build their Board.

In MKP we have a similar structure we call a Court of Support. Typically, there are four men - each selected by the novitiate. The four men signify the four quadrants from the Robert Moore and Doug Gillette devised "King, Warrior, Magician, Lover" wheel of archetypes and they play roles suitable to their station. The structure can be used for a man to get one-time counsel during an I-group meeting or can be used over a span of time to provide redress for any personal issues.

Though I've spoken about the different forms of modern day community, it's refreshing to hearken back to a simple (yet contemporary) tale of neighbors looking out for neighbors. It's a reminder how the unfussiness of good values overrides what could be relationship ending judgments, like "She's standoffish." By reaching out in the simplest, most direct ways to support each other, we create community.

> *My neighbor, an older lady new to the neighborhood, walks her dog all the time. Well, we noticed that she wasn't walking her dog and so another person who came to visit her was worried, so she called the police. They ended up going in and found her alive, but unconscious and in a coma. So, after she got back home - she is new, so she was kind of standoffish with everybody - I saw her coming down the street and I rolled my window down. I said, "I need to get my belt out on you," and she started laughing. I said, "You had everybody in the neighborhood concerned. That's it! I'm going to give you my number. I'm going to give you my mom's number. If you need anything, you call us." I said, "Next time, I will have my belt..." "I'm so sorry," she said, and then she told me what happened. But it's that kind of thing that's necessary to make the connections between our neighbors. We have to be neighborly. We start with us.* **Kwabena Terrence Shelton**

What You Need To Do *Now*

Short Term Ideas for Community Groups:
- Download our free ROP Guide for Community Groups at warriorfilms.org. In it you will find numerous helpful and practical suggestions for what community groups can do with kids.
- Model mentoring. Ask who's mentoring whom among administration, management and direct care staff. Encourage anyone interested to seek out mentors and mentees, whether within organizational boundaries

or outside. It will mean a lot to your staff and your served demographic to know the adults themselves are mentoring and being mentored.
- Create team building activities such as storytelling, sharing, and developing trust between peers, management and administration. The YES! manual, available below, offers tips on how to do this. https://drive.google.com/drive/folders/0Bw9epFCg15x_ODRzMkhsN252bEU
- Sit in Circle. Whether used as a tool for restorative justice or to simply foster more open communication, sitting in circle or "council" is increasingly practiced across the nation as a way to foster more productive and effective communities in and out of organizational settings. The link below is a very basic primer on Circle and effective groups as well as links to programs that specialize in ways to bring this to your organization or community. https://docs.google.com/document/d/19DEqMkPK0bJ395aPpBtTbwK7CtyfwSMNMzwUYa-XPnY/edit
- Make time for group nature-based experiences. Take time together in nearby woods, prairies, deserts, lakes, mountains or whatever's available. Whether it's a picnic lunch, a boating trip, a day hike, a weekend camping trip or something else - the more time you spend outdoors in natural surroundings, the better for everyone.

Long Term Ideas:

- Create norms within your organization that build concepts and language that facilitate the ideas of Whole Person Development and inclusive practices/rituals. For instance, what would happen if you started the day as an organization with a specific song or class pledge? In our Hollow Bones Zen Order, our Morning Service includes reciting our Mission Statement: *We are a sacred Order bringing into being a harmonious and loving world, through the practice of meditative, compassionate awareness and mindful stewardship.*
- Institute Organizational Emotional Literacy. Emotions are often the last thing that people think of when they think of the workplace. Yet as *human* beings, we are *feeling* beings. Emotions play a significant

role in the way an organization communicates internally as well as to the outside world. It is essential to well-functioning organizations that practices of healthy and straightforward emotional expression are institutionalized. Consider how to bring safe emotional expression into your organization's culture. Explore addressing the topics of power, the manners of praise, criticism, feedback, personal/professional relationship boundaries and office romances. See the Emotional Literacy exercise in the YES! Manual: https://drive.google.com/drive/folders/0Bw9epFCg15x_ODRzMkhsN252bEU

- Implement weekly group processing of organizational cohorts. For instance, pair specific staff members together to build emotionally open communication into the organization's core culture.
- Offer information to staff on the history, theory and practice of healthy initiation.
- Bring Whole Person Development into conversations at the administrative and management levels. Discuss organizational culture building, transmission and maintenance. How does your organization frame and manage the following questions?

1. When and how are changes in workplace culture addressed and implemented?
2. When and how is an employee quitting, being fired, injured, or dying addressed? Are there rituals around these transitions to provide closure?
3. When staff are groomed for advancement, how is this transition addressed and realized?
4. When and how are promotions addressed and enacted?
5. When and how is praise delivered and received?

- If there are unclear answers to these questions, perhaps it is time to address them.
- Make time to facilitate a staff retreat, even if it's a group meal at someone's house with a "no digital device" rule. It's not the number of

attendees or even the programming that is important. Instead, focus on real relationship building outside of the work environment. Consider utilizing the YES! Guide to planning and facilitating events and team-building exercises: https://drive.google.com/drive/folders/0Bw9epFCg15x_ODRzMkhsN252bEU

- Consider Rites of Passage programs for staff. People that work together can extend community building practices outside the workplace. Strengthening those relationships through setting and realizing collective goals or sharing new hurdles and tests will not only benefit the organization, but the lives of all individuals concerned. See Appendix II for a list of ROP programs.
- Organize an Annual Initiation Day in which staff celebrate their cultural heritage(s), openly share knowledge unique to their traditions and speak of their own journeys towards mature adulthood.
- Take inventory of employee skills and interests outside of the workplace. Create opportunities within the scope of the workplace for them to teach and learn from each other. Include clients if possible, perhaps using a job fair model. This will not only increase staff and staff/client rapport, it will foster meaningful, often unforeseen connections and collaborations that promote greater efficiency.
- Organize a neighborhood block party to create new relationships between your neighbors.

8

Nature

It doesn't matter if a spiritual tradition is wiped out because they all originate from the land. They all rose from being aware of the teaching and the movement of the cycles of the land itself. And each spiritual tradition found words for that and ways to speak about that wisdom in a way that they could hold them together as a community. There's something about nature, that by lying on the ground or digging a fire pit or walking on the land evokes qualities of us humans that nothing else will bring out of us. And so many of those qualities that the land itself brings out of us are healthy. They're needed qualities for the world today to see things differently. Unfortunately when we're raised just in civilization, the clues about what it means to be human or what it means about cooperation or communication or how to get though hard times are often very dysfunctional clues. And we naturally, from birth, pick up the clues about living from the world around us. I'm always amazed to just drop people onto the land for three of four days. It's right under the surface - the understanding of what it really means to be human. **Meredith Little**

When I toured Australia in 2011, I was struck by the way public meetings and ceremonies usually begin. There is always an honoring of the local people, the indigenous people who were the historical caretakers of the land. In Australia, they are the Aboriginal and Torres Strait Islander people. Whoever kicks off the gathering takes a minute to acknowledge those first inhabitants, saying in effect, if not literally, "If it weren't for them, we wouldn't be here today." It's a beautiful way to begin. It ties the land, the ancestors and the community into one whole and invites everyone attending to join in recognition of that. It underscores our interdependence – the present-day people to the previous people, and the people to the land. It also serves to establish a tone of gratitude at the beginning of every event.

This happens in meetings large and small, from a gathering of the local Cub Scouts to the prime minister giving a speech. It's a beautiful cultural practice that I would love to see imported and applied throughout the USA. We should express gratitude to the Native Americans for stewarding the land for centuries before European people arrived. Of course, we also have much to be ashamed of given how we stole that land and committed genocide against those same original caretakers. Instituting these culture-wide practices like the Australians have could go a long way in beginning to acknowledge those realities and making amends.

Like indigenous people everywhere, Native Americans understand that human life does not and cannot exist apart from the land - from nature. All the food we eat comes from this great Mother. The water we use for drinking, the supplies we use for shelter, the medicines we use to heal ourselves, the raw materials for communications, travel and technology, and the carbon we burn for energy all come from the Mother. The great furnace in the sky – the sun, the clouds that bring us rain, and the tides from the moon all come from this source. Although wealthy individuals and companies are already salivating over the prospect of exploiting resources from planets like Mars, that is not yet practical. But even there, as illustrated in the film *The Martian*, part of what made human life sustainable for Matt Damon's character was using Martian dirt coupled with human waste to create soil to grow food.

Most ROP practitioners would say that a deep experience of the outdoors, of nature, is required for ROP. It's hard to contemplate what initiation could mean if not a deepened awareness of the preciousness of the planet's natural resources – its abundant seas, its fresh waters, its rich soil and sunlight, its rainfalls and wind, its forests and stones, minerals and diverse plant and animal life. For thousands of years, humans left their villages and caves to return to the land for renewal. Alone. They made beds under trees or bushes, drank water from streams, sat, watched and wondered at passing birds, animals and insects. Their purpose was not to conquer anything. Their purpose was to find alignment, to live for some time in accord with the forces beyond their control - the weather, animal life, lack of food, night skies, blazing suns and passing clouds - all while separated from family, friends and all the ways of human community in order to reintegrate with time beyond time, with Kairos.

At least half of what they faced was the internal weather. The fears, doubts, uncertainties, regrets, unmet dreams and crushed hopes – the accumulated psychic detritus from years of living. We might call it an exercise in recycling. Recycling all that emotional and psychological baggage, pouring it back into the land, the Great Mother from which we all came and to which we all return, that can hold all the pain humans can offer.

We might also call it an exercise in remembering. Remembering all that is truly fundamental in our lives – the miracle of being alive, the joy of breathing, the endless bounty provided by the five senses, the beauty of this world of varied plant, animal and mineral life, the mystery of the stars and infinitude, the wonder of emotion and the heart as the seat of human feeling, the glory of food and water and the need for the body to expel waste. Rediscovering what is arguably life's greatest gift – gratitude. All of these are available to us only if we are willing to spend enough time alone and in silence on the land, fasting and remembering.

> People would come back from the fast and say something like: "It was as if there's always been a veil, or a barrier, some kind of obstacle between

me and nature." I'd say, "Well, it's the other than human world - the greater earth community..." "There's always this veil, this barrier and during my fast that lifted. And that really shocked me, because I hadn't known there was a veil. And when it lifted, there was a deep psyche shifting experience because I experienced for the first time in my life my natural membership in the earth community. And I felt like I was at home in the world in a way that I had never felt before." And people would say for months afterwards: "This has profoundly changed my experience of what life is." **Bill Plotkin**

It's a completely different orientation that comes from really learning human nature from the way that nature expresses itself. And that's what happens when we plunk people down onto the land, take them away from their parents, away from their culture, give them back to the land, and the only eyes that they see themselves through is the land. And to be open to the clues of healthy relationship. The clues that nature offers us of wisdom and health and communication and cooperation are all very healthy. It takes so little for we humans to bring together that split of human and nature. It's right under the surface. And to feel our relationship, not only with the land but with all creatures. That relationship with the wholeness. "It's one of thee." It's not rational. It's good to learn about how we are connected with everything in a rational way, but it's not enough. We have to be on the body of the land, away from our context, sleeping on the ground. It's so easy and quick. It evokes that sense of how important our place is in the scheme of things. And that's what a Rite of Passage is. **Meredith Little**

I'm reminded of what I experienced near the end of a three week retreat at Spirit Rock Meditation Center in West Marin County, California in February of 1999. I remember sitting on the grass outside the meditation hall for what seemed like an hour but was likely only 10-15 minutes, staring in wonder at growing blades of grass. I was blissed out. Such can be the experience of being on and with the land. Such can be the welling up of gratitude due only to the cultivation of awareness of residing on this Earth, of resting on the planet's green and supportive skin.

That said, it's good to remember that scenes like the one above are the stuff of easy parody. One retreat teacher commented how walking through the meditation grounds, with so many people standing still, looking at the earth or sky, or moving in slow motion could easily make an outsider question whether he landed in an insane asylum. Through the practiced cultivation of mindfulness, this ocean of appreciation - which exists in us all but tends to lie dormant - can easily be uncovered. At the same time, as paradoxical as it may sound, it's not uncommon for meditation practitioners on long-term retreat to start to experience boredom and even pain due to extended days of bliss. Even great happiness can become a burden if it's all we ever feel. We sometimes need the alternating flow of pain in order to recognize and appreciate joy.

Days of extended bliss are entirely possible in ROP set on the land too. They're just less likely due to constantly changing conditions. On meditation retreats, we're typically provided beds, showers, toilets and meals - most of the creature comforts Westerners are used to. Not so with land-based ROP. No one receives any of that. Silence and the lack of human interaction are two common features with meditation retreats, but that's about it. After all, it is an Ordeal. Hardship is necessary.

I've had the good fortune to partake in four different Vision Quest experiences. Three were short, mere tastes if you will; one was a full 12-day experience.

The first short one was in the summer of 2006 on the Pine Ridge Reservation in South Dakota. I experienced a mere fraction of what some of the young people from the Chicago group YSS (Youth Struggling for Survival) did. Consistent with the old ways, the young people spent up to four days and nights in a circle about six feet in diameter abstaining from food and water, praying for a vision to inform their lives. I experienced a truncated version of this myself and spent 12 hours in the brutalizing sun on a 100-degree day. I have lifelong respect for the young people who accomplish this Rite of Passage.

I don't recall any great revelations I had during my time on the hill. But it certainly renewed my respect for the power of the sun, the simple grace of trees providing shade and the deliverance of water.

In 2012 I did a 24-hour version of the same retreat at my friend Gigi Coyle's place in the rocky wash outside her "Three Creeks" ranch in Big Pine, CA. I have reprinted my entire journal entry from that experience in appendix VI so you can see in detail just how mundane and magical these adventures can be.

> *What is needed in today's world is a simple, bare bones form that people could bring their own values, their own religion, their own spiritual context, and bring it into that form. And it would deepen and bring understanding to them. The main teacher for us was nature itself. The main Initiator for us was the land and the ceremony itself, finding what the common elements of an initiation ceremony are that we could find in indigenous cultures around the world. And finding those key, common qualities and creating a container that just had that.* **Meredith Little**

When I set out on my 12-day ritual ("Vision Fast" is the term they use) in August of 2015 with Beyond Boundaries - a cousin organization to the School of Lost Borders co-founded by Meredith Little - I had the intention of reawakening joy in my life. Though I fought my way through a long and debilitating depression, complete with bouts of suicidal ideation, I had yet to reclaim a deep and abiding sense of gratitude and joy in my life. Something needed to die in me for enlivening to return. I suffered a string of career disappointments in prior years and I knew that I needed a new "something" to do with new goals and new visions, but I was clueless as to what it was. I finally worked out a strong statement of intention that I recited when I left base camp for my four-day solo fast: "I come in honor of my own life and in deepest gratitude for all beings."

All that I experienced during those four days and nights would be too long to recount here or even reprint in the appendix. I had interesting encounters with a garter snake, a rattlesnake, nighthawks, bees, nodding trees, the usual pesky flies and mosquitos, a potential voyeur with binoculars on the opposite ridge, even wonderful hallucinations in the night sky. I settled on a once and for all definition of "my people, my community" as nothing less than the human family, with a special place reserved for the poor, the exploited and the forgotten – the "Salt of the Earth." I did a Death Lodge. I invited in the spirits of all who wanted to be with me, living or dead, who had any unfinished business. I also spoke to those I myself needed closure with.

On the fourth night I built a Purpose Circle out of stones and sat awake all night in prayer. I named all my joys, said everything I felt was unsaid from previous rituals, asked for everything I needed in order to better serve my people and prayed for the well-being and happiness of all. I asked for a vision to guide the remainder of my life and direction from the ancestors to better understand how my life fit within the flow of time. Mostly I spent the night chanting sacred chants and singing songs from my youth.

I was somewhat ill. I had chills. Earlier, I puked out some electrolytes. Was it dehydration? Sun exposure? Coming flu? General weakness? Who knew? I spent most of the ten hours from sunset to sunrise on my back, wearing every piece of clothing I had, including three pairs of socks on my feet and one on my hands, staring into the vast night sky. My favorite hallucination was the one I mentioned in Chapter Three: that powerful, erotic female dancer leaping across the stars. But I also saw a vision of my elder years. In the trees to my right I saw the silhouettes of an elderly couple, leaning back together in wicker chairs, his arm around her shoulder, both doing as I was at that moment - enjoying the majesty of the night sky. Peace. Equanimity. Beauty.

After 12 days I left the entire process feeling both fulfilled and unfulfilled. I did what I set out to do. I experienced a lot of joy and I rediscovered many of the things that bring me joy in daily life (even though some took me a few years to fully recognize): service to the feminine, comedy, sex, self-acceptance, singing, and doing what I'm doing in writing this book – sharing with others what I have learned to be true about living a meaningful life.

But I also felt a twinge of disappointment. I hadn't had any supernatural events. No dazzling lightning bolt visitations from "The Great Mystery." No burning bushes. (I am, after all, still a drama queen!) I didn't receive the absolute clarity I was seeking about whether I should continue on as a filmmaker or give it up and try something altogether different. I left and returned with the same set of questions: With rapidly dwindling available resources, where was I to find the support I needed to continue my work? Should I even continue on the path I first set for myself back in my 20s?

Later I realized the universe had indeed delivered answers to these questions, just not in a form I remotely desired. Eleven months after my time on the mountain, my beloved wife died. I mention the time period because this particular Rite of Passage is intended to be a full year's duration. Though processes of closure and reincorporation must take place in the final four of the original 12 days, all that follows for a full year in a person's life is considered part of the ritual. All that occurs is considered fodder for the necessary death/rebirth cycle, regardless of whether it seems "good" or "bad." *Still very much in love with your wife, happy with your relationship? Welcome to her final demise through cancer and death. Picked up on a false outstanding warrant for your arrest? Welcome to four months in jail.*

One way to understand events subsequent to the 12-day ritual, both "good" and "bad," is through the lens of unresolved karma. My wife's death helped me resolve the sudden and inexplicable death of my father when I was nine. The months I spent escorting her to her death helped me put that lingering drama to rest – again, despite the fact that I never would have even remotely wished for that solution. In the second case above, of an African-American Veteran being put in jail for four months due to a clerical error, he - a subject in one of my *Veterans Journey Home* films - had finally to come to terms with, and to some degree, let go of the rage that he carried due to the racism he experienced from the white soldiers who screwed him while in the service, along with a government that arbitrarily and falsely imprisoned him afterward. In the simplest sense, these, like all ROP, challenge us to let go of the aspects of ourselves that no longer serve.

Of course, it's not only "bad" things that occur in the subsequent year. The stories of people experiencing sudden good fortune following a Vision Quest are legion. But they too can be seen as re-righting a karmic imbalance. Some good luck may well be overdue.

> *A dear friend of mine was an animal behaviorist and entomologist. He was fascinated by the work that we were doing. He said, "You know, there's a real difference when you study a caged animal and an animal in its own habitat. The behavior is completely different." He said, "My feeling is that modern psychology is the study of the caged human. And that's why it's problem oriented."*
>
> *Our culture tends to focus on "what's wrong." And in a lot of ways that has happened because we have taken the human out of its natural habitat. That creates problems. We forget how to support each other. We forget how to honor the qualities that we're capable of that need to be brought back into our culture. Indigenous people knew that their mentor was the land. Every manifestation of nature was a piece of wisdom. A human mentor was someone who helped bring the young person into context with the Great Teacher in ways that instilled and grew and developed these natural qualities of what it means to be a human in the world. We just don't have that today.* **Meredith Little**

Along with the myriad of ways our physical survival depends on the land, our natural landscape supports us in other, more mysterious ways. In the wake of my wife's death, I turned to the Redwoods to hold my grief. It was not planned. I found myself walking in Oakland's Redwood Regional Park with my brother and sister-in-law four days after she died. When we dropped down into the canyon's low-lying redwoods, I knew I needed the support of those Elders. I wrapped my arms around one and wailed. It was completely instinctive. There was some vital necessity for me to have the support of a living thing 1,000 or more years old, life that had seen it all, the comings and goings of entire civilizations - possibly including our own - that filled me with gratitude. I knew that whatever I had to release, to discharge, was going to be completely held, contained with absolute undemanding equanimity. "Grandfather, please hold my grief. I need your support," I sputtered. Those ancestors did not fail. They can hold it all. After that I didn't miss an opportunity to connect with these Elders. Two weeks later in Muir Woods with my sister I did the same, spending 15 minutes holding on to, weeping with, and talking to a majestic Redwood off the beaten path. I brought home a baby branch to place on Tracy's altar.

> *Our social identity is not our true and deepest identity. We have a place in the larger earth community that we're born to take. But we don't have words, we don't have language for that. So, what we've discovered, and this is completely consistent with the traditions with the healthy cultures that we know about, is that the way the human consciousness is able to begin to grasp its place in the earth community is through metaphor. It's essentially poetry, or through myth, personal myth. Because that's the way we have come to understand our deeper place in the world, we at Animas Valley Institute, have come to call our soul identity mytho-poetic. It's through metaphor that our deeper psyches show us our place in the larger world.* **Bill Plotkin**

Many ROP proponents would argue that without a deep experience of nature, no ROP will have the fundamental value of establishing a clear and deep connection with Mother Earth. Many teachers of this work - certainly Angeles Arrien, Meredith Little, and Bill Plotkin, to name only three - would agree. I deeply appreciate that perspective and I certainly advocate for wilderness and nature-based ROP, but I've also witnessed profound transformations of individuals in urban and indoor locations that have little or no direct connection to the natural world.

What we understand by the term "nature" is not limited to "outside" – to the flora and fauna, weather, skies and earth that surround us every time we step out of our homes. "Nature" exists within us. Though we commonly think and talk about "human nature," we rarely connect our internal weather to the environmental conditions that surround us.

What were traditionally referred to as the four Elements - Earth, Air, Fire and Water - are no longer considered especially relevant to modern science. Nonetheless, they are helpful in understanding how nature lives on in the bodies of individual humans. These four elements guided much of Western medicine for 2000 years, from the Greeks circa 500 BC to the Middle Ages. (They also form the basis of much of Eastern medicine in Tibet, China and India.) Also known as the Four Humours, the physical properties of the Elements are, to a high degree, replicated in the behaviors and psychology of humans and are still commonly featured in astrological readings. I myself have a pretty even mix of Air, Fire, and Water in my natal chart, but no Earth. If I'm not careful, I will spin out mentally with visions of films, writing, art and music, but not do the necessary, practical, arduous and "dirty" work - the work of Earth - to bring them to fruition.

Earlier I mentioned the Fire that burns so brightly in youth and the necessity for Elders to bring Water and Earth to cool the flames. The point here is to recognize that there are elements of our biology and physiology that integrate us with the natural world. The carbon, oxygen, nitrogen and hydrogen that make up 95% of the human body are four of the six key building blocks for all life on Earth. We are physically part of the living things that surround us, just as they are part of us. We share the same elements, minerals and even DNA. 99% of each individual's DNA is identical to every other human on the planet. That 1% is all that makes up every single known difference between human beings. Even more amazing, we share the same 99% with chimps and bonobos and the genetic difference between them and us is ten times *smaller* than that between mice and rats. We share over 60% of our DNA with chickens, fruit flies and bananas! Our "pride of place" as rulers of the natural world is completely misplaced. Rather, we should understand that we are *caretakers* of the natural world because we are a *byproduct* of that world. We should have the good sense to care equally for the life that is outside us – the very life that produced us and is part of us – as the life inside. That is our literal nature and it should be sufficient to make us stewards of Nature.

> *We spend much longer in childhood and adolescence than chimpanzees and apes do. This is a developmental and evolutionary advantage. Taking longer to mature allows us certain capacities to develop that couldn't develop otherwise, or not as well.* **Bill Plotkin**

I've seen powerful evidence of our "nature within" inside Sacramento's Folsom Prison. The personal transformations I've witnessed among inmates easily matches or surpasses the transformations I've witnessed among free people. I've seen an inmate put his life at risk by publicly hugging the warden and telling him he loved him. I've seen rival gang leaders tell one another they would lay down for each other in the yard, ie., should a fight break out they would not adhere to strict gang loyalty, but instead refuse to fight, putting their gang leadership and their very lives at risk. I saw a former Aryan gang member covered head to toe in Nazi tattoos cradle a sobbing Jewish man - a *free* Jewish man who chose to come into the prison to get healing from the men inside. I remember once looking up at the vaulted dome in the chapel where we worked, shocked to find the ceiling still there, amazed that the power of the miracles I witnessed somehow hadn't blown the roof off to expose the sky.

The way I see it, these processes allow Initiates to experience "nature within" – their deepest human nature. I've repeatedly seen murderers serving life sentences touch that deepest part of them that only wants to love and be loved – that part sometimes called Buddha nature, sometimes called the God within, or Source. Whatever its name, whether Initiates are conscious of it or not, that core is deeply tied to the natural world outside. The nature "out there" lives inside of them in a very real way. Since most have spent the vast majority of their lives behind bars, their experience of nature is not just metaphor. They've suffered the storms of rage and the roiling seas of abuse. They've known the deserts of isolation and the Arctic lack of human love. Fortunate ones have discovered how it can all give way to mountains of insight and sheltering forests of community.

Certainly gangs - whether in urban areas, in prisons or on reservations - do not require integration with the land for their initiations. Many would say that's exactly why they don't qualify as legitimate ROP. I disagree. I would say that although they are not *healthy* or *pro-social* initiations, they are nonetheless *effective* ROP. They quite effectively initiate members into a new community with its own unique sense of rights and responsibilities.

There are also those life circumstances "when Initiates are already cooking," as Michael Meade puts it, that can serve as initiations when coupled with proper mentorship. Furthermore, I've witnessed largely indoor workshops, hosted by MKP and other organizations like Melissa Michaels' Surfing the Creative, that have the soulful impact that ROP on the land do. So, I think there are effective ROP rituals that can and do take place "off the land."

> *So many of the young people that came into my life, starting with myself, didn't feel a sense of connection with the land necessarily, or a place, didn't feel a connection with a clan, and were looking for home. And the body became the doorway to home.*
>
> *An Elder in my life said, "All Rites of Passage are body based." It's true! You can't go into nature and go through the many moments of terror and death and return and be disconnected from your body. However, what's really different about my work is that rather than going onto the land, my body is the land. This is the sacred soil into which we dive very deeply to deconstruct the false senses of self and access the vast intelligence that's coded in our DNA that's available in our blood and our tissues and our cells.*
>
> *So, the body is the Sacred Ceremonial Dance Ground, where the Descent and the Return can all happen. And it can happen in an inner city and it can happen in the wilderness. Some of the real violation that happened for me as a child happened in nature when I was not being protected by other people. So, for me being in nature became a*

very dangerous place. I was safer in an inner city, where I grew up, in a dance studio with all kinds of strong emotions going on, because at least there was visibility. At least I was not alone. At least someone could find us. And so, it was just natural for me to want to come off the mountain, literally. I was going to meet the people where the people were and find a way to create these doorways with access to something beautiful and sacred in some of the places that are some of the outwardly ugliest on the planet. **Melissa Michaels**

I love that statement and I love the truth about the body that Melissa Michaels articulates. The body is and should be home. We need not look elsewhere, outside the body, for safety, fulfillment, truth or even for ROP. Melissa Michaels' teaching is also consistent with the teachings of the Buddha. To awaken, we need only to dive deeply into the body. All meditation teachings start with the body. All those things we seek outside ourselves, even the fulfillments and joys, are there to be uncovered through deep, ongoing awareness of the body. Our path begins by dropping into the body and searching for the deepest self. All that needs to be learned is there.

Initiation, whether on the land or not, presents no contradictions, no dichotomy. It's both/and. Certainly, most people living in Western society deeply benefit from more meaningful interaction with the natural world. The modern world, mainly the West, has reached the apex of its disconnection from the natural world. The stories are legion of young people who think that eggs come from the supermarket. They may never have seen a chicken, or imagined the lives of chickens – whether on industrial farms or pastoral, free range farms. They may never have made the connection when driving past fields of soybeans or wheat to the tofu or bread that awaits them on the dinner table. They may never have picked apples off a tree, milked cows or goats, gleaned potatoes, planted strawberries or foraged for fiddleheads, much less shot and skinned a deer, fished and deboned a salmon or fought off a coyote rummaging through garbage. They may never have hiked to the top of a mountain, canoed a lake, slept outdoors in the rain, been scorched by the sun, seen a shooting star, watched the Northern

Lights or gaped at a sun that never sets.

We could all benefit from spending more unstructured time on the land. Soon it may not be a choice as more and more social and economic systems begin to collapse. When we do so, it need not be with an eye solely toward harvesting nature's bounty, though that is essential for sustainable living. We can simply study and learn. There is all this talk in popular culture about Biomimicry and Green Tech. What's astonishing is that these ideas are in any way considered new. People have been observing the patterns and practices of all aspects of nature for thousands of years and implementing that knowledge into the way they do things. Nature designs its structures and mechanisms for good reasons, so they are maximally sustainable. Even disasters like forest fires, earthquakes, hurricanes, floods and tornadoes play their part in rebalancing Earth's natural systems. Ancient civilization would have never been possible without the flooding of the Nile bringing fresh nutrients to the soil making crop growth possible. The growth of new forests is not possible without the burning of dead trees and undergrowth. Earthquakes redesign coastal shorelines and waterways, bringing the ocean's rich minerals to the land and rebalancing flora and fauna.

Richard Louv has written extensively about the healing power of nature. "Nature Deficit Disorder" is his term for the condition affecting far too many of our children today.

> *The future will belong to the nature-smart—those individuals, families, businesses, and political leaders who develop a deeper understanding of the transformative power of the natural world and who balance the virtual with the real. The more high-tech we become, the more nature we need.* **Richard Louv**

Native peoples have known this for centuries but Louv has brought this understanding into the contemporary world of high tech and communications.

Human beings are innately attracted to nature. Biologically, we are all still hunters and gatherers, and there is something in us we do not fully understand that needs immersion in nature. We do know that when people talk about the disconnect between children and nature—if they are old enough to remember a time when outdoor play was the norm—they almost always tell stories about their own childhoods: this treehouse or fort, that special woods or ditch or creek or meadow. They recall those "places of initiation," in the words of naturalist Robert Michael Pyle, where they may have first sensed with awe and wonder the largeness of the world, seen and unseen. When people share these stories, their cultural, political and religious walls come tumbling down. **Richard Louv**

There's more inside of us to live from than what's in nature. Because nature by itself is only given as a prerequisite for asking: How do I have to now metabolize this? Transmute it into creative life? Because our creativity is really what's at risk, not the planet. The planet will recover from how we have misused it. But we may not recover from the lack of use of our inner life. **Orland Bishop**

What You Need To Do *Now*

- Take a backpacking trip of at least seven days.
- Do a 24-hour Vision Fast ceremony. Find a place in the wild you can get to with relative ease. Leave at dawn and return the following dawn. Bring at least one gallon of water and a journal, but minimal other

protective gear and no food. Spend the night in self-created ritual.
- Sign up for a Vision Fast with experienced guides: through School of Lost Borders, Veteran Rites, Weaving Earth, Animus Institute, etc.
- Check out what other Land Based Ceremonies exist near you through YouthPassageways.org.
- Spend an afternoon in contemplation in a nearby park. Observe how many of the forces of "the wild" are still at work.

9

You as an Individual

Ours is not the task of fixing the entire world all at once, but of stretching out to mend the part of the world that is within our reach. One of the most calming and powerful actions you can do to intervene in a stormy world is to stand up and show your soul. **Clarissa Pinkola-Estes**

Don't ask yourself what the world needs. Ask yourself what makes you come alive and then go do that. Because what the world needs is people who have come alive. **Howard Thurman**

Atta Dipa![12] **The Buddha**

Stand up and show your soul. Do what makes you come alive. How as individuals do we do that? The world certainly doesn't encourage those aims. Where do we find the wherewithal and the courage? Why would we even do such a thing when the world around us seems

---

[12] "Be a lamp unto yourself." (From the ancient language of Pali.) Said to be the Buddha's final words.

to target people like that, making them out to be ridiculous or grandiose, narcissistic or guilty of "TMI"[13] - over-sharing and boundary-less?

We do it because we have to. To do otherwise is to turn our back on what we know to be true about who we are and why we're here. We can't deny the power and potency of the gifts we've received from ROP, of the mentorship we've received or the divinity of our purpose. Living a lie is no longer an option.

Self-care is an important part of the equation. We have to be willing to do all that's necessary to keep our bodies humming in good order with our minds. A healthy diet, regular exercise, strong spiritual and/or meditative practice, sufficient sleep, minimizing "pollutants" and indulgences (alcohol, tobacco, drugs, TV, social media, porn, etc.) All of that is important. We don't need self-help books to tell us that.

I call myself a high maintenance individual. There are a lot of things I need to do to keep my mind/body in good order and to keep despair at bay. I begin every day with our ten-minute Hollow Bones "Morning Service," reciting the Heart Sutra, the "Awakened One's Vow," and many other sacred reminders of impermanence, "emptiness," and the illusion of self. Then I meditate for half an hour. I try to work out every day but always manage at least 3-4 days each week. I attend my men's support group meetings about twice each month. I have calls with mentors at least once a month. I also do my best to give my cat Beanie love for at least half an hour every day, whether during meals, morning chants, or watching sports or movies in the evening. I aim to schedule at least 1-2 weekly visits with my lover for intimacy and lovemaking. At least once each month, I try to spend a day outdoors. Besides my monthly calls with mentees, I schedule regular calls and lunches with friends. The luxury of my life is that I can schedule each and every day as I see fit. I'm my own boss. I tell people I take mini-vacations every day - an extended lunch, a massage, sitting in the hot tub at the gym, an evening get-together or a walk around the lake. I make up for it by basically working seven days per week. Why wouldn't I? My work is my play! How

---

[13] The standard online acronym these days for "Too Much Information."

can I do all this? I don't have children!

But that's me. For over 40 years I've largely structured my life around the creation of art. But even if you're not your own boss or you have two children there's plenty you can do for self-care. I recently worked with a mentee to restructure his daily schedule to allow for meditation, stretching and time devoted to his passion for sustainable farming. All he had to do was get up half an hour earlier than his young twins and replace one hour of evening TV and internet surfing with study. The quality of our lives is determined largely by the energy we put into quality creation.

Life is a marathon, not a sprint. I am very much the tortoise, never the hare. I pace myself and go slow. Since none of us know how long we'll have, it's imperative that we live measured lives in balanced, healthy ways. Ideally, each day is a microcosm of my optimum life. I often ask myself at the end of the day, "If I die tonight, can I go out happy, knowing that today I did at least some of what I feel most deeply called to do?" The answer most days is yes.

We must begin again to become human beings, and give up some of our human doings. Yes, there is much to be done in any given day. The challenge that this book represents is to do it in ways where we're fully present and open to all that life is offering. In those unexpected ways in the most everyday places - the laundromat, the grocery store or behind the computer - life and its biggest impacts can and will happen to us. Our task is to drop most fully into what's being offered and, when necessary, respond with rituals to acknowledge and consecrate those moments.

Don't give your power away to gurus, teachers, priests or whoever...
Meredith Little

Once we discover our source, what it is that sets us free, it's essential that we not give that power away to anyone, including those above, along with leaders, elected officials or experts. Or, in my case, give it away to TV networks and Hollywood studios, critics and awards panels, film festivals, or even paying customers. Ultimately, our affirmation must come from within. We must remain vigilant to the range of others who seek to take that power in self-knowing away from us, to try to sell us false identities: TV hucksters, the government, celebrities, the wealthy, and the know-it-alls, the seducers, the power mad and the salesmen. They can only take from us what we're complicit in giving. And we should never ever give away that willingness to enact what brings us most alive. Atta Dipa! Be a lamp unto yourself. You are your own guru.

> *Individuals should have an opportunity to go before a group of healers and Elders to expose all their deep secrets and be given sacrament. Those who have been wounded and those who been the perpetrators, like in South Africa. I think that*[14] *was a beautiful attempt to heal this breach, this fracture of the human spirit. We're not our experiences, you know. The things that have happened to us or things that we have perpetrated, they inform our life. They're not who we are.* **Aqeela Sherrills**

Standard Western practice these days, when someone is troubled, is to reach for a therapist. At least for people of higher socioeconomic class. For others it's a minister, a coach or a friend. Certainly, therapy has come a long way since the early 1900s to gain widespread social acceptance among Western people. I find this to be a mixed blessing. Many people can and do find relief from various forms of suffering through therapy. Many deepen their understanding of their own life and learn to recognize which of their present-day triggers are rooted in the distant past, in the wounds of childhood. I did with my therapist.

But over time I became cognizant of an astonishing truth. I felt comfortable baring my soul to her and her only. I didn't feel trust that I could share my deepest feelings, my most shameful confessions, my complex and contradictory interior life, with others, even including my best friends. I

---

[14] The Truth and Reconciliation Commission, South Africa, 1996-2003.

wondered: what is the point? I love my therapist. I feel safe with her. Her insights are revelatory. But if I'm only willing to be truly authentic solely with her what good is it? How can I broaden my soulful sharing to include others? What is it going to take?

As I later learned, it takes ritual, Rites of Passage and mentorship – a seeking to consecrate moments in time that can hold and support me and others in unfolding. It takes community. And it takes the courage to stand up and show my soul, like I did at Sundance in 1994, like I have with this book and my last.

Once we know deep in our bones who we are, it's up to us to do the work to heal our wounds. There are plenty of individuals, professionals and collectives who will support us in our journey toward wholeness and enlivened living. There are plenty of healers and Elders to give us sacrament. But it's us who must take the first step. The biggest challenge we face is ourselves, holding tenaciously to the stories we have about who we are. In greater and smaller ways, every day we circumscribe our capacities by telling ourselves lies. "This will never work." "I am not smart enough." "I don't have the skill set." "Everything I do turns to shit." "Nobody will respect or care about what I do." "Everything I touch turns to failure." "I'll never do it perfectly so what's the point?" All action starts with individual volition. Until we take steps to seize our own autonomy we will remain prey to those stories of the past. "I was sexually abused as a child, therefore I will be abused and exploited as an adult." "As an orphan I was unwanted and unloved, therefore I will be abandoned and unloved as an adult." Whatever those wounds are - and each of us, every one of us, carries some – they will not go away on their own. Without public transparency and sacrament, we are doomed to live our lives in shadow. Personal wounds require intentional, focused effort to lay to rest. That's the time when we require help.

But as Aqeela Sherrills reminds us, those stories are not who we are eternally. Every individual human being has a limitless capacity to transform. This has recently been confirmed by neuroscience. It used to be conventional wisdom that the brain was shaped and solidified in its capacities no later than late adolescence, certainly by the mid-20s. Now we know that not to be true.

Once I discovered filmmaking in my early 20s, I didn't hesitate to jump in and make films. I was on fire. I didn't have a backward glance. Back then, the stakes were small. I was only a student in a filmmaking program. It didn't really matter, not even to my teachers, whether my short films were good or not. The presumption was that few people outside the college would ever see them and that many of us would never create and sustain careers in film. They were wrong about me. I wanted to conquer the film world with my first film. I had a plan, albeit imprecise, for becoming a Hollywood success. I wasn't lacking in gumption.

As I grew older and matured artistically, my ambitions and reach grew. I wanted to make longer films, bigger budget films - films made from larger palettes on bigger canvases. I wanted to expand my storytelling in new directions. As I gained experience, I knew more of what the stakes were with each project. I knew how many hours, months or years it might take to finish a film. I knew how many thousands of dollars, then hundreds of thousands, then millions it might cost to make. The risks of potential failure grew greater. In my 20s I simply leaped, knowing that I'd find some way through the unknowns to a terminus - some path forward to the finish line. By the time I hit my 40s I was less sure, ironically, even after my greatest success: *Hoop Dreams*. Increasingly, that lack of assurance met something new that had escaped me earlier: critical and commercial failure. So for the last 20 years, every time I started a new film, I began a dialogue with myself that usually commenced with a single question rooted in fear. "Am I crazy?"

That internal dialogue grew increasingly familiar over the years. My ambitions became smaller. I began letting go of attachments to reaching a large audience, being critically recognized or receiving remuneration. I had to. I saw no other solution. Many times I lost faith. Many times I gave up hope. But I pushed through and continued the work.

Now, as I've passed the 45-year mark as a filmmaker, I can say that I have come full circle. I'm a student again. I'm back to where I started. Nothing else matters but the work itself. I get up every morning delighted that I get to make movies at all, overjoyed that I can share my life's journey through writing. I've taken a long journey back to myself, to where I started, with nothing else of consequence but the recognition that this is what I'm here for. To create, create, create. I've let go of most of my desires for impact of any kind, certainly of any expectation of large audiences, critical success and remuneration. I have returned to the source of what makes me come alive. That's something no one can ever take away. I am free.

What You Need To Do *Now*

- Think deeply about who you are. What stories have you been told about yourself by others in the past? What stories have you told yourself? Which of these stories do you continue to tell yourself today? Are these stories serving you? Is it time to let them go?
- Keep a journal. Writing about yourself and your life is a great way to discover who you truly are.
- Take a life inventory. List all your key joys, sadnesses, regrets, successes, etc. Can you honestly say your life is on the path that best serves your gifts and your growth? If not, what steps can be taken to steer you in the right direction? Remember: it's never too late!
- Do a timeline of your life to date, from birth to the present moment, with all the key events marked with your age at that time. Then do a similar timeline of each of your parents' lives. Compare them. This is an exercise I did with my therapist. It shocked me to realize how many of the dramatic key events in my father's life matched similar timelines to my own. You may discover something quite similar. But you may also discover how vastly different your life trajectory has been from your parents'.
- Ask yourself: What aspects of my life are living in shadow? What do I need to do to bring awareness to my shadows and live a more authentic and self-accepting life? How will it serve me and those who surround me?

10

Contemporary Challenges and Future Speculations

ROP has mostly disappeared around the world, which is interesting for something that is archetypal and that everybody has some understanding of and inkling towards. It has almost completely disappeared from tribal groups as well. I work with some tribal groups that are trying to reinstitute it and it is extremely difficult to do it in an honest way.

What is often missing, when I see people trying to put together a new form of initiation, is the real tradition. They'll come up with a form, but it won't have enough root, it won't have enough anchoring into the ground, and then it won't have enough resonance or strength to hold what's happening to the kids. **Michael Meade**

In the early 2000s, I started having conversations with people doing ROP work with teens. Spread out in different corners of the world and usually focused on one particular formula for ROP, they were some of the most inspiring conversations I've ever had. But after chatting for a while, almost every conversation would usually take one common turn. "You need to talk to so-and-so," I would say. These brilliant thinkers were completely unaware of ROP practitioners doing work very similar to theirs, sometimes in the same city! They were even less aware of others doing ROP work that was structurally the same, but using different methods. They were buried in their own silos, thinking they were some of the few to hit upon the pressing social need for this work. Invariably I would tell them, "You really should put together a gathering for your colleagues to come together and exchange best practices." It took a good ten more years for me to realize no one else was going to do it, so I did.

In April of 2012 in Oakland, California, I hosted about 30 founders of different ROP practices from around the world. I called it "The Teens Rites of Passage Summit." Many of those same people I had conversations with over the years attended, including some of the people quoted in this book. My hope was to found a "clearinghouse" organization to coordinate efforts and disseminate information from all the different ROP organizations worldwide. In 2013 that organization was born.

In the two years' run-up to the founding, I got an earful from many of the luminaries in the field expounding on what constitutes "pure" ROP, and, though they never used the word, what was sacrilege. Some of these concerns I have already shared in previous chapters, like whether it's even possible to initiate people in settings other than the wild outdoors. There remain plenty of disagreements and dividing lines in the theory and practice of ROP. What follows are the principal ones and my responses to them. I share them in the hope that they will bring the ROP story somewhat up to date and point, however uncertainly, to the future.

If you don't have functional *communities* to initiate young people into, can ROP *programs* really serve them? Or are they doing them a disservice? Should ROP based in unique cultures (or religions) be abandoned given the fluidities required by our present-day multi-cultural world? Are indoor and urban ROP truly effective if they don't connect Initiates with the natural world at a time when our planetary systems are so fragile and in need of attention? Given the different ages that unique individuals mature, does it even make sense anymore to limit ROP by age restrictions? Are gender specific ROP outdated, even destructive, if we're aiming to initiate young people into an increasingly genderfluid world? Since most ROP today function with heteronormative biases, how do we best accommodate LGBTQ people?

In the course of conversations with some ROP experts, these questions have been presented to me as great divides. Personally, I don't see them as oppositional or even dichotomous. They may form the substance of theoretical conflicts, but they need not represent irresolvable institutional and everyday practice divides. I've always taken an all-inclusive "both/and" approach, meaning that all of these - let's call them ideological differences - evaporate immediately once you accept them all. The position I take? In the right circumstances and under the right conditions, *all* of these different approaches can produce positive outcomes. Yes, you can initiate boys and girls separately *and* together; yes, you can offer culturally and religiously specific ROP *and* also offer ones that are pan-cultural, welcoming all beliefs and non-beliefs; yes, you can initiate with heteronormative ideology as long as the non-compliant are still welcome at ROP elsewhere; age restrictive ROP are still effective as long as exceptions can be made within them and by other ROP that cater to broad age ranges.

But those are my solutions and some say, "Hold on! Not so fast!" Some will say that if *any* cultural practice exists that doesn't make room for transgendered or queer people then that practice hurts everyone and perpetuates a societal shadow. I really understand and appreciate that point of view. Again, I'm all about inclusivity, but not to the point where it necessarily trumps another individual's cultural and religious practices. Consider a heteronormative ROP practitioner, let's say a Christian fundamentalist, who argues that to practice LGBTQ inclusion is to violate a fundament of his or her culture or religion. Though I don't personally subscribe to that viewpoint, I believe it deserves to be respected. (To be clear, I'm not talking about United States federal or state laws here. Fortunately, there are an increasing number of them that prohibit discrimination based on sexual orientation or gender status. I'm talking about cultural and religious practices of ROP, which the federal government has recently demonstrated it does not have a vested interest in.)

Many indigenous ROP practices are maintained on a basis of exclusivity for people of their own culture or ethnicity. To initiate outsiders is to risk betrayal of ancient ways, to risk cultural appropriation. I respect that too. Outsiders should be *invited* if they're to be included at all. If they're not invited then they have no right to participate, much less appropriate practices that they witness. Most progressive folks practicing ROP would say this is a no-brainer. But to return to the example above, why should an indigenous group's practice of exclusion be any more acceptable than a non-indigenous group's? What if that indigenous group says no to queer youth? And what about the many contemporary initiatory practices that already exist that include elements of historical indigenous practices? What do we do about those? Shut them down? ROP practitioners usually say they were blessed by Native Elders to share these practices. But different Native Elders might dispute that and say they were stolen and appropriated. Who's to decide? Do we leave it to the court of public opinion or do we make these decisions based on our deepest wisdom?

    I would argue that cultures are living things and, as such, will always grow and change. And they will grow and change all the faster in our increasingly interconnected and increasingly multicultural world. When it comes to status quo ROP practices that are already somewhat exclusionary, or to hybrids drawing partly from indigenous traditions, I say leave them be. As long as ROP leaders lovingly and diligently recognize their lineage(s) and teachers, as long as they are doing good work in a good way, serving the greater good and not just serving themselves, then leave them be. Jazz and hip-hop (and so much more art) began exclusively in African-American culture. Are we to create social norms that say non-African-Americans have no right to these art forms? That others cannot and should not learn from these cultural expressions, share and delight in them, and yes, "appropriate" them and make them their own? Cultural sovereignty has to be respected until times change and a threshold arrives making it clear that it no longer makes sense to hold something back from the wider public. Doing so will not serve the greater good. If a cultural practice gets widely adapted and starts becoming popular then it is clearly filling a deep human need beyond its smaller group of originally intended practitioners. Again I say, let it serve the greater good. ROP have to go through their own Rites of Passage; they have to grow and evolve.

> *To take initiation as Rites of Passage or rituals for awakening, then there are two main parts to it. One is that there be some traditional form, or some form, or formality that is known. And the other is that it be radically open to change.* **Michael Meade**

The point of all this "both/and" thinking, this inclusionary priority made paramount, is that if we don't embrace all the different expressions of ROP practice, we risk becoming our own worst enemies. We risk saying "You are welcome... But not *you*." We risk excluding some people and some groups from our community. Personally, I don't think absolutist approaches are constructive or effective. When utilized, we risk creating "the other." We do this through ideological means no less stringent than Christian or Muslim fundamentalism. "I work with *communities*. I'll join your organization but only if *programs* are excluded from it." "I won't be part of any organization that doesn't automatically exclude men or organizations that promote SSA.[15]" "Boys need initiation more than girls; we must focus on them." "Mixed gender initiation can't work." "You have a great ROP program but until you offer serious mentorship as part of aftercare for Initiates I won't take part." "If individual X who espouses Y is part of your gathering then I'm not participating." I've heard all these objections before from ROP leaders. Literally every single one. And every time I hear something like that, I see a wall go up and I see an "us vs. them" mentality take shape. Ideas harden into absolutist positions. "I'm right; they're wrong."

There's an old maxim for marriage that says, "You can be right or you can be happy." I see the choices here similarly. When it comes to some issues, we can be ideologically "right," trying to cross every T and dot every I. We can be politically correct, but both intentions and impacts have to be measured.

---

[15] Men who say they have "Same Sex Attraction" but are trying not to be gay.

Yes, it's important to try and make every effort to get things "right." But it's also important to measure impact: are we aiming to be maximally "pure" or are we aiming to be maximally inclusive and maximally effective? What exactly are we aiming for? Personally, I'm invested in maximal inclusion and maximal effectiveness.

I believe multiculturalism can be an ideology no less absolutist (and therefore exclusionary) than communism, Christian or Muslim orthodoxy or consumerist market capitalism. Ironic, I know, because on the face of it, multiculturalism places inclusion as its deepest value. But I've seen it have impacts in diverse circumstances where it drives people away. It makes them wrong. "You said such and such, therefore you clearly don't respect the rights and claims of so and so." "By not doing X…" or "by saying Y… you have demonstrated that you are Z…" [Fill in the blank: racist, sexist, homophobic, ageist, ableist, classist…] If we are to really grow the community of ROP advocates into a worldwide body of significance, we need to be able to accept every individual or group at their unique station of growth. Spiral dynamics has taught us that and expects nothing less of us: "Transcend and include."

What I'm arguing for here is an existential response to each ROP practice and policy with the highest priority placed on effectiveness. If a given ROP is effective and creates deep transformation for participants then I say, "Welcome!" I believe it is a waste of time to codify policies across different cultural ROP practices. It as a Sisyphean task that can and will consume huge resources and never achieve its aim of 100% "buy-in" from every potential ROP practitioner or group. No matter how good the languaging and no matter how inclusive the intentions, it's impossible *not* to offend some person's sense of identity at some time, however unintentionally. No matter what you say and do, at some point, somebody is going to get wounded. What do you do then? Refer them back to the written policies and codes? So, they can be taught exactly how they are "wrong?" No one responds positively to that. You have to be with them face to face and try to solve the conflict through deep listening and heart to heart contact. You have to practice listening modalities like Non-Violent Communication. Trying to codify ROP practices and policies is not only a waste of time, it runs counter to the spirit and practice of ROP themselves. They cannot and should not be codified. *What's even worse is that efforts to do so might actually inhibit creating real social change.*

There's a book called *Theory of Change* that aims to identify what social change-makers' core (and usually hidden) assumptions are. Carol Weiss popularized the term "Theory of Change" as a way to describe the set of assumptions that explain both the mini-steps that lead to the long-term goal and the connections between program activities and outcomes that occur at each step of the way. What makes for maximal effectiveness for whoever seeks it? Some people are naturally more process oriented. Others, like myself, are (slightly) more outcome oriented. Clearly both are important. What I hope to draw to people's attention is the need to understand what our primary assumptions are that drive our theories of change and to confirm whether those assumptions are in fact leading to the changes we want. I want to initiate and mentor every teen on the planet. How do we get there? That's what interests me. That means embracing all the different variants of ROP practice whether they fit our standards of social justice or not.

Tactically, it's smart to focus on youth ROP these days. For organizations that promote youth well-being, there are lots of support monies and resources available right now from status quo powers. No matter how politically conservative governmental, corporate or institutional bodies may be, they will usually support youth well-being and maturation.

One issue that is *not* a ROP fault line anymore seems to be the one reconciling the largely right-brain world of ROP field activities with the largely left-brain world of organizational administration. We are finally bringing rational, statistically based data and science together with the mysteries and miracles of ROP. For too long these worlds stood apart. ROP practitioners now increasingly use whole brain systems, linking left and right hemispheric thinking, taking the right brain world of ROP work – the intuitive, spiritual and sacred forces that "magically" coalesce to create human transformation – and translate them into the left-brain world of scientific explanations, statistical data and rational logic. Most people in the ROP world understand that generating rational explanations and data is fundamental when substantiating the value of their work, not to mention essential when securing funding! If we can't *prove* that initiating young people raises their grades, keeps them off medications, reduces delinquency and self-harming behaviors like reckless drinking, drugging and driving, what use is it?

> *We have to keep asking ourselves: "What are the qualities that our people need in order to live in the world today?" That's what small communities did way back. It used to be that what was needed for the survival and the health of those small communities were warriors who would protect the village from the animals and from other tribes. The needs to instill the qualities of "warriorship" were very real. And so often initiations were when they were dropped into nature alone. Sometimes it was "go out and kill a lion." When you've killed that lion then you can come back and we'll celebrate your initiation. So, they were bringing experiences to those people that developed the qualities needed for that community. So again, it was: what to do we need to instill?* **Meredith Little**

I've long marveled at so-called futurists. People who can extrapolate from present trends into the future and bear witness, however speculative, to what might come. I never considered myself one of them. Many native peoples had social roles for folks like these and called them oracles. I am not an oracle. But recently I have found myself receiving insights, however small, into what might come. Most of that thinking is not remotely mystical, but a plain byproduct of research. I'm told it's a patriarchal assumption to prognosticate in an authoritative way since it can be received as overbearing, like, "God has spoken!" So, I offer these subsequent reflections humbly, merely as thoughts that have occurred to me. I offer them intuitively, in the collaborative spirit of sharing, not as declarations from the mountaintop.

I expect the ROP practices of the near future will continue to grow in size and impact and become more "multi:" multi-cultural, multi-gendered, multinational, multi-religious. ISIS, Al-Qaeda, Boko Haram and the Taliban are some of the greatest arguments for ROP on the planet right now. What are all those men (and yes, a few women) from around the world being drawn to if not the opportunity to live a life of mission and purpose (contrary to what capitalism teaches), to be of service to something greater than themselves (contrary to what consumerism teaches), to function as a team, as a community working together for a "noble" purpose (contrary to what individualism offers), to be empowered and have impact (contrary to what Western countries offer them due to racial and ethnic discrimination)? In short, they offer initiation. Who else is offering that to Muslim youth in the East or the West?

I spoke with an Imam in Detroit in 2001 about what teen initiation looks like for contemporary Muslims. I was shocked to hear him say there is no such thing. He did speak to the strong community values, service missions and mentoring practices that mosques offer. But clearly that's not enough for many Muslim youth. It appears they need something more powerful, more transformative.

ISIS and other forms of Muslim extremism are only one manifestation of the global dysfunction of communities that lack healthy teen initiation. Certainly there are similar manifestations in fundamentalist branches of Christianity and Judaism too. I've already spoken about how reform Bar Mitzvah practice can easily be subverted by consumer culture. Too many fundamentalist Jewish and Christian sects can easily initiate young people into an "us vs. them" worldview - where outsiders are marked as "other," the enemy - no less pernicious than indoctrination by street gangs.

> *When most youth do not reach true maturity, the whole culture begins to decay and degrade. And many observers, like myself, have been noting that for quite a number of years; it certainly seems that Western culture at least, maybe some other cultures too, are in the terminal phases of unraveling, of collapse. And of course, there are many of us that are rooting for that collapse to complete itself as soon possible.*

CONTEMPORARY CHALLENGES AND FUTURE SPECULATIONS

And simultaneously, we're supporting and doing our best to be among those who are creating the infrastructure for a healthy culture. And the contemporary Rites of Passage movement is certainly one of the most exciting dimensions of what we're seeing. **Bill Plotkin**

The picture for the future is not rosy. No later than the end of this century, I foresee the beginning of neo-feudal dark ages dominated by autocrats and dictators. Every day the list grows longer of countries turning to, or perpetuating, autocratic or even totalitarian rule: Turkey, China, Iran, Hungary, Russia, Syria, Egypt, Venezuela, North Korea, Brazil, Yemen, Cuba, Saudi Arabia, Kuwait, Burundi, Libya, Chad, Congo, India, Indonesia and Poland... The list goes on and might soon include the U.S as the January 6, 2021 assault on the Capitol attests. Similar non-governmental power blocs like U.S. Militias, Mexico's drug cartels, gangs in El Salvador, paramilitaries in Colombia, and many more, will assert more and more influence and control. Like ISIS and Al-qaeda, these heavily armed gangs might soon rule large swaths of the planet.

Due to environmental and economic catastrophes - the scale of which is difficult to imagine - mass migrations and wars for scarce resources like water, food, arable land and carbon could kill up to 80% of the world's population by the end of the century. That's the bad news. But the remaining 20% will increasingly turn towards ROP practices. That's the good news. Those practices may, for a time, be less multicultural than those in our lifetimes but they will deepen their *individual* cultural footprints. Indigenous people, who hopefully will be able to safeguard the continuity of their practices, will certainly strengthen them. Survival of the village may well depend on it. Like Meredith Little mentioned, a "warrior class" may again be necessary to defend and protect semi-autonomous communities, whether from neighboring villages, warlords, drug lords, feudal lords, corporate armies or from oppressive government armies and police. Unlike our historical epoch, those warriors may not be gender determined, but they will require initiation. (Not to mention post-war rituals of Reintegration.)

My guess is that many communities will re-establish two stages of adolescent initiation – a universal one for all those entering puberty (11-13) and ones, perhaps elective or "chosen," at the end of adolescence (16-21) for warriors and all the other key role players in community life.

The ROP social inventions that exist and are still spreading today – processes, workshops, and organizations like MKP, Boys to Men, Rite of Passage Journeys, School of Lost Borders and so many more - will have likely disappeared. They will be forgotten. Instead, what I expect you will find are communities which have adopted the practices from those and other ROP organizations and woven them into the fabric of everyday community life. Eventually, as information resources become limited and unreliable, they'll explain it by saying, "This is how we've always done it." I see that as a good thing.

> *When you have Elders, they are going to tell you how to actually behave. Right? They're not just nice, wise people sitting there going, "Oh you're wonderful." They're actually going to chew you out and tell you what you need to be doing and bursting your little bubbles. And so, I think sometimes when younger people actually have functional Elders in the community, they're not too happy with it.* **Starhawk**

I turned 65 in October, 2020. In the last few years, the social role of Eldership has increasingly been thrust upon me. I never wanted it or asked for a seat at this particular table but there it is - life demands from us what it seems to want. So, I've been thrust into positions of honor and basically asked to be wise. I do my best to speak my truth and quickly sit down.

Eldership is often spoken about in various networks but how often is it *practiced*? Are Elders really sought out? Is there real respect for Elders who may have different points of view than youngers? It takes real humility to hear something you don't want to hear or hear something that triggers you, especially if you hear it from someone who you think is full of shit. That's the real test of hearing Elders, of hearing anyone. Not when they bless you and acknowledge you and hold your hand in support. Don't get me wrong. Those things are absolutely necessary and are huge aspects of an Elder's role. But naming hard truths can often be just as valuable. Do you have the real humility to listen and not immediately defend, argue or dismiss? The cultural ethos of today is that it's impolite or somehow wrong - or worse, a micro-aggression - to call someone on their shit. I find this deeply problematic. One of the great revelations of my life came from doing "men's work" which taught me that this is one of the powerful ways men in fact love each other. Some men care enough to honestly tell each other what they think, even if it's not always pretty. If someone really wants you to grow into your greatest self, they'll do that. If they don't care and don't really love you, they'll stay silent, or worse, they'll disconnect and leave you to sow your own chaos and confusion. Certainly, different genders, cultures and age groups have different styles of communication. But the purpose of learning cross-cultural ways is partly so we can learn to hear difficult things from each other without reacting defensively. When the Elders give up and walk away because nobody's listening, that should send a huge red flag to any person or organization that's paying attention. Sadly, I've seen a lot of Elders walk away from the organization I co-founded. I am one.

I was well into my 40s before I became truly capable of listening to hard truths that I didn't want to hear. It's not easy. It takes real skill and practice. Sitting in discomfort is a skill I learned only by allowing myself to be hammered again and again by wise mentors. I needed it! I can be a stubborn SOB with a thick head! Hours and hours of meditation practice and dharma study helped too…

ROP work is not about singing Kumbaya and dancing the Hora together - or not *only* about that, about celebration. Though I believe *violence* is not inevitable, I do believe that *conflict* is inevitable. As long as humans are around, conflict will not go away. Conflict creates change. Dialectics are the motor force of change. Thesis, when met with antithesis, becomes synthesis. This synthesis eventually becomes a new thesis, which is inevitably met with a new antithesis, and we reach the point of a new synthesis, and so the cycle endlessly repeats. The question is: how are we going to deal with conflict when it arises? Are we going to shut it down? Are we going to disconnect and drop out? Or are we going to learn to accept it - to sit in the heat that's generated - and listen carefully to what the situation may be trying to tell us? "Welcome Fear! You bring excitement and challenge!" "Welcome Anger! You bring fierce clarity and deep passion!" These are the lessons Zen has taught me. Can we hear messages like anger and fear in ourselves and still stay in good relations with each other? I know we can. It's been proven to me again and again through situations like the one I mentioned in Chapter Seven with MKP. It's important to learn how not to shrink from it. What we can do is change our relationship to it. One of the purposes of ROP is to create fierce warriors for justice, not wimps. Mahatma Gandhi, Dr. Martin Luther King Jr. and Nelson Mandela, just to name three, were lots of things, but they were not wimps who shrank in the face of conflict.

Life initiates us every day. We're always being initiated. And for us to recognize that this is a part of living and dying, that we must do this, and that this is natural to our nature. And to honor those and to know that when we are initiated, sometimes, you know in many big ways, that that means we are dying to something. And to honor that death. And to turn toward how to incorporate and integrate this new knowing that we have because of something that has initiated us. That's a part of the fabric of what I hope we bring back into our culture. **Meredith Little**

We're creating the new paradigm right now so that we can capture the imagination of the right individuals and be able to present, "This is the new way we're going." But it requires a strategic investment in people. We still live in a culture that wants to give money to things and brick and mortar projects and all that kind of stuff, and not invest in the human capacity, in our ability to change and transform. **Aqeela Sherrills**

ROP happen over and over again in the course of a normal 80-100 year life span. It's not one and done. We need to learn to recognize the signs. It's easy when we do a structured ROP process. We need to become equally adept at recognizing Rites of Passage when life forces them upon us. "Oh my god, the doctor says my wife is dying. This must be Separation. I must be entering Descent." "I'm broke. I've lost my job. Now I'm living in my car. I have no clue where to turn or what to do next. This must be my Ordeal." "My partner has put together a surprise party for my 60th birthday. Our whole community is here. This must be my Homecoming." The more we familiarize ourselves with the archetypal components of ROP, the more we will drive these lessons into our bones. We will also learn to fear life less. "This ROP, however painful, has something to teach me. Last time, I learned an important lesson about living. What is it I need to learn now?"

Picture a planet where there are only healthy, prosocial and productive ROP and every young person is initiated. Where we no longer have dysfunctional or incomplete initiations into gangs, into military service, via suicide or murder, via unsupervised, excessive drinking and drugging, via sexual violence or bullying, via school dropouts and homelessness, via cutting, depression or hate crimes, via anorexia or bulimia. Imagine a planet where we no longer have uninitiated, suspended adolescents running our institutions, corporations and countries, consumed by their own unconscious fears and appetites, becoming addicts to money or power because their own lives feel so meaningless and unfulfilled.

Imagine a world where the ceremonies that we regularly practice are ritualized to deepen their impact and meaning. Imagine at every birthday party that each celebrant is tasked with naming the things that most challenged them in the last year and to state what lessons they learned. Imagine that every Memorial Day we not only put flowers and flags on graves but we invite our extended families to speak publicly to the grief of their losses. Imagine if every Valentine's Day we share with our beloved all that we most treasure in them and speak those truths to their face.

ROP might well be the grand unifying field theory of human development. Imagine a world in which all people have a deep sense of purpose for their life and are connected to their deepest passions. Imagine how much happier people would be knowing their own physical, mental, spiritual and emotional limits so they don't have to seek them out through unconscious trials. Imagine how much happier people will be not fearing serious trial and discomfort, knowing there is meaning to be harvested in their pain, so they don't seek to drown their unhappiness in forms of addiction. Imagine that all citizens know the rights and responsibilities of adulthood and feel welcome and accepted by other adults in their communities as coequals. Imagine that all parents know when it is time to let their teens go forth on their own as co-equal adults and are culturally and institutionally supported in doing so. Imagine that all people are supported through all the challenging phases of their life: puberty, menstruation, first time having sex, partnering and getting married, having children, facing loss of loved ones, illness, divorce, job loss, retirement and death. Imagine how everyone can become skilled in recognizing and performing rituals at any given moment for any particular purpose, not just parties and wakes. "Oh, my girlfriend just left me. I need to do a grief ritual." "My cherished bike was stolen. I need a ritual to acknowledge and release the shock and the anger." "I just got my first job on my new career path. I'm going to mark the occasion with a ritual." "My husband was robbed and beaten. I'm going to do a cleansing ritual to allow him space for release and remind him I love him." This is that world. We are those people. This is that time.

Sound like utopia? It does to me. But don't worry, there would still be plenty of human suffering to go around. There would still be conflict, sickness, old age and death, broken hearts and broken bones.

> *I do not root my moral choices either in fear of eternal punishment or in hope of eternal reward. Instead, I recognize the divinity of the world and every being in it and respond to everyone and everything as though they were God — because they are. So, make your choice. Eat the forbidden fruit. Don't fear God. You are God.* **Reza Aslan**

Sarai Shapiro, one of my ROP colleagues and the founder of Gaia Girls Passages, introduced me to the idea that the story of Adam and Eve can be viewed as an initiation story. Before rolling out that thought experiment, I first want to acknowledge how offensive it may be for some, particularly so for Christians, and ask for forbearance. I recognize that the traditional reading of The Fall is purely negative, where Adam and Eve are seduced by Satan and introduced to evil. Based on what Sarai shared with me, I'm inclined to speculate that it may be a more mixed, perhaps even positive tale.

All of us are similar to Adam and Eve. (Of course, scriptures insist we are all their progeny!) Perhaps the fall from grace is merely the end of innocence. Perhaps we will never grow up unless and until we leave our father's home. We will stay eternally young and innocent. We will think it's all about us. We will not begin our journey into deep morality. We will not begin to know good from evil and develop the capacity to choose wisely.

Perhaps the story is also about the benign indifference of knowledge, that our trust in it has to be measured. If knowledge tells us we're sinful, that we must feel shame at our nakedness – maybe not just of body but of mind, of our authentic self – then maybe it's the knowledge of sin itself that is suspect. Maybe we have both good and evil in us. Maybe sin isn't the absolute, 100% unconditional evil we're told. Maybe we can learn from sin as much as we can learn from good. One thing that all ROP Initiates have to learn is to trust *themselves*, no matter how precarious the circumstances and no matter the cost. Book learning is important, but experiential learning - all the good and bad experiences of a lifetime - is arguably more so.

Maybe to leave the garden is a necessity, essential for the founding and sustainability of community. Otherwise, we will not know standards beyond our own desires. We will not know how to live in good relations with others. Until individuals are forced to leave paradise and enter "the marketplace," they will not take on the challenges of negotiating differences. They will not learn how to seek consensus, which is one of the hallmarks of maturity and a pillar of community wellbeing. Who knows? What's really in that apple may just be the knowledge of Rites of Passage.

What You Need To Do *Now*

- What *contemporary* challenges do you see your community faced with? What challenges do you see your community faced with *in the future*? What can you do to bring positive change to meet these challenges? Remember, the challenges you faced when you were younger and the challenges the youth face today may be very different.
- Are there times in your life when you shy away from speaking the difficult truth that someone needs to hear? That someone could benefit from hearing? Do you shy away from hearing difficult truths yourself? From who? From peers? Elders? What about from young people? Notice the gaps and resolve to make up for them.
- Seek out one or more young person. Make one simple request. Tell them you will sit with them in silence if need be, or at most asking clarifying questions, for as long as they want to speak: *Please share with me all your concerns about the future.* If some of what I wrote about the future in the chapter above comes as a shock, brace yourself. It feels far worse to many young people.
- In what ways can you facilitate multicultural learning experiences in an increasingly global world? The contemporary challenges faced today are challenges that are very rarely specific to just one culture. The more we facilitate these multicultural learning experiences, the greater chance we have of coming together as one human species (as opposed to "us vs. them") and solving the issues of today and tomorrow.
- Go to a church or synagogue or mosque near you with people practicing a different belief system from yours. Listen and learn.
- Do the same in a park or museum or cultural center in an unfamiliar neighborhood. You get bonus points if the people there have different skin color from you!
- Attend an induction ceremony for new citizens to your country.
- Complete this thought exercise: imagine what daily life will be like for children, especially for *your* children if you have them, in the year 2050. Write it down in the form of a short story or essay.

CONTEMPORARY CHALLENGES AND FUTURE SPECULATIONS

- Native Americans often consider how their actions will impact people seven generations from now. What practical steps can you commit to to leave the world a better place for the next generations? Recycling? Composting? Starting a garden? Driving less? Flying less? Taking your own bags to the grocery store for reuse? Young people tend to note these behaviors scrupulously and appreciate them.
- What can you do to facilitate Elders in your community meeting more regularly with youngers? How can you model dialoguing with people in different generations to exchange perspectives and wisdom?

11

Covid-19 and our Planetary Rite of Passage

I've been writing, making films and giving talks about the archetype of initiation, of Rites of Passage, for 20 years, but I never expected what happened in 2020! The entire *planet* going through a Rite of Passage?! Certainly, in history there were single years, or 2-3-year periods, when the entire planet confronted cataclysmic change: the World Wars, perhaps the Great Depression and the Plague years. Even though I have studied, and to some degree, prepared for so-called "collapse," I never in my lifetime imagined I would experience anything like the number and degree of economic, social, environmental and political shockwaves that occurred in 2020. Though far from over, I will now write about this planetary ROP in order to extract what I see as some key lessons from this time and offer it as a present-day teaching to contemporary readers. If you encounter this chapter in the future when Covid-19 is a distant memory, you will experience something of what it was like to live through it and can take it as a prototype of what could well happen again.

For most of the world, the official beginning of Separation (or Severance) began in March 2020. China was already locked down to a great degree by then but the rest of the world, perhaps especially the U.S., was slow to act. March 2020 was like watching a house of cards collapse in slow motion as country after country took steps to limit the free circulation of its citizens. Normal work life? Gone. Normal patterns of shopping, socializing, exercising, entertainment, spiritual or religious practice? All gone. Sense of safety? Gone. Our once familiar world was immediately and irrevocably unfamiliar. We were forced to let go of all our traditional ways of being. Just like indigenous Initiates who are suddenly, even violently separated from their everyday life and taken to the sacred sites of initiation, we were forced into wearing masks, told to limit our time outside - basically locked down in our homes. No less wrenching than if we were boys from the tribe spirited away to the forest, the jungle, the outback or the desert, escorted by Elders into the complete, and completely fear inducing unknown.

Now, as I write this at the end of 2020, we find ourselves in Ordeal – that Liminal Space between the worlds. Like most ROP, we Initiates – now the entirety of the human race – did not overtly ask for this. But it is worth reflecting upon that it was not some random act of a wrathful God. Personally, I feel like it's our collective human karma - paying the piper. It's the simple law of cause and effect. For too long we've lived disconnected from nature and each other, driven by shadow and an isolated sense of self – looking out for #1 – and not acting from a deep-seated awareness of how we're all connected to each other. So, I view this time as a logical outcome of our historical human choices and behaviors. No, we didn't ask for it, but in many ways, we deserve it.

Ultimately, how it got here is less important than the fact of its arrival. Our task starts with accepting these shocking new realities, doing whatever we need to grieve the passing of our old way of life. All emotions - anger, rage, grief and fear at losing loved ones, life savings, a much-needed job or worse, a home, shame at all the bad prior life choices - are to be welcomed. But then they need to be safely and consciously offloaded and put to rest. After that, we can try to resist – we can scream, moan, stay in bed, medicate ourselves with drugs, alcohol, TV and movies, repeating the mantra over and over in our heads "this shouldn't be happening, this shouldn't be happening…" None of it will do a damn bit of good. Resistance is futile. The new reality is here.

We are now on a collective journey through the Underworld. We are in the belly of the whale, the Dark Night of the Soul. Phase Two of initiation is upon us. We are in Kairos time. Who hasn't lost track of the days? I recently forgot what month it was. That sense of dislocation, that severance from Chronos, from "the normal flow of time," feels absolute. After Phase One has stripped everything inessential away, the Ordeal fundamentally tests everything we have left – everything we are as human beings: our morals and values, our belief systems and our understanding of the meaning of life and death. Even though we didn't choose this ROP, we nonetheless have important choices to make. "What do I need to let go of in order to live most meaningfully? What in me needs to die in order to be reborn?"

As we've discussed, initiation confronts us with death. It forces us to wake to the preciousness of life by threatening our life, sometimes even taking it away. Is there anybody you know right now who is not concerned about their health? Not obsessed with their health care providers? Not losing sleep over the insurance they have or worse, *don't* have?

Along with the possibility of real death, we have to face metaphoric death. All the systems of human interaction and belief are now up for grabs, hanging in the balance. Politics? Democracies are shaky and some are crumbling. "Neo-feudalism" is ascendant. Dictators and plutocrats worldwide are seizing power. Economics? The inherent inequities of winner-take-all capitalism have never been clearer. Poor people are dying in greater numbers because they don't have health care, sufficient living space to social distance, jobs, money in the bank or food to put on the table. They don't even have schools to put their kids in. And the homeless? Indigenous people like the Navajo? Situation desperate. For years, the oppressive social realities of millions of indigenous and homeless people have been ignored. This new reality may mean a death sentence for many. Religion? Some say these are the end times. I disagree. Despite the environmental crises that have already arrived – desertification, hurricanes, tornadoes, fires and droughts – and worse that may still come in the way of vastly rising sea levels flooding coastal cities worldwide, I'm confident human life on the planet will survive. The question becomes what kind of world do we want to live in?

The dominant ethos of Western society for hundreds of years has been "me, me, me." "I'm looking out for #1. To hell with the other guy." We can try to persist with this worldview, but COVID-19 has already exposed its illogical and harmful impracticality. Just look at how connected every human being on the planet became in a brief few weeks to a wholesale food market in Wuhan, China! Whatever might have happened there is impacting us all. The speed of that is breathtaking.

To deny the reality of our interconnection and interdependence going forward is downright dangerous. I heard stories in the 1980s, perhaps apocryphal, of people infected with AIDS taking out their frustration on others by infecting them. That is extreme shadow behavior. "I'm hurt; therefore, I'm going to hurt others." Yet that's how many of us live our lives. Revenge, whether on individuals or institutions that have hurt us, is an ever-present temptation. We have to grow up. We have to make wiser, more compassionate choices. The choices we make with COVID-19 are a matter of life and death for others and the choices others make could mean life or death for us. We simply and literally cannot survive without each other. "Us, us, us" is the only way forward. Through initiation, the universe has graciously, if painfully, invited us to grow up and to step into full adult maturity and adopt this way of living that indigenous people practiced for thousands of years – oneness with the environment and all living things. Health care workers, having already accepted the credo of "us, us, us," are dying by the thousands. I call that service to the greater good deep maturity. What about you? Do you accept the invitation?

Homecoming, the final phase of the archetype of Rite of Passage, may still be a long way off. Even with the vaccines, COVID-19 could be with us for another year or two. The economic and political fallout will likely last much longer. And then there could be other viruses to come. So, our present Phase Two, Ordeal, is not going away anytime soon. That's the bad news. But the new world is here now. The time to grow up is now. The stakes are too high. To persist otherwise is not only to remain in our suspended adolescence, it is to risk killing most of us. We don't have to wait for ceremonial closure, for things to become less chaotic, less insecure. So, how are we to behave?

The good news is that we have time to contemplate essential life questions. "What kind of world do I want to live in? What brings most meaning to my life?"

In our old world, too many lived disconnected from their true purpose - their greater calling. It's partly for that reason that planetary life got so out of balance. As geodesic dome popularizer Buckminster Fuller noted, "When everyone on the planet does exactly what they're called to do, the world will live in perfect harmony."

So, what are you called to do? What are you passionate about that you may not be doing already? What is it you've always wanted to do that you told yourself before was unrealistic, unachievable, or a mere fantasy? For many it's making some kind of art - being a writer, a musician, a painter or a filmmaker. It could be a profession you've felt called to but thought would be too expensive, time consuming or difficult to learn: becoming a doctor, an engineer, a hairdresser, an auto mechanic, a quilter or a therapist. Now is the time to think through what you most yearn to do and start doing it. Most likely it won't take a lot of thought. Think back to your childhood and the dreams you had. What excited you? Lay out plans and make it happen. Your gift(s), your talent(s) or your discovery(s) might just be the very thing that helps save the planet.

Though it may not lead you to doing that particular thing full time, that passion will lead you where you need to go, fulfilling your destiny. Once you open one door, you will find the universe responds by opening others. I never imagined that my own initiation into Mature Masculinity would later lead me to making films on Rites of Passage and writing books like this one. I never imagined that turning to Buddhism to alleviate my own suffering would later lead me to teaching meditation and dharma. As my friend Mark Oravsky put it: "Not being able to answer the questions, 'Who am I?' 'What is my purpose?' and 'What gifts do I have to share with my community…?' is a very, very dark place." This planetary initiation extends a clear invitation to us out of that dark place.

The glimmering shape of the world that could be is already coming into view. Smog shrouding the city of Delhi has disappeared, offering residents their first view of the Himalayas in years. Air pollution levels are down worldwide. The ozone layer is repairing itself. Bears are returning to the forests and hillsides where they haven't been seen in years. People are taking daily long walks, many for the first time ever, awakening to the splendors of our natural world. Though these changes may only be temporary, they serve as models for what could take place long-term if we make the right choices.

The pace of modern life has stopped accelerating and slowed way down. People are less hurried; they're spending less time *doing* and more time *being*. Many are long overdue for catching up on rest and finally getting the sleep they need. I love taking naps and for the first time ever, I feel less guilty doing so. For many, the perpetual rush - from place to place and task to task - that was so much a feature of the old world, has stopped. People are opening their eyes to the painful realities of an old world ruled by constant stress. People like me who already move at a tortoise pace are especially pleased. Neighbors are looking out for neighbors, some maybe for the first time. Couples, many of whom have lived together for years, are reconnecting and rediscovering their beloved without the perpetual demands of work or children. Those who have young children are recognizing the true impracticalities and immaturity of impatience, maybe seeing their children in all their depth and complexity for the first time. Forced to become teachers, many are awakening to the coach within - their own previously unrecognized capacity to mentor. People are discovering the joys of gardening, the joys of cooking, the joys of service. Since my girlfriend's lunch kitchen for the homeless closed, she has taken to delivering food packages to the aged, infirm and hungry. Strangers are singing to strangers from open windows and fire escapes, on city sidewalks and across open fields.

What might it look like – a world that works for all? It's time to build that vision and set an intention to make it so. It might mean guaranteed, cradle to grave health care for everyone. It might mean governments run not by the power hungry, by tyrant kings, but by true servant leaders, ready, to paraphrase Gandhi, "to make every decision based on how it might impact the poorest of the poor." It might mean that billionaires share their wealth, becoming "only" millionaires. It might mean nations make constitutional pledges of peace, like Japan's Article 9 – renouncing war and the sovereign right of belligerency. It might mean that we put the long-term wellbeing of the planet first, to shift from a carbon-based economy to sustainable energies, to become true caretakers of our precious land and water resources as big sisters and brothers to all living things. These are just a few upside possibilities.

Of course, things could get a whole lot worse. The U.S., which has been teetering on fascism, could resume that downward spiral. For President Biden's inauguration, Washington D.C. was turned into an armed camp. U.S. Homeland Security might start gunning down anyone trying to cross the border. Martial law could be declared at any time, with demonstrators thrown into detention centers like those presently run by ICE. We might continue gutting our national air, water, soil and species protections and open our remaining national parks and wilderness areas to carbon extraction. The rain forests in the Amazon could continue to burn, passing a permanent threshold beyond any possible return. Rubber gloves used during the pandemic that were tossed into the sea in Hong Kong have already shown up on the beaches of Long Island.

There are never any guarantees how things will turn out with ROP. Though we have wise Elders all across the planet, very few power brokers actually listen to them. As you now know, Elders safeguard ROP to make sure the Initiate grows up and inhabits a more advanced stage of human development. But too many people on the planet today are not humble enough to listen. Overly willful, stuck in hubris and convinced that they've got it all figured out, they'll continue blaming "the other" for all their woes, whether they be immigrants, gays, socialists, Jews, Muslims, Democrats, men, women, "the privileged," police, people of color, capitalists, whomever. It's always more convenient and simpler to blame others, even colleagues and friends "who just don't get it." That behavior has to change.

For the record, I share these shadows. Though I refrain from targeting groups, I have a default tendency to project all that is wrong in the world on certain individuals who make life hard for me. I can become a know-it-all, stuck in self-righteousness. But I can't do that anymore. None of us can. We have to grow up. Each of us has to accept some share of responsibility for all that occurs and we have to make decisions on our own and collectively, *for ourselves and for the collective*. We have to stand up and accept the depth and true meaning of inter-independence. We are both independent and interdependent. Everything we say, do and even think affects everything and everyone.

This is the choice the universe is outlining for us. When Rites of Passage like this occur, just like when Elders show up to initiate teen boys for the sake of community, it is the universe's way of saying, "I want this for you. I need this for you." It's on us to do the hard, necessary work to get it done. We cannot let fear stop us.

The logic of Rites of Passage is to make us move beyond our fears. Most people live with two broad types of fear: fear of continuing the status quo and fear of the unknown - the new. For most people fear of the unknown is greater. The status quo, the present norm, may contain lots of fears ("If I keep slacking off on my job will my boss fire me?" "Will my husband treat me badly when he comes home if he's in a bad mood?") But those fears are usually secondary, less scary, than the fear of real change ("I hate my job but what will happen to me if I quit?" "I hate my marriage but what will happen to me if I leave my husband?") The fear of anything remotely predictable is preferable to the fear of unpredictable unknowns.

How do Rites of Passage move us beyond our fears? By making us move *toward* them. It takes us directly and thoroughly into those deepest fears, both the fear of the present status quo and the fear of change. Then it pummels the shit out of us. We have to be pummeled to move away from old bad habits. Feeling fear helps expedite change. Feeling extreme fear helps expedite extreme change. If you're feeling extreme fear these days, you're right where you need to be. We won't let go of our old behaviors, thoughts and beliefs unless we get scared down to our bones. It's similar in some ways to what Twelve Step practitioners call "hitting rock bottom." We have to be stripped to the core. Until we do, a familiar dysfunctional pattern will be preferable to facing the fear of something functional but unfamiliar -

some new way of being that's healthier and more wholesome than the old ways. Only when we are scared shitless, maybe faced with death, maybe even wanting to die, will we summon the courage to move through our fear into the unknown.

Then what? Fortunately, it's usually not that hard to answer. In our heart of hearts, in our conscience, we already know. "I need to quit drinking." "I've got to stop spanking my children." "I need to move out." "I need to quit my job." "I need to divorce my husband." "I need to start exercising." A recent one for me is "I need to stop eating sugar." Once we've put our finger on a particular source of misery in our lives, the path ahead becomes clear. We can step into the fear of change with a roadmap, and hopefully, some guides - mentors, close friends, support groups, anyone who will keep us on track.

If you're unwilling to step into your fears and face the unknown, you might want to stop reading here. The remainder of this chapter is devoted to practices you might implement or strengthen to find your way through this ROP. It's up to us to do the hard, necessary work to be reborn. It's time to face our shadows and do the work to build a world that works for all.

If you don't already have one or more mentors, make a list now. Put down the name of every person who has ever had a strong, positive impact on your growth and development. It can be a teacher, colleague, coach, neighbor, boss or friend - anyone who has had a positive influence in your life who caused you to say, "I want to be like her (or him)." Someone who inspires you, who seems like they "have it all together." (Of course, no one has it *all* together, but being deceived by appearances can sometimes be a good thing if it gets you to seek what they have to offer!) In my experience, it can be helpful if it's someone of the same gender (or non-gender) as you, but it doesn't have to be.

Having mentors may never be more important than during this time of planetary Rite of Passage. Friends are great, but mentors are better. AA sponsors can become the best mentors a person might ever have. Sometimes a compassionate witness and a calming, wise voice are all we really need.

But you must also mentor others. Reach out to those you already know and love, especially if you suspect they might be struggling. Ask them how they're doing and listen deeply to their answers. People will usually lead you straight to what they need most IF you do the necessary work of gently prying them open with thoughtful, compassionate questions. If they're still not ready to share then simply remind them you're there and available whenever needed. You might extend a formal invitation of mentorship if it feels right, but you may not need to. It may suffice to say, "I'm going to give you a call once a month just to check in." Simply showing up regularly for another person is all that's generally needed. Even in this extreme time - *especially* during this time - we can use mentoring to restore the fabric of fragmented community and bring comfort and understanding to this unique Threshold we're in. Even though we're physically separated, we don't need to be emotionally apart. Mentorship drives connection even deeper.

Robert Moore, Douglas Gillette and others have taught us that mentorship is a function of the Healthy Sovereign[16]. It can be thought of as "practice" Eldership. The time we find ourselves in now is a time of the Shadow Sovereign. Take a look around. Official planetary leadership is mostly shadow driven and dysfunctional. True Sovereign energy is hard to find in the public arena. We are ruled by children grabbing for the spoils. Few demonstrate the necessary understanding of true adulthood: "us, us, us." Calling forth and acting on our most Sovereign impulses has never been more necessary. "What does the world need the most right now?" is itself a Sovereign question.

But don't let yourself get caught up in unnecessary self-questioning like, "What is enough? Is what I'm doing making a difference? If I just do what I'm passionate about, won't that be self-serving?"[17] In Zen we call that "wrong thinking." It's a waste of time.

Many people think they can't effect change unless they hold powerful positions in government, corporations or large institutions. They feel that unless they are policy makers, like benevolent dictators ruling the world,

---

[16] If you're not yet familiar with the neo-Jungian archetypes of Sovereign, Warrior, Magician, Lover, I refer you to Robert Moore's, Douglas Gillette's, and others' work.

[17] Not if you give it away freely!

nothing will make a difference. Nonsense. This misunderstanding discounts the nature of interdependence. There are few who are called to that kind of large-scale power brokering, whether in public or private service. It's fine if you are, but most are not and that's fine too. Because we're all interconnected and everything we do has ripple effects that unfold throughout each and every one of us - whether seen or unseen, with impacts known and unknown - then it becomes clear that we don't have to be capital L Leaders. We are, all of us, small l leaders. We are the leaders of our own lives. Or, as Joseph Campbell might put it, the Heroes of our own Life Story.

Popular pictorial representations of society underscore the misperception that only capital L Leaders matter. Most people tend to think of society as a pyramid with the wealthy and powerful at the top and the poor and powerless at the bottom. Everybody is placed somewhere on a vertical continuum - a hierarchical ladder of importance and influence. Though I don't want to discount the outsized influence of the wealthy and powerful - the capital L shadow leaders, those tyrant kings - it is wrong to assume their influence is absolute or even decisive. A far more useful image is that of a web.

That is what in Buddhism and Hinduism is referred to as "Indra's Net." Here is how Alan Watts described it: "Imagine a multidimensional spider's web in the early morning covered with dew drops. And every dew drop contains the reflection of all the other dew drops. And, in each reflected dew drop, the reflections of all the other dew drops in that reflection. And so on, ad infinitum. That is the Buddhist conception of the universe in an image." Each one of us is a dew drop, or if you prefer the more common metaphor, a jewel. Each of us is a jewel situated at the junction of other strands reflected in turn by other jewels. When they shine, we shine. When they are dull or overwhelmed with fear, we are affected.

This image is helpful to understand interconnection, how one thing that one person does affects the entirety of the web. There is no independent origination. Nothing can exist that is not sourced in some other already existing sources. Take an example starting with the smallest matter known – atoms. Huge atomic explosions start with sub-atomic particles. These bombs unleash the potential of an unlimited chain reaction by tapping into nuclear fission – the splitting of atomic nuclei. Within seconds, something happening on the sub-atomic level expands and grows to an explosion of almost planetary proportions.

Take a more prosaic and contemporary example. I was scolded or yelled at by strangers four times in the early weeks of Covid for not wearing a facemask or for passing too close to them[18] when I was out riding my bike or taking a walk. I get it. They're afraid. But trying to shame a stranger is usually ineffective. Doing it face to face in public is bad enough. But social media and the internet have exacerbated it exponentially and it's now common for someone to receive death threats online for not wearing a mask (in some places) and for wearing one (in other places). People don't pause and reflect how transmitting their fear through anger might be counterproductive. As for me, my body tenses; I feel attacked. My instinct is to lash out. Instead, I took to saying, "Take care of yourself and I'll take care of me." Just think how much more effective their approach might be if they sourced their fear in what is likely their deeper sadness, or their love. "I love my children so much that I'm terrified for their safety." Or, "My uncle died in a hospital two weeks ago and I couldn't even say goodbye. Please help me honor his life by staying at least six feet away and wearing a mask." Since we're going to impact each other one way or another, why not make that impact positive?

Neuroscience is now beginning to understand that the brain functions in ways similar to Indra's Net. Trauma to one area of the brain through stroke or physical injury can often lead to another part being trained to fulfill those or similar functions.

As is the case in a healthy community. When one person falters or falls, others in the community step forward with what's needed. All forms of service harmonize with the rest of the web. We shouldn't be concerned with questions like, "Who's controlling the web? Where is it going? Why is it so big? What happens if the strand next to me breaks down?" Our job is

---

[18] For the record, I was not within six feet of these people.

to make sure our strand is well tended to, that we understand our unique role in the web and are living that out to the best of our ability, bringing our gifts and passion, delivered with our most skillful means. We can't break or weaken the web of life. Indra's Net holds us in connection regardless of what we do. We can only create rippling impacts that are positive or negative. So why not polish the jewel that we are and make all the other jewels shine that much more?

Who would have imagined in 2019 that wage laborers like grocery clerks, auto mechanics, postal carriers, delivery workers, garbage collectors and others would one day come to the forefront of our awareness, making Indra's Net shine? Not to mention health care workers, including janitorial and food service staff. Talk about jewels!

Mutual-aid networks are no less impressive, mini Indra's Nets of their own. Self-starting, self-regulating groups of volunteers like Invisible Hand, Service Workers Coalition, Mask Oakland, Bed-Stuy Strong and Minnesota COVID-sitters are springing up across the country to meet the needs of those around them: feeding and handing out masks to the homeless, providing child care for health care workers' children and organizing groups to resist tenant eviction. They serve as models for the grassroots structures that we will increasingly need to put in place as governmental and institutional structures collapse.

That is Warriorship. Doing what needs to be done no matter what. And in case you were wondering, this ROP is also the time of the Warrior. This is not the time of the Magician or Lover. It is the time to stay strong and be particularly disciplined. Not only in observing social rules of safety for yourself and others but in our daily habits. It's not the time to overindulge in the gifts of the sensual world - excess food, alcohol, drugs and TV. That's Inflated Lover. It's the time to stay strict and observe (or create for the first time!) strong habits of meditation or prayer, martial arts practice, exercise and study. It's a great time for a disciplined, self-designed and implemented meditation retreat, like the one I did for seven days in June 2020 alone in my own home. It's a great time to begin that new course on painting or chemistry. If you're lucky like me, it's a great time to continue your daily work of art and inspiration making the world more comprehensible and secure. That's your biggest job right now. Put yourself into a service role that makes you come alive.

For much of 2020, I have been happy. Before telling other people that – friends and family, my men's group and others – I used to preface it by saying, "I feel guilty, even ashamed, to say this…" This is a world crisis! How can I be so damned happy right now?! It felt blasphemous. Like I was making light of all the tremendous suffering going on. Not so. I know there are parents terrified right now they won't be able to feed their kids. I know people are dying right now without a chance to look one last time into the eyes of their most beloved and say goodbye. I know children and teens are committing suicide because they can't take another day locked down in their homes. I know adults young and old are ending their own lives because they see no future. I sat at my desk in the early days of Covid and watched a homeless man walk through Oakland's deserted streets howling in misery.

Does this make me happy? Of course not. My heart is open and I feel the pain of commiseration. I also feel my own waves of sadness, anger and fear. I remain aware of it all. (And if you prefer to think of it this way – yes, I'm extremely privileged.) But in my appreciation of the minutiae, of warming my heart in gratitude for my girlfriend, of riding my bike around Lake Merritt and hiking in the Berkeley hills, of continuing the film work and writing that means so much to me, of drawing on 30+ years of Zen, men's work and other training to share some of what I've learned, my gifts, with the world, I feel a deep satisfaction and yes, even happiness. Like a Warrior, I know and accept that I may die tomorrow. But I will die a happy man, knowing I did what I came here to do.

Thank You For Reading My Book

I hope you've appreciated *Rites to a Good Life*. It was a labor of love to condense all this wisdom from my teachers into one book. Before you go and start applying what you've learned, I have a small favor to ask:

Could you please write an Amazon review?
Even if it's only 1 or 2 sentences, your review would mean a lot.

Simply go to this book's Amazon page, scroll down, and click "Write a customer review." Even if you did not buy the book from Amazon, you can still leave a review there.

Reviews are the best way for an independent book — like this one — to get noticed and reach a wider audience. For this reason, your support really does make a difference.

Thanks again for reading. I wish you much success in your journey, especially now that you have rites to a good life!

Sincerely,
  Frederick Marx

Acknowledgements

There are hundreds of people who deserve my thanks. For a complete list of all my beloved supporters, I refer you to the credits of my recent films. I'm reserving this space for the career game changers.

First and foremost, I bow to John and Barbara Crary who have provided the single biggest boost *ever* to my entire 45 year career. Without their steadfast love and devotion, the world might not discover any more Frederick Marx books and movies. If you appreciate my work please don't thank me, thank them.

For standing by me in dark times and good, I salute Joel Bluestein, Michael Bonahan, Ann Down, David and Janet Peshkin, Rich Robinson, John Sklar, Warren Walters, Brian Zanze, and the entire Seibold family - Ellie, Fred, Mark, and Amy.

For jumping into the fray to support this book and for steering the small but nonetheless seaworthy ship that is Warrior Films, I thank the Board: John Crary, Brad Michaels, and Anna Nicholls.

For manifesting support in every possible way, including reminding me daily that neuroses can be as amusing as a beloved pet, I give eternal thanks to and for Maggie Perkins.

Appendix I: My ROP Teachers

My ROP Teachers

Adge Tucker
  Andy Mecca
  Angeles Arrien
  Anita Sanchez
  Arne Rubenstein
  Aqeela Sherrills
  Bill Kauth
  Bill Plotkin
  Brad Leslie
  Briony Greenhill
  Chike Nwoffiah
  Christopher Kuntzsch
  Clarissa Pinkola-Estes
  Craig Glass
  Craig McClain
  David Blumenkrantz
  David Lindgren
  Darcy Ottey
  Diana Sterling
  Diane Kamaolipua
  Douglas Gillette
  Ed Tick
  Fugen Tom Pitner

APPENDIX I: MY ROP TEACHERS

Gigi Coyle
Howard Thurman
Jack Kornfield
Jack Zimmerman
Jerry Kwame Williams
Jim Horton
Jim Mitchell
John Gaughan
Kalani Souza
Kate Dahlstedt
Kwabena Terrence Shelton
Kwame Scruggs
Joe Sigurdson
Laurence Steinberg
Luis Rodriguez
Mark Schillinger
Melissa Michaels
Meredith Little
Michael Greenwald
Michael Meade
Mircea Eliade
Orland Bishop
Patricia Clason
Rich Tosi
Richard Louv
Robert Bly
Robert Moore
Sarai Shapiro
Searle Wailana Grace
Snake Bloomstrand
Sobonfu and Malidoma Some
Starhawk
Terry Larkin

Tony LoRe

Appendix II: Rites of Passage for Teen Boys in the United States

Please Note:

- This list is by no means definitive or exhaustive. It was first created in 2008 and has not been thoroughly updated. A more thorough, updated and user-friendly list of ROP can be found at **YouthPassageways.org**.
- As these are mostly underfunded non-profit groups. Some of them may in fact now be defunct.
- Many of these organizations are only *based* at the addresses below but may actually hold events nationally or even internationally.
- Many also hold events for girls, with or without boys.
- I'm inclusive in what are called Rites of Passage here. Some of them would not refer to themselves this way.

Wilderness (non-denominational)

- Rites of Passage Journeys, Seattle, WA http://riteofpassagejourneys.org/
- School of Lost Borders, Big Pine, CA http://schooloflostborders.org/
- Wilderness Reflections, Fairfax, CA http://www.wildernessreflections.com/
- Stepping Stones, Mill Valley, CA http://www.steppingstonesproject.org/
- Men's Leadership Alliance, Boulder, CO www.mensleadershipalliance.org

- Rites of Passage VisionQuest http://ritesofpassagevisionquest.org/

African-American

- Rites of Passage Institute, Cleveland, OH http://eenh.org
- Oriki Theater, Mountain View, CA http://www.oriki.org
- Alchemy, Akron OH http://alchemyinc.net/

Native-American

- Ed Featherman, Kyle, South Dakota
- Buffalo Visions, Montana http://www.visionsserviceadventures.com/
- Youth Struggling for Survival, Chicago, IL http://tekpatzin.proboards.com/index.cgi
- La Plazita Institute, Albuquerque, NM http://laplazitainstitute.org

Christian

- Passage to Manhood, Peregrine Ministries, Colorado Springs, CO http://www.peregrineministries.org
- Band of Brothers, Colorado Springs, CO http://www.bandofbrothers.org

Jewish (Rabbis reinvigorating Bar/Bat Mitzvah practice with true initiatory intent)

- Rabbi Goldie Milgram, Philadelphia, PA http://www.reclaimingjudaism.org/node/47
- Rabbi Stephen Booth-Nadav, Denver, CO
- Rabbi Mandel Dubrowsky, Dallas, TX
- Rabbi Steven Gross, Houston, TX
- Rabbi Gary Gerson, Oak Park, IL

All or any tradition

- Rite of Passage Experience, Glastonbury, CT http://www.rope.org/

Weekend workshops (non-denominational)

- Boys to Men, San Diego, CA http://www.boystomen.org/
- Young Men's Ultimate Weekend, San Rafael, CA http://www.ymuw.org/
- Spiritual Warfare Effectiveness Training, Philadelphia, PA
- http://www.swet.org/

Public School Programs (non-denominational)

- Challenge Day, San Rafael, CA http://www.challengeday.org/
- Lifeplan Institute, Tiburon, CA http://www.lifeplaninstitute.org/
- Community Matters, Santa Rosa, CA http://www.community-matters.org/

Freelance initiators of boys

- Luis Rodriguez http://www.luisjrodriguez.com/
- Malidoma Some http://malidoma.com/main/
- Michael Meade http://www.mosaicvoices.org/
- Orland Bishop http://www.globalonenessproject.org/people/orland-bishop
- Imam Dawud Walid http://dawudwalid.wordpress.com/
- John Eldredge http://ransomedheart.com/
- Dr. Maka'ala Yates http://www.manalomi.com/
- Kalani Souza http://www.youtube.com/watch?v=am7-OGnGhis
- Aaron Ortega

Appendix III: The Ten Best Practices of Mentorship

1. Observe the 80/20 rule: Mentees speak 80% of the time, mentors 20%.
2. Don't give advice! (Unless specifically and directly asked.)
3. Be *empathetic*, not *sympathetic*. Listen compassionately. Pity is completely counter-productive. Mentors must only share what similar problems they've faced and how they dealt with them. But the mentee must always make key decisions for her/himself.
4. Mentees must choose their own mentors. Mentors can not be forced on mentees. Mentees must feel a pull or draw toward the mentor.
5. In order for the relationship to succeed and become sustainable, mentors must learn, grow or gain something too. If mentors are getting nothing from the relationship, something is wrong. (Usually, the problem is with them, often due to their arrogance. Mentors may not be sensitive and open to what the relationship is offering them. Often that offering can appear in the form of challenges from mentees.) AND: mentors must stand in service to the mentee; the relationship cannot be about serving the mentor's (usually unconscious) emotional or psychological needs.
6. Mentors must acknowledge and bless. They must call out and name, in detailed and specific ways, what they see happening with mentees. If mentees are lost and confused, acknowledge and honor them even for that, for staying in the fire and not forcing a premature decision. Every moment presents a new opportunity to see a mentee wherever they are in their journey, to call it out and speak it honestly.

7. Model accountability. Show up. Mentors signal their respect for mentees by treating them no differently than they would anyone of great eminence.
8. Mentors should honor mentees by asking them for input on their own challenges. Nothing better signals to them they have arrived and are worthy of providing counsel - that they have become peers.
9. When the time is right, the greatest blessing a mentor can give a mentee is severing the mentorship bond, ie., "You have learned what I can offer. Now it's time for you to move on. First, to become a mentor yourself (if you're not already) and second, to seek out others for new learning."
10. Mentees need to learn how and when to acknowledge and appreciate mentors. They must understand and be able to name their "lineage," who their teachers and best role models were.

Appendix IV: Desired Qualities of a Mentor

- Have a strong desire to support young leaders.
- It helps to have what's called process or emotional work experience along with your business/professional experience.
- Be able to hold the space for others to make mistakes and shine without needing to be noticed yourself. If you want recognition, go elsewhere to get it. Don't bring your own needs and wounds to the relationship, however unconsciously, hoping for a fix.
- Understand the act of "blessing" through actions, words or energy.
- Understand how to extend your energy and intent without speaking.
- Show up in service to the process.
- Risk reaching out to the mentee rather than she/he always reaching out to you.
- Respond with intuition.
- Be in the moment. A wandering mind only creates lost opportunities.
- Do not be concerned if it seems like you aren't doing much… Presence is strong! Being witnessed is sometimes the greatest gift we can give!
- Do not act in "rescue" mode unless there is truly some danger.
- Be humble enough to recognize and admit you aren't a saint. Teach through awareness and admission of your flaws.
- Understand that mentorship creates generativity. It restores links in the chain of time, guaranteeing that cultural wisdom is passed *through you* to future generations.
- Be willing to add your personal experience and reflections to these

APPENDIX IV: DESIRED QUALITIES OF A MENTOR

Guidelines!

Appendix V: My Mentor Harold Ramis

I feel compelled to share with you what Harold Ramis meant to me. He was such a wonderful human being and such an inspiration to me I feel that to do anything less would dishonor his memory. For those of you unfamiliar with his life and work, just google him.

People everywhere know his genius from the films he made. I was privileged to know the man - always generous, compassionate, supportive, inclusive, humble, wise... He was my mentor and friend - a pillar of strength and integrity, his voice a beacon for how to face a world of deceit and lies and hurt. The sadness I feel at his passing is immense.

I first met Harold in his office in a northern Chicago suburb in the summer of 2003. We were introduced by a friend of mine – an attorney who seems to know everyone in Chicago. We had such a pleasant conversation that only afterwards did I realize how strange it was – Harold spent well over an hour chatting with my wife and me, simply getting to know us. It's hard to imagine many Hollywood celebrities spending that kind of time making leisurely inquiries, serving tea and cookies, and being equally interested in my wife and her work as a writer and English professor as in mine.

I don't remember now whether it was that first conversation when I asked him to mentor me. Given my usual chutzpah it's entirely possible. But most likely it was a year or two later. I do remember his answer though. Not a yes or a no, more "let's just wait and see how things go." I think Harold preferred to leave things like that unsaid. But the truth is from that first meeting forward he did whatever he could to make himself available to me and to be of service in whatever ways he could. That willingness to benefit others, to put oneself at the service of another's development and well-being is a fundamental pillar of mentorship.

Another pillar of mentorship is simply showing up - spending the time, making yourself available. Not long after we met, I did a presentation for the Chicago branch of the Young Presidents Association on the importance of Rites of Passage for youth. Harold came to the event in a private home in the same wealthy, north side Chicago suburb where he lived. He publicly thanked me for coming to his community to bring the message, implicitly recognizing that this wasn't an issue just for "them" – "at risk youth," the low-income folks of color in the city – but for white suburbanites too. He had the courage to say, however sweetly, "Wake up folks. It's our kids too!"

Harold demonstrated another fundamental principle of mentorship - open your contacts and integrate mentees into your professional network. He went out of his way to introduce me to two of his old friends from college – George Zimmer, founder of Men's Wearhouse, and Ben Zaricor, founder of the Good Earth Tea Company. In time, both men came to be supporters of my work.

Harold told me, as he's publicly told many, he considered himself "Buddhish." Something like, but not quite a Jewish-Buddhist. "Buddhish"... a term far superior to the more commonly used "Jew-Bu" or "Bu-Jew." No doubt because of the humor brought by the "ish" and its colloquial meaning from Jewish culture as "sort of" or "approximately." The truth is that many of his family members are practicing Buddhists and that Harold himself was deeply impacted by Buddhist thought. I think he was one of those rare minds who could be introduced to the main principles of Buddhism and subsequently spend an entire lifetime observing them without, to my knowledge, ever formally practicing. The man lived the Eight Fold Path: Right View, Right Intention, Right Speech, Right Action, Right Livelihood, Right Effort, Right Mindfulness, Right Concentration. He embodied the principles that so many of my teachers emphasize: "Don't talk about Buddhism. Be a Buddha." Or, as the Dalai Lama has put it: "The world doesn't need more Buddhists. What the world needs is kindness." Harold embodied kindness.

And generosity. When he turned up with his wife at a Chicago fundraiser to support my Buddhist film Journey from Zanskar, it wasn't enough for him to show up and be the celebrity co-host – to pose for pictures and sign autographs. He circulated and made sure everyone had a chance to say hello. He and his wife donated their own money too.

The connection he had to my Boys to Men? film and its sequel, now in production, called Rites of Passage: Mentoring the Future, was even more personal. He sat in regular men's circles in LA in the 80s and 90s. He knew first-hand there was something that men needed from each other in order to become the men they always wanted to be. He also implicitly understood the importance of pro-social Rites of Passage for youth to help them transition into young adulthood. He was proud of the fact that both his sons had Bar Mitzvah.

Harold served for four years as an advisor and two years formally on my Warrior Films Board. Even with his very full schedule he attended meetings regularly and offered everything he could. I had the bad sense to schedule our yearly in person meetings in Chicago in December. Harold always drove downtown without complaint - during rush hour in the worst conceivable weather - to attend our dinnertime meetings. Every year he offered to pay the bill and I always refused. Finally, he took to surreptitiously paying the bill in advance.

One of his great gifts was turning public events into seemingly personal encounters. He turned up yearly at a fundraiser in San Francisco to support the Zen Hospice Center. The year I went, what he said from the dais magically seemed to address all the personal questions I had for him. His warmth and self-effacing openness never betrayed the fact that he must have made dozens of presentations at similar events. He was so generous with his time and his self-effacing humor.

One tremendous gift I received from him was his mentorship

APPENDIX V: MY MENTOR HAROLD RAMIS

regarding my career. I've long been troubled by wounds dating back to the making of Hoop Dreams. The pain recurs regularly, even to this day. Talk about Groundhog Day! Sometimes I do feel stuck waking to the same circumstances in an endless loop. Harold helped me sort through a workable strategy toward reconciliation and acceptance of one particular issue.

Perhaps the greatest gift I received from him was when he sent me a script of his based on his personal life after college. He'd worked on it off and on for many years. It was a sweet story about a young man seeking to find himself - working through family and relationship issues - while working in a hospital mental ward. I told him there was potential there – a small scale, coming of age drama – but it still needed a lot of work. We talked about the difficulties of making effective drama when you're still too identified with the primary character and his experiences. A challenge I know from years of making a script based on my family's life reach its full potential.

But the gift was that he saw fit to send me the script and solicit my opinion. Mentors understand that seeking a mentee's honest feedback is one of the greatest ways they can honor them. It's a way of blessing them into a recognition and acceptance of their own greatness. It's a way of acknowledging them as a peer. Harold did this time and time again with me.

He always welcomed me to visit him on set. I visited the set for Ice Harvest north of Chicago and for Year One in the desert sands of New Mexico. Like a documentary filmmaker, I think he was partially interested to see what might emerge from the chemistry of personalities interacting. He introduced me to John Cusack and Randy Quaid from the former film and Jack Black and Michael Cera from the latter. I also think that inviting friends to his sets were his way of normalizing the extraordinary process of filmmaking, of humanizing it. Over the years I too have sought ways to turn the sometimes-brutalizing process of filmmaking into its own voyage of discovery, not sacrificing even the film's smallest means to the film's greater end. Though we never *discussed it I sensed that Harold shared this aim.*

He embodied another fundamental principle of mentorship – the mentor must be fed alongside the mentee. The relationship has to be reciprocal. Whether it was my comments on his script, my enthusiastic appreciation for his films, the satisfaction he took in my films, or the simple joy he got out of being helpful to me, I do believe our relationship fed him in some small way.

I think Harold sensed how disappointed I was in myself for not being a Hollywood success. When he was finishing Year One my wife and I visited him on the Sony lot. He bought us lunch, brought us to the editing suite to show us some scenes he was working on, and then brought us to the mixing soundstage where they were adding and polishing sound effects. I believe he wanted me to feel comfortable and at home – to make me feel like I belonged. For that gift alone I can weep with gratitude even now.

That was the last time I saw him. He said that he was going to take some time off. I didn't know then that he already knew about his illness and that he'd spend the next four years fighting it.

His example was the closest I've come in my life - in the literal sense of physical proximity - to a single human being who seemed the complete realization of both his artistic goals and his personal behavior. He was successful both in what he did and who he was. Both the artist and the man were all they could be, and in sync. A true Laughing Buddha. I miss him already and the grief that I feel is real. But the gratitude for having had him in my life as a mentor and friend is real too and is boundless.

I also feel complete, with no regrets. The last few years, as I knew he was sick and dying, I emailed him occasionally when I thought of him – to thank him for all he did for me, to acknowledge what a profound impact he'd made, and to bless him on his own journey. Which brings me to an essential lesson for the mentee – remember the teacher!

Now with him gone, I've already started asking myself, "What would Harold do?" I wish I could channel him to help solve a thorny problem

I'm facing right now. Or maybe it is his voice I can hear telling me not to react. "Let it be." Maybe. All I know is when I grow up, I want to be like Harold.

Appendix VI: 2012 Mini Vision Fast at 3 Creeks - FM Journal

I left Gigi and Win's place ~ 12:30. The sun was already hot, but I was glad to be wearing jeans as protection from the sun and mosquitoes. I thought as I was walking "What if I could make every step a blessing? Every breath?" I'm a profane man spending his life in search of the holy...

Heard the sound of the high tension wires. Surprisingly, not a thrum, nothing electric. More like the sound of wooden barrels stretching. I couldn't believe it was coming from the wires... Who knows?

I stopped at the gate for water and a rest. I like to push on to certain goals and "arrive" before resting. Yes, this is the attitude that partly made me diabetic – pushing on (and on and on) while working, not stopping to feed and nurture myself. Then almost crawling to the fridge to down juice, peanuts, chocolate... anything I could quickly and easily get my hands on and down my gullet. Of course this was also the pattern set by Mom in my pre- and adolescent years – coming home late and me climbing the walls with hunger. But I won't blame it on her. I'm an adventurer. I like to push my limits and see how far I can go.

So I walk into the wash, perhaps only 100-150 meters from where I rested and I immediately realize I don't need to carry my things further as long as I'm just scouting out a Power place. So I leave my things on a rock, calculating that I'll be back in 40 minutes – 20 minutes up the wash, 20 minutes on the return loop on the road. No need to take sun lotion with me for my exposed arms and neck. No need to even put it on. So I just take my water bottle. I check my phone – 1:15 pm. It will be at least 75 minutes until I return.

So I start up the wash, enjoying considering different boulders to partner with for the night for shelter and support. I immediately see a place that could work.

But I want to explore so I push on. Not long thereafter I see another perfect place, a soft sandy bed right up against a flat wall of rock 20 feet high. It's ideal, and in fact will serve as my spot later. But I push on wanting to see all my surroundings, getting the full lay of the area.

Before long I start to get impatient with how long it's taking. This is a long, winding wash! I pay less and less attention to my surroundings and just push on. On the verge of a funk, no doubt impatient and inattentive, a flock of about ten quail startle me as they suddenly squeal and flap out of a nearby bush. From dead silence to that sudden squawk sends a sharp shiver of fear down my spine. I wonder what it all means.

I keep on walking. Earlier parts of the wash with higher and curvy rim walls were interesting. Lots of cool rock striations. For a while I forget what petroglyphs are and assume these cool combo rocks are them. A couple times I have to leave the wash floor and scramble around some rocks up in the brush. Eventually, I take to the top of the ridge just to expedite walking. I keep thinking of turning back but always say no, just this much further, just up to that next bend... Soon enough I come across a road, then a fork in the road, then the circle Gigi drew on the map. End of the wash. Amen. I check my phone 1:59. It's taken me 45 minutes to get there. For whatever reason I decide then and there I won't look at my phone anymore to track time. "Get lost in time. Have the experience." Kairos time for me.

I'm now sunburned and know it. I really need to get back to my stuff. I have my hat on but it's a small one Gigi loaned me and barely keeps sun off my face, much less anything else. I think about taking off my sleeveless t-shirt and putting it on my shoulders but don't, thinking it won't help much and just expose more of my chest and back to sun. I probably should have. "Tough it out, tough it out," goes the interior voice.

I follow the road. It quickly comes to a couple forks. I tell myself always take the right fork which will wind me around to the start of the wash. That seems to work until I take one that seems to lead me to a high flat ground in the back of the big right tit. It's a dead end. OK, I think, I'll just take the gully back down into the wash. It's not too steep, nothing like dropping off one of the sheer drop walls. It's a little scary and I get in too much of a hurry at times. I remind myself to slow down, focus on footing. Soon enough I'm back in the wash thinking "Now, how far am I from my bags?" I don't recognize anything and fear it'll be a while. Nope. Ten minutes, maybe five.

I'm surprised and glad when I see my stuff. I look around for the nearest boulder offering shade and collapse under it. I drink, take my shoes and socks off to kick out sand and rocks, and lean back on a not very comfortable rock. I meditate and doze. I sit up, drink more water, and lay back again. Maybe for an hour, maybe even two. "What's the hurry?"

I do call out my intention to the land. Asking for support, asking for guidance. I figure, "I'm here. I need to let the land know why." As with other times that I do it later, it lands in my body well, reminding me that "Yes, this is why it is good to be here."

I put sunblock on my face and shoulders. Then lay down again and doze. I can't summon the energy to go to the spot I picked. Should I? Yeah, but why now? Why not wait til the sun is lower or down. It is blazing right down the center of the wash, right in the direction I need to go.

I go back and forth. One moment I'm resolved to go. The next, "Fuck it, I'm staying." Eventually, I start chanting "Om mane padme om." I've never actually done this chant before for very long. It's good. I soon find my own rhythm and sing-song. I shut my eyes. I get high. It's taking me somewhere. I open my eyes and enjoy the sites, fearing embarrassment at the thought of someone happening along, and keep chanting. I stop to drink now and then but keep going. I have to pee but I keep chanting and imagine that my body is sucking the fluid in my bladder back into my system. Eventually, I rock a little, back and forth, to the chant. It's good.

I check on the sun a few times. It's still too high, too damn hot, and I keep chanting. I do it for two hours maybe. Finally, I say this is ridiculous, I can take a little sun and get up and put on my backpack and grab my gear. I start up the wash. I get only maybe 25 meters before I'm looking around for another boulder offering shade. I find one and practically dive for it. This is an even better one than the last. Comfortable. There's a smooth rock to lay back on. Better yet I can place my foam pad under my lumbar and get good sitting support. So I do and chant some more. Maybe another two hours. Again it's good. I feel occasionally ridiculous but know it's OK. Now I'm really resolved to wait out the sun.

I watch the shadows grow longer and longer. I'm not so impatient. Plus there are what look like interesting rock carvings on rocks opposite me. I enjoy thinking they are petroglyphs but soon decide it's just my eyes playing tricks. Over time I do watch them change and recede until they no longer resemble human figures when I get up to leave.

Around maybe 7 pm I thank the rock for the wonderful shade (as I did the earlier boulder) and move on, resolved to make it now no matter what. It takes me maybe five minutes to reach my spot! I feel somewhat ashamed but it is soon replaced by joy in being there. Such a perfect place. I'm sure other vision fasters must've used the same spot. I lay down the tarp on the soft sand, anchoring it easily with nearby rocks. The rock wall makes a perfect backrest. In front of me is a lovely display of rocks on the opposite ridge nearby. Lots to look at. I'm protected somewhat from the wind and definitely from the sun. I realize the spot was probably in the shade hours ago but am not bothered by not having come earlier.

I set up home. Putting out my stuff, taking off my shoes. Again, the rolled pad makes a perfect backrest, one that I sometimes use as a lumbar roll. Other times I sit on top of it and lean against the perfect, smooth rock. I chant again. This time "Nam Myoho Renge Kyo." I am reminded how this chant is very "yang," not yin and trippy like the earlier Tibetan one, and yin and spacey like many of the Theravadan ones. I chant for maybe two hours, occasionally appreciating the sun going down and the interesting shapes of all the rocks standing and watching me on my sunken stage in my little theater. There's an especially humanoid boulder with a smiling face and wide eyes that I resolve not to look at at night for fear it'll freak me out despite the fact that it seems affirming and positive. No matter. Once the sun drops and the dusk really sets in all the features of the rocks dissolve into nothing anyway.

I resolve to do my death lodge after the sun falls behind the mountains in the Eastern valley. It takes a while. But finally it does. Fearful, I start anyway.

I look through my bag for items I can destroy in the process. I find some outdated car insurance cards and some business cards. I begin by asking the rocks and plants to be my witness, to participate by observing my process and holding me to my commitments. I name all those things about me that want to die, what drives that urge to death: my impatience, both with the world and with myself, mostly myself; my self-hatred - how I can't seem to accomplish much of what I seek to do, how I'm a fuck-up, etc.; my self-consciousness, my endless second-guessing – how I often don't feel comfortable in my own body being who I am, struggling to arrive at "what's natural;" the anger that grows out of the impatience – having so little tolerance for all the most minor things in life; my victim psychology – everything bad that's happened to me is because others have fucked me over, etc. I go on, putting energy into it, yelling sometimes, trying hard to rip the cards apart. When two of them don't tear since covered in plastic I take my pen out and stab them. It's good to release the energy yelling a few times. I cry too.

When I feel complete I take all the pieces and walk away to bury them. I first pick a spot that I judge is too close, then a further one. It seems like a nice protected little graveyard. I dig a hole and drop the pieces in, placing a small rock as the headstone. I say a little prayer, not especially kind and gentle, that says here lays that part of me that was so unhappy and so wanted to die. I remind the rocks and plants that they are witnesses.

Then I return to my tarp. I know it's essential to fill up what's just been emptied but at first I'm at a loss. And now in this moment of writing I'm not exactly sure what was said and done. I think I said some prayers for myself, inviting in patience, tolerance, acceptance, generosity, humility. Though I feel calm I also have thoughts that are reminders of what just died and was buried, that somehow I didn't do it right. So I look over there and remind myself that's gone. I will do this a few times in the coming hour. I thank the land for supporting me and say the process is now finished. I sit back, relax, and enjoy the view.

Soon it's deep dusk. Out of nowhere, suddenly one bat, then a second, and finally two more swoosh by in front of my seat, feeding. They look like small birds. A couple times they come so close I fear they might hit me but then they veer off. It's a real treat to watch them. They swoop and feed for ~ 15 minutes then just as suddenly as they appear they are gone. It's dark. There are bright, early evening stars.

I fall into a groove of chanting/silent meditation that I'll largely maintain throughout the night. It's lovely to hear the silence once I've stopped chanting. The regular gusts of wind subside a bit and I feel I can hear for miles. In fact I actually can, given that what I first believe to be wind noise actually turns out to be cars and trucks on the distant highway. Come midnight onward the occasional "gusts" dwindle down to almost none. That's when I finally know for sure - traffic.

I haven't really thought about food. When my stomach occasionally growled I thought "Oh, my stomach's growling." Felt it and then watched it quickly fade away. I never really felt bothered by not eating. (At least until the next morning when the diarrhea started.) Keep in mind too I was consuming 2-3 glucose tabs every 2-3 hours as I kept testing my blood sugar and finding them low.

It's dark. At one moment, what seems like a leaf drops down almost directly in front of me. Scares the shit out of me. Where did that come from? I look up. There is a bush growing out of the rock not too far above me and on that same angle. Still, what fell down didn't seem to be a branch or leaf from it. I look around in the dark on the tarp but can't seem to locate anything. I didn't search in the morning to see what was there. But I also don't recall noticing anything like a leaf being there. Who knows what it was, where it came from, or where it went.

I'm settled into the night. I start chanting Hare Krishna. Always loved that chant. After an hour or so I stand up and start moving to create some warmth. It works. I chant for another hour or so then sit down to meditate. I'm warm and relaxed.

Man, the silence is incredible. I've never heard silence like this. No wind, no animals, no traffic, nothing. Around maybe 3 am I hear a lone grasshopper or cricket but only for about an hour, maybe less. From silence back to silence. Weird.

I also am visited by one lone mosquito. She buzzes along maybe at 2 or so. It's comical. One mosquito, the middle of the night, desert, in the middle of nowhere. I have to laugh. But I also waste no time applying repellant to every exposed surface. I hear an additional buzz or two, then gone, forever.

I can't get over the quiet. It's immense. How can a space this vast be completely soundless? Even if it is the middle of the night. I'm reminded of my song from many years ago "Silence of the Night," how I used to return home as a teen, drunk and stoned, and sit on the back porch and meditate (without knowing that's what it was), trying so hard to hear the silence of the night above the ringing in my ears.

I've put on all my clothes, turned my jacket collar up, and wrapped the blanket round me. Though I've cooled off now I'm just warm enough. I'm so grateful.

Later I figure out to use my empty backpack as a place to put my feet inside for extra warmth.

After a couple rounds of chanting and silent meditation I feel tired and roll out the foam pad and lay down. It takes a while to get comfortable and to get myself mostly covered. I use the pad itself slightly rolled at one end as a pillow. It amuses me to have my feet in my backpack but it's damn practical since the blanket won't cover me down there. I don't sleep but lay there and rest. After an hour or so I get up from the discomfort of being locked in one position. I sit and meditate some more.

More chanting, more meditating. I've appreciated charting the movement of the few constellations I recognize across the sky. Some move recognizably from West to East, others spin in a smaller loop then disappear behind the ridge.

As fearful as my mind was when night first settled in, I'm glad to note it's calmed during the night. Mostly because I simply wouldn't allow myself to go to the fear. Which in most cases is thoroughly irrational: maybe I'll be visited by ghosts? Maybe my dead father will come? Maybe some crooks will come, knock me out and steal my stuff!

I do look to the East to search for signs of morning light occasionally. But not with much real expectation or enthusiasm. Finally, when it first starts to get light it surprises me. I meditate and chant some more but I'm already chafing at the bit to get home. I want very much to see the bristlecones. But I'm also clear on how that's a convenient "out" from the wash.

I start to break camp. I hardly make a move before I realize I've got to crap quick. So I find a spot not too close but not as secluded and remote as would be ideal. Feeling a bit queasy but much better I bury it all under handfuls of sand, then scrub, and finally a rock. Creepy-crawlies... have at it.

I thank the land, the rocks, and the bushes and plants for being my protectors. I thank them all for being so kind and gentle with me. I'm really sincere. The night, the whole experience, feels easy and uneventful to me. I do feel like I was gently held. Though I don't regret leaving, it's a good spot. I'm grateful for it and would return anytime.

So I wait for more substantive light, then decide it'll be wise to leave before the actual sun crests over the Eastern mountains. That way I won't have it in my eyes walking home, nor have to bother with putting on sun protection. In fact, the plan works perfectly. As I leave the wash it seems just about to crest. But as I keep walking down the hill it stays just below the mountain ridge, and in fact doesn't "rise" all the time I'm walking until about 15 minutes after I return to 3 creeks. It's a fun game to play and I enjoy it.

Nobody seems to be stirring at 3 creeks. I put my gear back near the shed for Gigi since I'm unclear as to where it all goes. It's fun to peer in through the yurt window at Tracy sleeping. But it seems she wasn't sleeping, or at least not deeply, and she quickly stirs. It's fun to see her and not speak.

www.ingramcontent.com/pod-product-compliance
Lightning Source LLC
Chambersburg PA
CBHW031432160426

43195CB00010BB/704